TORAH MYSTERIES ILLUMINATED

INTRIGUING INSIGHTS INTO
THE ESSENCE OF MAJOR TORAH TOPICS
OF CONTEMPORARY RELEVANCE

Thomas Furst

URIM PUBLICATIONS
Jerusalem • New York

Torah Mysteries Illuminated:
Intriguing Insights into
the Essence of Major Torah Topics
of Contemporary Relevance
by Thomas Furst

Copyright © 2022, 2015 Thomas Furst

Typeset by Ariel Walden

Printed in Israel

Second Revised Edition

ISBN 978-965-524-194-5

Urim Publications
P.O. Box 52287
Jerusalem 9152102 Israel
www.UrimPublications.com

Library of Congress Cataloging-in-Publication Data

Furst, Thomas, author.
   Torah mysteries illuminated : intriguing insights
into the essence of major Torah topics of contemporary
relevance / Thomas Furst. — First edition.
       pages   cm
   ISBN 978-965-524-194-5 (hardback)
1. Judaism.   I. Title.
   BM562.F87 2015
   296—dc23   2015000691

To DEBBIE, my dear wife and best friend,
for her inspiration, insights, and encouragement,
and for always being there for me
with unlimited
love, energy, and devotion.

CONTENTS

INTRODUCTION

This *sefer* is a compendium of the author's *divrei Torah*, with the intention to present original, thought-provoking, and practical perspectives on major Torah topics.

This project began many years ago when our family was about to embark on a Pesach vacation. We received a mailing which invited guests to volunteer as participants in the program. My wife, Debbie, enthusiastically encouraged me to volunteer as a speaker, but I initially rejected the idea as I never viewed myself as being so qualified.

As *Hashgacha* would have it, an idea came to me, centered around the concept of why we refer to our holidays as Yom Tov, despite the fact that the Torah calls them by every name but that one. Giving this question a great deal of thought, I came up with what I believed to be an original concept, based on what is frequently a deeper secondary meaning of the word *tov* in Tanach, and I decided to give speaking a try. The talk was very well-received and the audience response, together with tremendous encouragement and inspiration from my wife, gave me great *chizuk* to speak and write again. And so, as the years went on, I repeated the process with other topics, including Shabbos, Rosh Chodesh, Amalek, Shevet Levi, Parshas Balak, and others, and also wrote several shorter articles.

With each *d'var*, my objective is to introduce ideas which are both original and relevant to our everyday lives. My methodology is to think of questions that are often overlooked because certain concepts are frequently taken for granted. For example, why is *hachnasas orchim* such a significant mitzvah and how did Avraham know it to be so, to the extent that he knew he had the right to put Hashem on hold while attending to his guests? Is it credible that Moshe Rabbeinu so strongly resisted the historic mission of redeeming our people simply because he stuttered, and what important lessons can we derive from this episode about the special character of *Shevet Levi* and the reason for its bifurcation into *Kohanim* and *Levi'im*? Why is the *Hallel* on Rosh Chodesh only a half-*Hallel* and how do we understand the tremendous significance of this day? Why are the many *mitzvos* which permeate the first night of Pesach (limitless discussion, *arba kosos*, etc.) not applicable to any other day or night of Pesach?

In this *d'var Torah*, I will suggest certain *chiddushim* – novel ideas – which do not appear to be cited by the traditional commentaries. On the one hand, it is a bit daunting to suggest that there may be novel insights which do not appear to be explicitly cited by the numerous and significant commentaries already published. It seems logical, however, that Hashem intended this outcome, as we will now explain.

Clearly, if everything worth saying can be found explicitly in our traditional commentaries, then no-one would ever make the attempt to come up with something original (yet rooted in our tradition) – everyone would simply consult the commentaries. I believe, however, that Hashem wants each of us to be motivated to make the effort and that is why there are, and probably always will be, many original ideas out there waiting to be discovered.

*

Over the years, I received a great deal of very positive feedback and much encouragement to publish, which culminated in this *sefer*. I owe a great deal of thanks to the myriad of people who have encouraged me and, not least, to Tzvi Mauer, Batsheva Pomerantz, and the staff at Urim Publications, who have proven to be an invaluable resource and a true pleasure to work with.

In many important ways, this is a family project. Aside from my wife Debbie's incredible support every step of the way, she contributed much insightful editing and organizational advice. My daughter Rina and her husband Zach were very helpful in the surprisingly difficult task of preparing a descriptive, yet concise, table of contents. My daughter Ariella's input and her notes from Midreshet Moriah got me thinking in the right direction when I was preparing the Amalek article. My son David, over the years, organized learning sessions with some of his friends where, in the course of my preparation, I somehow came up with the ideas for several of the articles in this *sefer*. My *mechutan*, Jerry Kestenbaum, suggested the very apt title of this *sefer*.

I would also like to add my thanks to Yeshivat Kerem B'Yavneh for creating, in my formative years, a terrific atmosphere of love of the Land of Israel and love of Torah, and to Yeshivat Reishit Yerusha-layim, which my son David attended, for providing me with great *chizuk* in various ways.

I would also like to acknowledge my learning *chabura* over the past several years at Meridian Mortgage, where I attend *Mincha* most weekdays, and whose principals have graciously permitted my learn-ing partners to take a bit of precious time out of the working day to learn Torah. It has been an honor to learn with Jacob Nefoussi, Asher Haft, Shmuel Teichman, and more recently, Mordechai Beren and Sam Schonfeld, as well as Chaim Schreck. They have each helped me crystallize a number of my ideas.

Rabbi Evan Hoffman helped me track down several sources. My dear friend, Chazzan Ze'ev Kron, helped me proofread the Hebrew quotes. I received valuable typing assistance – for the Hebrew quotes – from Ortal Koma.

And I would be remiss in not adding a word about *yichus*. In many ways, a person is a product of their ancestors, and I am extremely proud to be descended from the Chasam Sofer, and that my dear wife is descended from the Magen Avraham and related to the Gerrer Rebbes. The inspiration of their heritage, and perhaps a tiny dose of their genes, constitute an essential element of this project. More contemporaneously, my late father, Harry Furst, and my late father-in-law, Aryeh Eliezer Kaminer, *ztz"l*. Each had a very sincere and abiding love for Torah and personified its moral principles – their powerful and treasured impact on our family is enduring. We have also benefitted tremendouslyfrom the wisdom and moral strength of the patriarchs and matriarchs of our extended family, namely Leon-ard and Aliza Kestenbaum, and Irwin (*a"h*) and Bea Peyser.

As a final note, *chiddushim* do not come about without a great deal of *siyata d'Shmaya*. I would like to express my extreme gratitude to Hashem for gracing me with a number of original ideas, as well as the *ma'aneh lashon* to express them, thereby permitting me to share these concepts with others.

THE HIDDEN ESSENCE OF SHABBOS ᗌ

Shabbos is a *mitzvah* which is all too familiar to most of us, making it difficult to step back and get a better perspective of the essence of this *mitzvah*. The purpose of this *d'var* is to explore the mitzvah of Shabbos in depth, with the hope of gaining a perspective which I believe is novel and exciting and which I hope you will find to be both enlightening and of significant practical value.

Let us begin by listing a number of aspects of the mitzvah of Shabbos which illustrate its enormous significance (we will elaborate on these points momentarily):

(1)   Shabbos is one of only a handful of *mitzvos aseh* which are weighed against all *mitzvos* of the Torah;

(2)   Shabbos is one of only three *mitzvos* which are expressly classified by the Torah as an אות;

(3)   Shabbos has boundless reward for its observance as well as very harsh penalties for its transgression;

(4)   Shabbos was selected by Hashem to be among the exclusive group of the *Aseres HaDibros*;

(5)   Shabbos is perhaps the only mitzvah whose observance raises a person to a level which is analogized by the Midrash to a quasi-state of *Olam HaBo*;

(6)   Shabbos is the only mitzvah which is viewed as the bride of Bnei Yisrael (as in *Lecha dodi likras kalla*); and

(7)   Shabbos is the only mitzvah whose observance twice consecutively would bring about the coming of Moshiach (according to the Midrash).

How do we understand the exalted status of this mitzvah?

❧ PURPOSE OF THE MITZVAH OF SHABBOS

IS SHABBOS ALL ABOUT REFRAINING FROM WORK?

Most people, if they were asked about the essence of Shabbos, would probably phrase their response in terms of some sort of physical rest and recharging of batteries. This response is quite logical, and is no doubt at least partially correct, in light of the following words in the *Aseres HaDibros* (Shemos 20:10, 11):

ויום השביעי שבת לד׳-אלקיך לא־תעשה כל־מלאכה . . . כי ששת ימים
עשה ד׳ את־השמים ואת־הארץ את הים ואת־כל־אשר בם, וינח ביום
השביעי, על כן ברך ד׳ את־יום השבת ויקדשהו.

And the seventh day is dedicated to G-d. Do not do any work . . . because G-d created the heaven, earth, and the seas in six days and "rested" (וינח) on the seventh day, that is why G-d sanctified Shabbos.

And so it appears that a central aspect of Shabbos is refraining from work. It is apparent, however, that such a limited view of Shabbos does not come close to explaining the sublime essence of Shabbos. Consider the following:

(1)   Why would Shabbos be a day which is sanctified only for Bnei Yisrael, in light of the fact that a weekly day of rest is a universal concept and, moreover, our nation was millennia away from even being formed when Shabbos was first sanctified at the time of Creation?

(2)   Why is resting *per se* on Shabbos such a major mitzvah? Hashem created an entire world during the first six days – an accomplishment that is monumental beyond description. Why then is it specifically the cessation from work on Shabbos that is sanctified, and not Creation itself?

(3)   If Shabbos is about refraining from work, how do we understand the concept of a day of rest in the case of (a) someone who is not working, such as someone who is on vacation and spends all week on the beach, sightseeing and going to shows; (b) someone who is in the hospital and is unable to engage in any meaningful kind of work or creative activity, or (c) a student in an advanced yeshiva (i.e., no tests or homework)

who spends all his time learning, even on Shabbos, and who engages in minimal *melacha* throughout the entire week?

(4) At the time of the *manna*, we note that Bnei Yisrael were for all practical purposes not working at all, having been provided by Hashem with food, water, clothes, and physical protection, all the while having to do virtually nothing to sustain themselves, and therefore having no real need to rest up on Shabbos. If Shabbos is about resting up from six days of work, why does the Shabbos test of the *manna* become one of the ten tests of Bnei Yisrael in the dessert, featured so prominently in the Torah? Furthermore, why is the *manna* incident of such significance as to form the basis for the sacred mitzvah of *lechem mishna*, observed at every single Shabbos meal thereafter down through the ages?

(5) Lastly, if Shabbos is primarily about refraining from work one day each week, which is a practice that virtually all humans would adopt in some manner through the exercise of logic and common sense, why are the consequences for violation of Shabbos so draconian? The Torah states (Shemos 31:14):

ושמרתם את־השבת כי קודש הוא לכם מחלליה מות יומת, כי כל העושה
בה מלאכה ונכרתה הנפש ההוא מקרב עמיה.

And you shall guard the Shabbos because it is holy. Whoever desecrates the Shabbos shall be put to death. Whoever works on Shabbos will be cut off from his people.

The mirror image of this question is: If Shabbos is mostly about the practical and logical concept of refraining from work one day each week, why is the reward for sanctifying Shabbos so enormous? The Rambam makes the following astonishing statement at the very end of his exposition of *Hilchos Shabbos* (30:15):

וכל השומר את השבת כהלכתה ומכבדה ומעונגה כפי כוחו כבר מפורש
בקבלה שכרו בעולם הזה יתר על השכר הצפון לעולם הבא.

Every person who observes Shabbos in accordance with halacha, and honors and makes the Shabbos as pleasurable as possible according to his power, such person's reward in this world is greater than the hidden reward of *Olam HaBo*.

This seems like giving students in school a huge reward for going to recess. Could such enormous reward be reserved for a mitzvah that primarily involves refraining from work for a day each week?

IS SHABBOS ALL ABOUT RECOGNIZING HASHEM'S ROLE IN CREATION?

Another possible purpose of Shabbos, as indicated by the *pesukim*, is recognition of Hashem's role in Creation. In the Friday night *Kiddush*, we talk about Shabbos as זכרון למעשה בראשית. The following *pesukim* (Shemos 31:16, 17), which seem to echo this theme, are incorporated into our *Kabolas Shabbos* davening as well as in *Kiddush* on the Shabbos day:

> ושמרו בני ישראל את־השבת לעשות את השבת לדורותם ברית עולם.
> ביני ובין בני ישראל אות הוא לעולם כי־ששת ימים עשה ד' את־השמים
> ואת־הארץ וביום השביעי שבת וינפש.
>
> And Bnei Yisrael shall observe Shabbos as an eternal covenant. Between Me and Bnei Yisrael it is an eternal sign that G-d created the heaven and earth and rested on the seventh day

But if a central theme of Shabbos is recognizing Hashem's role in Creation, consider the following:

(1)   Just as cessation of work is a concept which has universal (and not specifically Jewish) significance, the very same is true for Creation of the world. Why would this make Shabbos a sign between G-d and the Jews, to the exclusion of all other nations?

(2)   Every single mitzvah we perform, and not exclusively Shabbos, signifies our firm belief that the Torah is authentic and therefore that G-d created the world. Why is Shabbos specifically designated as a symbol of G-d's Creation?

WHY IS SHMITTA CALLED "SHABBOS" BY THE TORAH?

Another interesting question, relevant to our analysis, is why *shmitta* is called Shabbos – in light of the fact that *shmitta* does not represent the act of resting by a person? If one argues that the Jewish farmer is resting during the *shmitta* year, the farmer is in fact permitted to do all kinds of other work. Moreover, the Torah explicitly states that it is *the land, and not the farmer*, which is resting at such time (ושבתה הארץ שבת לד', Vayikra 25:2). The fact that the Torah applies the term Shabbos to an inanimate object which does not "work" in the sense that a human works, and the fact that *shmitta* has nothing to do with the account of Creation, shows that we need to probe much more deeply in order to understand the concept of Shabbos.

✍ UNIQUE ELEMENTS OF THE MITZVAH OF SHABBOS

In order to achieve an understanding of the essence of Shabbos, we will first deepen the mystery by reviewing a number of unique features of Shabbos (some of which were briefly noted at the outset of this *d'var*) which illustrate in a number of different ways that Shabbos is in a category of its own amongst *mitzvos*, although we do not yet understand why this should be so.

ONE OF THE ASERES HADIBROS

The first three of the *Aseres HaDibros* deal expressly with loyalty to and reverence towards Hashem's Oneness and *Kedusha*. Aside from these three, Shabbos is the only mitzvah בין אדם למקום included among the *Aseres HaDibros*. We note that there are a number of major *mitzvos* in the same category as Shabbos, such as *tefillin*, Yom Kippur, *bris milah*, *kashrus*, Pesach, and others, any of which could seemingly have been selected for inclusion among the *Aseres HaDibros*? Why was Shabbos selected to be a part of this exalted group?

WE ARE DESERVING OF MOSHIACH IF WE KEEP TWO SHABBOSIM PROPERLY

Shabbos has the extraordinary power to bring about the coming of Moshiach. In *Maseches Shabbos* (118b), we find the following statement:

אמר רבי יוחנן משום רבי שמעון בן יוחאי. משמרין ישראל שתי שבתות כהלכתן, מיד נגאלים.

Rebbe Yochanan said in the name of Rebbe Shimon ben Yochai: "If Bnei Yisrael were to keep two [presumably consecutive] Shabbosim, they would immediately be redeemed."

Why is Shabbos the only mitzvah to which this concept applies? And why indeed should keeping two consecutive Shabbosim trigger the coming of Moshiach?

COUNTING DOWN TO SHABBOS

Shabbos is a very powerful mitzvah, as exemplified by the manner in which Shabbos exerts its influence over every other day in the calendar. We see an excellent example of this in *tefillah*. On each non-Shabbos day of the year (even on a Yom Tov!), we refer to Shabbos in the *Shir Shel Yom*, as we count down to Shabbos, a feature which is unique among *mitzvos*.[1] The Mechilta d'Rebbe Yishmael states that this practice is actually a positive Torah commandment, derived from the *pasuk* זכור את יום השבת לקדשו in the *Aseres HaDibros* (Shemos 20:8):

> רבי יצחק אומר לא אתה מונה כדרך שאחרים מונין אלא אתה מונה
> לשם שבת.
> Rebbe Yitzchak says: "Do not count the days in the manner that the rest of the world counts them [i.e., giving each day a distinct name], but rather count the days with reference to Shabbos."

Rebbe Yitzchak construes the word *zachor* to mean that we need to remember Shabbos on each non-Shabbos day. But we cannot help but ask why the word *zachor* should not be construed simply to require that we remember Shabbos on the day itself, as we do by saying *Kiddush*. Why are we required to go much further so as to remember Shabbos on each weekday?

---

1. In the case of Shavuos, we are not so much counting down towards Shavuos as we are linking Pesach and Shavuos.

CONNECTION TO YETZIAS MITZRAYIM

Shabbos has a seemingly close connection to *Yetzias Mitzrayim*. For instance, in the Friday night *Kiddush*, we state that Shabbos is a *Zecher L'Yetzias Mitzrayim*. This connection is also made in the second *Aseres HaDibros*, as we will see in a moment. However, while the relationship of Shabbos to *Yetzias Mitzrayim* is very familiar to us, its rationale is not at all apparent. Consider the following:

(1) Shabbos was sanctified by Hashem in the very first week of Creation. Why would Shabbos be a reminder of an event which occurred thousands of years later?

(2) The connection between Shabbos and *Yetzias Mitzrayim* is found in the *Aseres HaDibros* in Va'Eschanan, where the *pasuk* states as follows (Devarim: 5:15):

וזכרת כי עבד היית בארץ מצרים ויצאך ד' אלקיך משם ביד חזקה ובזרוע
נטויה על כן צוך ד' אלקיך לעשות את יום השבת.

And you shall remember that you were slaves in Mitzrayim and Hashem redeemed you with His strong hand and outstretched arm and that is why Hashem commanded you to observe the day of Shabbos.

This *pasuk* tells us that G-d brought us out of Mitzrayim and that is why Hashem commanded us to keep Shabbos. Rashi comments:

על מנת כן פדאך, שתהיה לו עבד ותשמור מצוותיו.

It is on this condition that I (Hashem) redeemed you (from Mitzrayim), so that you would be His servant and observe the *mitzvos*.

We note that Rashi, while purportedly explaining why *Yetzias Mitzrayim and Shabbos* are closely linked, does not link *Yetzias Mitzrayim and Shabbos* but rather makes a connection instead between *Yetzias Mitzrayim* and *all of the mitzvos*. How do we understand this Rashi?

SHABBOS AS BRIDE AND QUEEN OF BNEI YISRAEL

Yet another mysterious aspect of Shabbos is why, of all 613 *mitzvos*, Shabbos is the only one which is likened to a bride (to Bnei Yisrael as *chasan*), and a queen to Bnei Yisrael as king.

Shabbos as Bride

Perhaps the basis for the author of *Lecha Dodi* conjuring up the image of Shabbos as a bride to Bnei Yisrael is the following Midrash (Bereishis Rabba 11:9).

> תני רשב״י: אמרה שבת לפני הקב״ה, רבש״ע ולכולן יש בן זוג ולי אין בן
> זוג. אמר לה הקב״ה: כנסת ישראל היא בן זוגך וכיון שעמדו ישראל לפני
> הר סיני אמר להם הקב״ה, זכרו הדבר שאמרתי לשבת, כנסת ישראל
> היא בן זוגך, היינו דבור: זכור את יום השבת לקדשו.

Rebbe Shimon ben Yochai taught: Shabbos approached Hashem and stated, "Each day has a partner [the first day of the week has the second, the third has the fourth, the fifth has the sixth, but the Sabbath has no partner]." Hashem responded, "Bnei Yisrael is your partner." And when they stood before the mountain of Sinai, G-d said to Bnei Yisrael, "Remember what I said to the Sabbath, that Bnei Yisrael is your partner, Therefore, Remember the Sabbath day, to keep it holy" (Shemos 20:8).

Shabbos as Queen

The Talmud (*Shabbos* 119a) relates that every Friday night, Rebbe Chanina would dress himself in his finest garments and declare: "Come, let us go out to meet Shabbos, the Queen."

> רבי חנינא מיעטף וקאי אפניא דמעלי שבתא אמר בואו ונצא לקראת
> שבת המלכה.

Rav Yannai would act similarly, as also stated in this Gemara.

The imagery of Shabbos as a bride and as a queen exemplifies the tremendous affection that we as a people display towards Shabbos, although we have not yet offered an explanation of why this should be so.

WEIGHED AGAINST ALL MITZVOS

A very powerful indicator of the supreme status of Shabbos among *mitzvos* is the fact that the mitzvah of Shabbos is weighed against all of the other *mitzvos*. We find the following Midrash (Shemos Rabba 25:16):

> שקולה השבת כנגד כל המצוות . . . א״ל הקב״ה לישראל אם תזכו לשמור
> שבת מעלה אני עליכם כאילו שמרתם כל המצוות שבתורה ואם חללתם
> אותה מעלה אני עליכם כאילו חללתם כל המצוות.
> Shabbos has the weight of all the other *mitzvos* combined.
> "If you shall observe Shabbos, I [G-d] will consider it as if
> you have observed all the *mitzvos* of the Torah. And if you
> violate Shabbos, I will consider it as if you have violated
> all the *mitzvos* of the Torah."

Two other *mitzvos* in this category are *Talmud Torah* and *yishuv Eretz Yisrael*. *Talmud Torah* is a pre-requisite to performing all other *mitzvos* and, in that sense, it can be said to be weighed against all of them. Similarly, Eretz Yisrael is the place of the Beis HaMikdosh and Yerushalayim, and has many important *mitzvos* which can only be performed there, so it is also understandable why *yishuv Eretz Yisrael* would be weighed against all *mitzvos*. But why Shabbos?

IT IS A CAPITAL OFFENSE FOR A NON-JEW TO OBSERVE SHABBOS

Another deep mystery of Shabbos is why Hashem decided to safe-guard Shabbos exclusively for our people. The Talmud states as follows (*Sanhedrin* 58b):

> עובד כוכבים ששבת חייב מיתה.
> An idol-worshipper [this may be a euphemism] who
> observes Shabbos is *chayav misa*.

Along the same lines, Shemos Rabba (25:15) states as follows:

> אם יבואו מבני נח וישמרו את השבת לא דיים שאין מקבלים שכר אלא
> שחייבים מיתה.
> If a non-Jew observes Shabbos [presumably with all its

halachic elements], not only does such person not receive a reward, but it is a capital offense.

Why, of all *mitzvos*, is it only Shabbos that has this adverse consequence for a non-Jewish person who observes the mitzvah?

◆§ THE HIDDEN ESSENCE OF SHABBOS

In order to unlock the essence of Shabbos, we need to first perceive the inextricable link between the observance of Shabbos and our conduct during the first six days of the week. We note that the Torah, when emphasizing to us the holiness of Shabbos, instead of focusing exclusively on Shabbos, repeatedly and prominently refers to the first six days of the week, seemingly for no reason. We will quote a few *pesukim* which illustrate this point. For example, the Torah, in the first *Aseres HaDibros* speaks about Shabbos in the following eloquent terms (Shemos 31:17):

ביני ובין בני ישראל אות הוא לעלם כי־ששת ימים עשה ד' את־השמים
ואת־הארץ וביום השביעי שבת וינפש.

Shabbos is an eternal sign between Me and Bnei Yisrael because I created the heaven and earth in six days and rested on the seventh day.

In this *pasuk*, Hashem states that Shabbos is an eternal sign between Him and Bnei Yisrael *because*. . . . Stop in the middle of this *pasuk* for a moment. Because what? You would think that the next words refer to Shabbos. In fact, the immediately following words are:

ששת ימים עשה ד' את־השמים ואת־הארץ.

. . . . G-d created the heaven and earth in six days.

Let us now examine a few *pesukim* where our working during the first six days of the week is linked to Shabbos by context and placement in the *pasuk*:

First *Aseres HaDibros* (Shemos 20:9, 10):

ששת ימים תעבוד ועשית כל־מלאכתך ויום השביעי שבת לד'־אלקיך.

Six days you shall do all your work and the seventh day
is Shabbos for your G-d.

In Shemos 23:12 (Mishpatim):

שֵׁשֶׁת יָמִים תַּעֲשֶׂה מַעֲשֶׂיךָ וּבַיּוֹם הַשְּׁבִיעִי תִּשְׁבּוֹת.

Six days you shall do your work and on the seventh day
you shall rest.

Similarly in the case of the following three *pesukim*:
Shemos 35:2 (Vayakhel):

שֵׁשֶׁת יָמִים תֵּעָשֶׂה מְלָאכָה וּבַיּוֹם הַשְּׁבִיעִי יִהְיֶה לָכֶם קֹדֶשׁ.

Six days you shall do your work and the seventh day
will be holy for you.

Again in Vayikra 23:3 (Emor):

שֵׁשֶׁת יָמִים תֵּעָשֶׂה מְלָאכָה וּבַיּוֹם הַשְּׁבִיעִי שַׁבַּת שַׁבָּתוֹן.

Six days you shall do your work and the seventh day
will be Shabbos.

And again in the second *Aseres HaDibros*: Devarim 5:13, 14 (Va'-
Eschanan):

. . . שֵׁשֶׁת יָמִים תַּעֲבֹד וְעָשִׂיתָ כָּל מְלַאכְתֶּךָ וְיוֹם הַשְּׁבִיעִי שַׁבָּת לַד' אלקיך

Six days you shall toil and do all your work, and the
seventh day is for Hashem, your G-d.

What is particularly striking about all these *pesukim* is that the Torah
seems to repeatedly connect the observance of Shabbos to the six days
of work that precede it. These *pesukim* all seem to say that Shabbos
does not become sanctified by itself and that the *kedusha* of Shabbos does not materialize unless something very significant happens
during the week. What is that important "something?"

CRITICAL IMPORTANCE OF KIDDUSH HASHEM

In order to understand not only the close relationship of Shabbos
to the preceding six days of the week, but also the reason for the
enormous importance of the mitzvah of Shabbos, we need to perceive
how and why the concept of *Kiddush Hashem* must govern every facet
of our lives. There is a *pasuk* in Isaiah (43:7), read not surprisingly in

the very first *haftora* of the year, following Parshas Bereishis, which
states as follows:

כל הנקרא בשמי ולכבודי בראתיו.

I created everything for My Glory.

This *pasuk* signals to us the fundamental and overriding importance of
Kiddush Hashem. It follows that we would see practical manifestations
of this in halacha and *hashkafa* and we will now illustrate that this is
in fact the case:

(1) Yom Kippur as a day of forgiveness: Although Yom Kippur is
    specifically designated by the Torah as a day of forgiveness for
    all our sins, there is an exception. The Rambam states (*Hilchos
    Teshuva* 1:4):

אבל המחלל את השם אע"פ שעשה תשובה והגיע יום הכפורים, והוא
עומד בתשובתו ובאו עליו יסורין אינו מתכפר לו כפרה גמורה עד שימות,
אלא תשובה יום הכפורים ויסורין שלשתן תולין ומיתה מכפרת.

But the person who is מחלל שם שמים, even though such
person did *teshuva* and Yom Kippur has arrived, and the
person has suffered punishment, that person's atonement is incomplete until he dies.

(2) Obligation to give one's life for *Kiddush Hashem*: Despite the
    Torah's extreme concern for preservation of human life, we
    are all familiar with the obligation to surrender one's life for
    the sake of *Kiddush Hashem*, so as not to violate one of the three
    cardinal sins.

(3) Episode of the *meraglim*: After the episode of the *meraglim*,
    Moshe pleads for Bnei Yisrael and, as a last resort, uses the
    argument that if G-d were to destroy the Jews on account of
    the transgression of the *meraglim*, the nations of the world
    would believe that Hashem did not have the power to take
    the Jews out of Mitzrayim. Moshe's resort to a *Kiddush Hashem*
    argument succeeded despite the fact that it had nothing at all
    to do with the merits.

(4) *Talmid chacham* with a grease stain on his clothing: As a final

example, we now turn to what seems to be a somewhat radical statement in the Gemara (*Shabbos* 114a):

אמר ר' יוחנן, תלמיד חכם שנמצא רבב על בגדו חייב מיתה.

Rav Yochanan said, "Any *talmid chacham* who has a grease stain on his clothing is liable to death."

Rashi explains that a *talmid chacham* is supposed to be circumspect about the respect and reputation of the Torah which he represents. The fact that a simple grease stain can make a *talmid chacham* deserving of the ultimate punishment is remarkable but, in view of our discussion, it only reinforces everything we have said about the exceptional significance of *Kiddush Hashem*.

CREATION IS, BY DESIGN, IN AND OF ITSELF AN INSTRUMENT OF KIDDUSH HASHEM

Now that we have demonstrated the overriding importance of *Kiddush Hashem*, we need to fill in one more piece of the puzzle in our quest to understand the essence of Shabbos, by demonstrating that the world which Hashem created was, by design, in and of itself an instrument of *Kiddush Hashem*. To illustrate, Rambam (*Yesodei HaTorah* 2:2) states that the way to fulfill the Torah's command to love G-d (ואהבת את ד' אלקיך) is to study Hashem's creations. The Rambam states:

והיאך היא הדרך לאהבתו ויראתו? בשעה שיתבונן האדם במעשיו
וברואיו הנפלאים הגדולים ויראה מהן חכמתו שאין לה ערך ולא קץ,
מיד הוא אוהב ומשבח ומפאר ומתאוה תאוה גדולה לידע השם הגדול.

What is the path to love and fear Hashem? As a person contemplates Hashem's wondrous creations, and appreciates the unparalleled and infinite wisdom embodied in these creations, a person will love, praise, and have a very strong desire to know and better understand the *Shem HaGadol*.

In confirmation of the Rambam's statement, each of us can surely name his or her own list of items which inspire awe and admiration of the Creator, such as the miracle of birth, the incredible intricacy of the human body, the awesome scope and beauty of the oceans and nature generally, and the incredible variety of animals, fish, birds, and insects – each with its own distinct, fascinating, and intricate habits and survival modes.

EXPLAINING THE LINK BETWEEN SHABBOS AND THE FIRST SIX DAYS OF THE WEEK

Now that we understand not only the fundamental importance of *Kiddush Hashem* but also that Creation was itself a powerful instrument of *Kiddush Hashem*, we are ready to unlock the true meaning of the exalted mitzvah of Shabbos. At the end of the account of Creation, the *pasuk* reads (Bereishis 2:2):

ויכל אלקים ביום השביעי מלאכתו אשר עשה וישבות ביום השביעי מכל
מלאכתו אשר עשה.

G-d finished His work on the seventh day, and G-d rested on the seventh day from His work.

This *pasuk* juxtaposes the fact of the six days of Creation with the *kedusha* of the first Shabbos. And, I believe, in light of our discussion, conveys a clear message to Bnei Yisrael that the very reason G-d was able to "rest" on the seventh day, investing Shabbos with its enormous *kedusha*, was because the Creation of the first six days was an embodiment of *Kiddush Hashem*, thus fulfilling Hashem's primary objective in creating the world.

Similarly, this is precisely why, as we have seen in a number of the *pesukim* we reviewed earlier, the Torah juxtaposes the *kedusha* of our Shabbos with the preceding six days of *melacha*. I submit that the Torah, by doing so, is sending us a strong signal that, just as the *Kiddush Hashem* of the six days of Creation gave meaning to the original Shabbos, so too does our Shabbos achieve its sublime *kedusha* only if the preceding six days are permeated with acts of *Kiddush Hashem*.

This is our central thesis, namely that (1) Shabbos is not a standalone holy day, but is inextricably linked with our behavior during the first six days of the week, and (2) the fact that Shabbos is in a category of its own in the realm of *mitzvos* is precisely because *Kiddush Hashem* is the very reason G-d created the world, and Shabbos, as we have discussed in detail, is a powerful symbol (אות) of our partnering with Hashem in suffusing the world with *Kiddush Hashem*.

Accordingly, as we direct ourselves towards Shabbos each week, our objective must be much more profound than merely earning a living or keeping busy. It is imperative that we work and interact with others generally in a manner which accomplishes the maximum *Kiddush Hashem* that we can achieve. Each of us, in the course of the work week, interacts with dozens if not hundreds of people – co-workers, clients, service workers, people on the street, family, friends, etc. In order for our *neshamos* to benefit from Shabbos in accordance with the true meaning and purpose of this very special day, it is imperative that each of the people with whom we interact is able to praise Hashem and the Torah on account of the way in which we conduct ourselves.

A COUNTEREXAMPLE

To use a specific example, which actually demonstrates the converse, I suggest that if a recent notorious Ponzi-schemer, who worked extremely hard during the first six days of the week destroying people's lives, had paused for Shabbos and scrupulously kept all its *halachos*, Shabbos for him would nevertheless have been a meaningless sham and travesty. His body would be at rest on Shabbos but the pure soul that he was given at birth, deeply mired now in *chillul Hashem*, would be in extreme turmoil, engaged in utter subversion of Hashem's purpose in creating the world. Similarly, Shabbos would be meaningless to a person who spends his or her entire week acting in a harsh and oppressive manner towards family, co-workers, or others. Another striking counterexample involved four accused drug-dealers who were scrupulous to shut down their operations on Shabbos.

HOW TO ACHIEVE TRUE MENUCHA ON SHABBOS

In sharp contrast, if a person manages to accomplish a *Kiddush Hashem* with every action, then such person's soul earns true *menucha* on Shabbos because such person, during the preceding six days, has accomplished Hashem's highest purpose. The Rambam states as follows (*Yesodei HaTorah* 5:11):

> If the *talmid chacham* does the reverse of the person who commits a *chillul Hashem* and shows a great deal of respect and courtesy to others; does business with *emuna*;

and is generally scrupulous in his performance of *mitz-vos*; all of which is done to a degree where he is loved and imitated, such person performs a *Kiddush Hashem* and it is about such a person that the *pasuk* in Isaiah refers when it says (Isaiah 49:3):

ויאמר לי עבדי אתה ישראל אשר בך אתפאר.
"And you are My servant Israel in whom I am glorified."

PROOF OF OUR THESIS FROM THE SHABBOS TEFILLOS

The Shabbos *tefillos* support our thesis and provide us with strong evidence that Shabbos was designed specifically for a person who is a walking *Kiddush Hashem*. Although the text of the four *Shemoneh Esrei tefillos* of Shabbos (*Maariv*, *Shacharis*, *Musaf*, and *Mincha*) vary from each other, the following words are common to all four:

וינוחו בו ישראל מקדשי שמך.
Those of Bnei Yisrael who are engaged in *Kiddush Hashem* will have *menucha* on Shabbos.

This *tefillah* could simply have stated וינוחו בו ישראל, omitting מקדשי שמך, but that would not be factual. I submit that this *tefillah* reflects the fact that the only way for a person's soul (as opposed to their body) to have *menucha* on Shabbos is for such person to be regularly engaged in *Kiddush Hashem* during the week.

✺ EXPLAINING VARIOUS SHABBOS MYSTERIES

With this construct, we can solve many of the Shabbos mysteries we have been discussing.

(1)   Power to bring Moshiach: The Midrash says that Moshiach would come if all of Bnei Yisrael kept two Shabbosim properly. We suggested that keeping Shabbos is much more than observing the *halachos* of the Shabbos day itself in that it also

requires making a *Kiddush Hashem* every step along the way during the week. Accordingly, if every single Jew kept two Shabbosim in a row, it would mean that, for two weeks, every member of Bnei Yisrael throughout the world would act in such a manner as to create a constant *Kiddush Hashem*. The Midrash is telling us, I believe, that the impact on our world would be so enormous that we would be instantly deserving of Moshiach.

(2) *Shir Shel Yom*: We can also now understand why the *Shir Shel Yom* is linked to Shabbos. This is a strong reminder to ourselves that we are partners with Hashem in bringing *Kiddush Hashem* to the world and that each weekday fulfilling this mission propels us towards the holiness of the upcoming Shabbos.

(3) Shabbos as part of the *Aseres HaDibros*; Shabbos weighed against all other *mitzvos*: The reason why Shabbos was chosen as part of the *Aseres HaDibros* and why Shabbos is weighed against all of the other *mitzvos* is one and the same and should be evident now from our discussion. It's all about the paramount impact of *Kiddush Hashem*. Shabbos is not an isolated day of observance but embodies daily observance of each of the Torah's *mitzvos*.

(4) Mitzvah reserved exclusively for the Jews; Shabbos as bride: We also asked why Shabbos is reserved for the Jews, despite the fact that the Creation of the world is a universal event. We now see, however, that observance of Shabbos is integrally tied to being *Mekadesh Shem Shomayim* during the week. And we know that it is specifically the Jewish people who were granted the unique mission of being a ממלכת כהנים וגוי קדוש (Shemos 19:6) and to be an אור לגוים – a light unto the nations (Isaiah 49:6), to spread *Kiddush Hashem* throughout the world. So this nicely explains why Shabbos is a uniquely Jewish mitzvah and also why Shabbos is considered the bride of Bnei Yisrael.

(5) *Yetzias Mitzrayim* and Shabbos: We can also now understand why Rashi, when explaining the Torah's connecting *Yetzias Mitzrayim* and Shabbos, states that Hashem took us out of Mitzrayim so that we would observe *all the mitzvos* (not just Shabbos). We know that the enslavement in Mitzrayim, as painful as it was, had the effect of refining our national charac-

ter (see reference to *kur habarzel*, the iron furnace, in Devarim 4:20). The Torah tells us a number of times to be compassionate in our observance of specific *mitzvos* (e.g., loving the convert, treating the disadvantaged such as a widow with compassion) by remembering our own subservient position in Mitzrayim. Since an integral aspect of performing *Kiddush Hashem* properly during the week consists of how we treat those who are vulnerable, and since such behavior is what makes or breaks the way we enter Shabbos, we can now better understand the connection between *Yetzias Mitzrayim* and Shabbos.

(6)   Reward and Punishment: We asked why there is endless reward for observing Shabbos and such great punishment for *chillul* Shabbos. Given that Shabbos is really all about accomplishing the very mission for which Hashem put us on this earth, we can understand why the reward and punishment associated with Shabbos are each so extreme.

(7)   Why Celebrate Resting Rather than Creation: As we have seen, Shabbos in fact is far more than just resting. Shabbos commemorates not only the *Kiddush Hashem* of Creation but also our perpetuation of this *Kiddush Hashem* on a daily basis.

(8)   Person who is not working: Since all people have many opportunities during the week to be *mekadesh shem shomayim*, it is apparent that working is not a pre-requisite to achieving, by the onset of Shabbos, the *menucha* of knowing that such person has conducted himself or herself impeccably during the week.

(9)   Shmitta: We wondered why the Torah referred to the *shmitta* year as Shabbos. The *shmitta* year, if observed properly, constitutes testimony of G-d's miraculous accomplishment in the sixth year, when the Torah promises us the land will produce food in extraordinary abundance. Those who cease working the land in the *shmitta* year highlight the *Kiddush Hashem* so manifest by the wonders of the sixth year. I suggest that the *shmitta* year is called Shabbos precisely because the resting of the land for a full year, a practice unique among the world's farmers, gives eloquent testimony to Hashem's miraculous powers, just as our resting on Shabbos is testimony to the *Kiddush Hashem* of Creation itself and the *Kiddush Hashem* we perform during the week. By contrast, a farmer who works

the land in the *shmitta* year in effect presents false testimony that nothing unusual occurred in the sixth year and, by doing so, subverts Hashem's great miracles of the sixth year. Presumably, this is why the Torah, in the *tochacha* of Bechukosai, singles out the transgression of *shmitta* for special mention as the cause of the most dire consequences for Bnei Yisrael.

(10) Manna: We asked why the Shabbos test of the *manna* became one of the ten tests of Bnei Yisrael in the desert, featured so prominently in the Torah, considering that Bnei Yisrael for all practical purposes had all their needs provided for them at such time and did no real work from which they needed to rest. The answer, I suggest, is similar to that of *shmitta*. Just as not working the land in the *shmitta* year is testimony to the miraculous produce of the sixth year, so too with the *manna*, where not venturing out on Shabbos is testimony to the miraculous double portion of the sixth day. The *lechem mishneh* of each Shabbos meal reminds us to this very day that the essence of Shabbos is *Kiddush Hashem*.

THE HALACHOS AND MINHAGIM OF THE SHABBOS DAY

PURPOSE OF THE HEIGHTENED STATE OF PHYSICAL AND SPIRITUAL JOY ON SHABBOS

Now that we understand that the Shabbos day derives meaning only from our acting during the week in a manner which maximizes *Kiddush Hashem*, what do we make of the Shabbos day itself? I would suggest that the *halachos* and *minhagim* of the Shabbos day are designed to maximize both our physical and spiritual joy (far beyond mere abstention from work) in order to serve the following purposes:

(1) Ensure that Shabbos represents a day that itself spreads *Kiddush Hashem* by demonstrating to all the virtual *Olam HaBo*-like peace and tranquility brought about by (a) our complete removal from the financial and other worries of this world; (b) instituting what is in effect a family day, and (c)

the multiple spiritual pursuits of *tefillah*, *zemiros* and Torah learning.[2]

(2)   Reward us greatly for being a partner with Hashem during our activity of the prior six days in spreading *Kiddush Hashem* far and wide.

(3)   Refresh us for the upcoming week so that we can accomplish our important goals with renewed vigor and enthusiasm.

MAXIMIZING PHYSICAL ENJOYMENT

So much has been written about Shabbos as a day of rest that it is easy to lose sight of the extent to which our *halachos* and *minhagim* go to ensure that our physical enjoyment generally, of which rest is only one of many components, is maximized on Shabbos.

If, as we have been discussing, a Jew's objective is to maximize *Kiddush Hashem* during the week, it seems that Hashem returns the favor by going to surprising lengths to ensure that such person's physical and spiritual enjoyment on Shabbos is maximized. Let us review some specific examples of this:

Food and Drink

The Gemara tells us that a person's allocation of his or her annual income, which is made on Rosh Hashana, does not apply when it comes to expenditures made for the honor of Shabbos. The Gemara states (*Beitza* 16a):

ואם הוסיף, מוסיפין לו.

If a person increases his Shabbos expenditures, such person's assets will be increased accordingly.

And just in case a person thinks that his or her limited capacity for food and drink places a cap on such person's enjoyment of Shabbos

---

2. This aspect of Shabbos gives us a new slant on the Torah words ביני ובין בני ישראל אות הוא לעולם, which are usually translated as "Shabbos is an eternal sign between G-d and the Jews," but I believe אות הוא לעולם can also be construed to mean that Shabbos is a sign for the entire world as to our exclusive and special role as a ממלכת כהנים וגוי קדוש.

food, Hashem takes care of that as well. The Talmud states as follows (*Beitza* 16a):

אמר ר' שמעון בן לקיש נשמה יתירה נותן הקדוש ברוך הוא באדם ערב
שבת, ולמוצאי שבת נוטלין אותה הימנו.

Rav Shimon ben Lakish stated that Hashem injects a *neshama yeseira* into a person at the outset of Shabbos and then removes it when Shabbos is over.

One would think that the *neshama yeseira* is an added spiritual dimension but Rashi provides a very surprising explanation:

רוחב לב למנוחה ולשמחה ולהיות פתוח לרווחה ויאכל וישתה ואין נפשו
קצה עליו.

Neshama yeseira is the capacity to eat and drink in much greater quantities than one is accustomed, without the body being repulsed by these amounts [loosely translated].

There are a number of *midrashim* and *halachos* which place very great emphasis on the merits of eating three meals on Shabbos, and particularly *seuda shlishis*. *A priori*, one could wonder why the halacha is force-feeding a person, so to speak. But it may well be that our eating *seuda shlishis* is so praiseworthy because it constitutes our acknowledgement of Hashem's miracle of the *neshama yeseira*.

Other Ways that Halacha Works to Maximize Our Physical Enjoyment and Mental Relaxation on Shabbos

There are so many other ways that halacha works to maximize our physical enjoyment and mental relaxation on Shabbos and we will briefly review a number of them:

- Minimizing personal requests in *tefillah*: The Midrash Tanchuma (Vayera 1) explains why we omit on Shabbos the middle blessings of the *Shemoneh Esrei*:

  The [other] twelve blessings are all for man's needs. Therefore, we do not pray eighteen [blessings] on Shab-

bos, because if one has a sick person in his house, he will
be mindful of him during the *bracha* of *Refa'einu* and will
feel distressed, for Shabbos was given to Bnei Yisrael for
holiness, pleasure, and tranquility and not for suffering.

- Clean house (table set, etc.), clean and groomed body, clean
clothes: No need to elaborate here, as everyone is familiar with
these *halachos*, including the objective if possible to have finer
clothes and utensils dedicated to Shabbos.
- Visiting the sick: One must use tempered language when visiting
the sick on Shabbos so as to keep the conversation as upbeat as
possible (*Shabbos* 12a).
- Marital relations on Shabbos: The Gemara (*Kesuvos* 62b) states
that Rav Yehuda said in the name of Shmuel that the conjugal
obligation of a *talmid chacham* is from one Friday night to the other
because, as Rashi explains, this is an evening of pleasure and rest.
- Shabbos gait: Even the way in which we walk needs to be tem-
pered on Shabbos (*Shabbos* 113a).
- Shabbos conversation: Shabbos conversation should be on a higher
plane than weekday conversation (*Shabbos* 113a, b).
- Refraining from weekday thoughts: A person is supposed to
refrain not only from work but also from thinking about work
(*Yalkut*, Yisro 296).
- Sleep: Sleep on Shabbos is a special pleasure (Aruch Hashulchan,
Shabbos 281:1).
- *Aveilus*: Public *aveilus* is not permitted on Shabbos (*Moed Katan* 24a).

SPIRITUAL PURSUITS ON SHABBOS

It makes perfect sense that Shabbos cannot be viewed solely in terms
of maximization of physical pleasures. The Talmud Yerushalmi (*Shabbos* 15:3) says that Shabbos was given to us not only to indulge in food
and drink, but also to be steeped in Torah learning.

Me'ein Olam HaBo

The Talmud (*Berachos* 57b) says that Shabbos is מעין עולם הבא – a fac-
simile of *Olam HaBo*. I believe we can understand this description in
light of what we have learned so far about various aspects of Shabbos,
namely (1) removal, as much as possible, from preoccupation with

stressful matters such as, but not exclusively, those which are work-related; (2) maximum physical pleasure, enhanced by the *neshama yeseira*; (3) various spiritual pursuits, including learning of Torah, extra *tefillos*, *zemiros*, and family time, and (4) important changes in our environment, including a clean body, neat house, special clothes, different manner of walking and conversation.

But the important underpinning to all these features, I believe, and what truly makes Shabbos into a מעין עולם הבא, is if we have partnered with Hashem during the week and maximized *Kiddush Hashem* to the best of our abilities. This is what makes Shabbos so special and so unique and why Shabbos is the only mitzvah which permits us to achieve such lofty spiritual heights, almost as if we were sitting side by side with Hashem, proclaiming true satisfaction with our activities of the prior week.

☙ CONCLUSION

Our thesis in this *d'var* is that Shabbos is a mitzvah of enormous importance precisely because it represents our fulfillment, during the entire week, of Hashem's primary objective of filling this world with *Kiddush Hashem*. I believe that the incredible reward for observing Shabbos reflects the overriding significance of this objective. We earlier discussed the Rambam's remarkable statement that "Every person who observes Shabbos in accordance with halacha, and honors and makes the Shabbos as pleasurable as possible according to his power, such person's reward in this world is greater than the hidden reward of *Olam HaBo*." We will now conclude with a number of other descriptions of the extreme rewards for Shabbos observance:

Pesikta Rabbati 23

כל שהוא מתענג בשבת שואל והקב״ה נותן לו משאלותיו.
Whoever makes the Shabbos a delight, makes a request and Hashem fulfills it.

Mechilta Beshalach 16

אם תזכו לשמור את השבת עתיד הקב״ה ליתן לכם ו׳ מידות טובות: א״יי
ועוה״ב ועולם חדש, ומלכות דוד, וכהונה, ולוייה.
If you keep Shabbos, Hashem will give you six good

measures: Eretz Yisrael, *Olam HaBo*, New World [presumably this refers to ימות המשיח], the kingdom of David, the privileged status of Kohen, and Levi.

Tanchuma Bereishis 3

כבוד שבת עדיף מאלף תעניות.

The honor of Shabbos is more worthy than 1,000 fast days.

Shabbos 118a

כל המענג את השבת נותנין לו נחלה בלי מצרים.

Whoever makes the Shabbos a delight is granted a limitless heritage.

Shabbos 119a

[עשירים] שבשאר ארצות במה הן זוכין, א״ל בשביל שמכבדין את השבת.

What makes the wealthy in lands outside Eretz Yisrael deserve the wealth [since they cannot give *maaser* as can those in Eretz Yisrael, who get wealthy from giving this *tzedaka*]? Because they honor the Shabbos.

Mechilta Ki Tisa 1:4

כל המשמר שבת אחת כתקנה, מעלה עליו הכתוב כאילו שימר שבתות מיום שברא הקב״ה את עולמו עד שיחיו מתים.

Any person who keeps one Shabbos properly is regarded as if he kept every single Shabbos from the time of Creation until תחיית המתים.

It is clear that Shabbos is a truly remarkable day, and I hope that by our delving into its essence, the observance and honoring of Shabbos will be more meaningful to all of us.

ROSH CHODESH: UNRAVELING THE MYSTERIES OF A MOST SIGNIFICANT DAY ෨෴

෴ INTRODUCTION

In the course of my preparation for this *d'var*, I discovered that Rosh Chodesh appears to be a day of great mystery and, in fact, may be one of the least understood of *mitzvos*, particularly considering its importance.

I hope that this *d'var*, to the extent it helps explain the profound significance of Rosh Chodesh, will make this very special mitzvah much more meaningful for each of us. Many ideas which I will present are original, so far as I am aware, and I am very grateful to the kindness of Hashem for permitting me to gain some insight into this topic. I hope that you will enjoy the exhilaration of discovery as much as I did during my preparation.

Our subject is a bit complex. So this may be a good time to keep in mind the traditional saying of our *Chachamim*: לפום צערא אגרא, which means that the reward for Torah learning is directly proportional to the effort. I will begin this *d'var* the same way I started thinking about this topic – by focusing on different aspects of Rosh Chodesh which seem to be very puzzling.

In order to frame our discussion, let us start with eight questions.

(1) CONNECTION BETWEEN ROSH CHODESH AND PESACH

The first question, appropriately enough, centers on the seemingly close connection of Rosh Chodesh to Pesach and to *Yetzias Mitzrayim*. We see this in two ways. First of all, G-d apparently felt that the mitzvah of Rosh Chodesh, represented by the words החדש הזה לכם, in Parshas Bo, had to be the first mitzvah given to Bnei Yisrael just as they were about to leave Mitzrayim, and could not wait even a mere two months until the Torah was given to us. This fact must surely have great significance.

Secondly, there is a statement in the Haggadah which clearly links the *mitzvos* of Haggadah and Rosh Chodesh. Immediately following the discussion with the Four Sons, we read:

> יכול מראש חדש, תלמוד לומר ביום ההוא.
> We would have thought that the mitzvah of Haggadah
> – the retelling of the story of *Yetzias Mitzrayim* – should
> begin on Rosh Chodesh (Nisan). Therefore, the Torah
> has to use specific words (ביום ההוא) to tell us that the
> mitzvah of Haggadah is to be performed on the first day
> of Pesach.

Now, you might ask, why would we have thought that the retelling of *Yetzias Mitzrayim* should begin on Rosh Chodesh? Rav Yosef Dov Soloveitchik, *zt"l*, in his Haggadah, asks this question and answers that the miracle of *Yetzias Mitzrayim* began on Rosh Chodesh. But he does not elaborate and so we are still looking for an explanation.

(2) YOM KIPPUR KATAN

Our second question relates to Yom Kippur Katan. While we tend to think of Rosh Chodesh as a one- or two-day event, in reality our observance of Rosh Chodesh begins with special *tefillos* on the preceding Shabbos – which we call Shabbos Mevarchim – and concludes with *Kiddush Levana* several days after Rosh Chodesh.

While we are all familiar with Shabbos Mevarchim and *Kiddush Levana*, not many are familiar with a *minhag* known as Yom Kippur Katan, observed by some, on the afternoon preceding Rosh Chodesh, with fasting and special *tefillos*. In this regard, let me read an excerpt from an email I received on December 1, 2000 from Midreshet Moriah, the seminary in Yerushalayim which one of my daughters then attended:

> A day that has seldom been noted on the calendar is Erev
> Rosh Chodesh . . . In halacha, it is seen as a mini Yom

Kippur. This year, because of the *matzav* [the difficult situation], many – both in Israel and in *Chutz la'Aretz* – kept this day as a partial fast, with *Selichot* said at *Mincha* time. Midreshet Moriah students joined the many who came to the Kotel on Monday afternoon for the Seder Yom Kippur Katan that was called by the Chief Rabbis and many prominent Rabbanim.

The significance of Yom Kippur Katan, and indeed the very fact that the observance of Rosh Chodesh has the name Yom Kippur attached to it, is another of the many mysteries related to Rosh Chodesh.

(3) MIDRASH – החדש הזה לכם ראש חדשים

A third Rosh Chodesh mystery centers on a fascinating Gemara on the *pasuk* in Shemos (12:2) which introduces the mitzvah of Rosh Chodesh. The *pasuk* reads, in part:

החדש הזה לכם ראש חדשים.

This month shall be for you the head of the months.

The Gemara (*Menachos* 29a) focuses on the use of the word הזה. As paraphrased by Rashi:

נתקשה משה על מולד הלבנה, באיזו שיעור תראה ותהיה ראויה לקדש
והראה לו באצבע את הלבנה ברקיע ואמר לו כזה ראה וקדש.

The literal translation of this Gemara is as follows:

Moshe had difficulty understanding the configuration of the new moon [meaning its size and shape]. So Hashem had to point out the new moon to Moshe with Hashem's Finger, and Hashem said to Moshe: "When you see the moon in this configuration, you shall sanctify it."

The Gemara lists two other things which Moshe had "difficulty" understanding and for which Moshe therefore required Hashem's assistance, namely, the Menorah and the *shemona shratzim* (the eight rodents enumerated in Vayikra [11:29, 30] which cause impurity).

All of the commentators which I have seen on this Gemara interpret it literally, in other words that Moshe really had difficulty conceptualizing the new moon, the Menorah, and the *shemona shratzim*,
and that Hashem had to somehow, presumably through the use of
visual aids, clarify Moshe's understanding of these items. There are,
however, many problems with interpreting the Gemara in this literal
manner:

(1) First of all, does it really stand to reason that, of all the *halachos*
     (many of which are very complex) which Moshe was taught
     at Har Sinai, these were the only three that were so difficult
     that Hashem had to give Moshe special instruction?

(2) Secondly, if we believe that Moshe had difficulty visualizing
     the appearance of the new moon, how is it possible that, there-
     after, down through the ages, any admissible witness could
     testify as to the appearance of the new moon – no special
     expertise was required?

(3) And why should the identity of the *shemona shratzim* be any
     more difficult a concept than the identity of the many other
     kosher and non-kosher animals and birds mentioned in the
     Torah?

Moreover, what is the significance of Hashem showing Moshe the
new moon with His אצבע (Finger)? Why could the Midrash simply not
have said that Hashem showed Moshe the new moon?

So, the deeper meaning of this Gemara is another mystery regarding Rosh Chodesh, to be added to those mysteries we noted
earlier – namely, the significance of Yom Kippur Katan as well as the
connection between Rosh Chodesh and Pesach.

(4) ROSH CHODESH AND WOMEN

A fourth question: Why is Rosh Chodesh a particularly significant
day for women? The Aruch Hashulchan states (*Hilchos Rosh Chodesh*
417:10):

רי״ח מותר במלאכה, והנשים שנוהגות שלא לעשות מלאכה בר״ח איתא
בירושלמי פי״א דתענית ובפרקי דר״א, שהוא מנהג טוב לפי שלא רצו ליתן
נזמיהן לבעליהן על עשיית העגל לפיכך ניתנה להן תוספת יו״ט בר״ח.

It is permitted to work on Rosh Chodesh, but women

have a custom not to work on Rosh Chodesh. The Yerushalmi Gemara states that this is a worthy *minhag*, because the women were unwilling to give their jewelry to their husbands for the purpose of building the *egel*, the Golden Calf, and that is why they were given an additional Yom Tov on Rosh Chodesh.

The Yerushalmi does not, however, explain why halacha seems to connect Rosh Chodesh with the refusal of the women to participate in *chet ha'egel* and so we add this question to our list.

(5) שבכל דור ודור עומדים עלינו לכלותינו

Another puzzle which we will try to solve in this *d'var*, although its relationship to Rosh Chodesh is not immediately apparent, is the statement in the Haggadah:

שבכל דור ודור עומדים עלינו לכלותינו.
In each generation they attempt to destroy us.

Why is this statement included in the Haggadah at all, since it seems to completely undermine our celebration of freedom by highlighting the fact that the slavery of Mitzrayim was only the first in a long line of attempts to destroy us – attempts which continue to this very day.

(6) חוקי ראשי חדשים

Our sixth question: Why, in the *Musaf* for Rosh Chodesh, do we refer to חוקי ראשי חדשים, which literally means that the laws of Rosh Chodesh are *chukim*, with no stated or obvious purpose?

(7) HALLEL

Our seventh question relates to *Hallel* which, the Mishna Berura tells us, is only a *minhag* on Rosh Chodesh. Why indeed do we say *Hallel* on Rosh Chodesh and why is it only a *minhag* to do so? And why do we only say half-*Hallel* on Rosh Chodesh?

(8) WHY A LUNAR CALENDAR

And finally, we note that the entire concept of Rosh Chodesh, and the lunar calendar upon which it is based, appears to be dysfunctional and illogical, since Rosh Chodesh is the mechanism by which we establish the Yomim Tovim, yet the occurrence of the Yomim Tovim are governed by the solar calendar. To illustrate, the Aruch Hashulchan, at the very beginning of *Hilchos Rosh Chodesh* states (417:2):

> והשנים שאנו מחשבים בהם הם שני החמה, שנאמר בפסח חדש האביב
> ובשבועות כתיב חג הקציר ובסכות כתיב חג האסיף וגידול התבואות
> וקצירתן ואסיפתן אינו תלויה רק בחדשי החמה שבחמה תלויה השתנות
> העיתים, הקור והחום הקיץ והחורף.

> We reckon holidays according to the solar year, as it says, in connection with Pesach, Chodesh HaAviv (spring time), and in connection with Shavuos, Chag HaKatzir (the holiday of gathering the fruit), and in connection with Sukkos, Chag HaAsif (the holiday of gathering the crops). The timing of the seasons and of the growth and gathering of fruit and other crops, are all dependent only upon the sun.

So, our eighth question is: Why did Hashem impose upon us a lunar year, with Rosh Chodesh marking the beginning of each lunar month, when our Yomim Tovim are dependent only upon the sun and when a lunar calendar system only forces us to be forever scrambling, by having to add a month every two or three years, to adjust our calendar to catch up to the solar year, so that the Yomim Tovim occur in their proper season?

To quickly recap our eight questions:

(1)   Why the close connection between Rosh Chodesh and Pesach, as evidenced by the mitzvah of Rosh Chodesh being given to us just before we left Mitzrayim and by the words of the Haggadah יכול מראש חדש?

(2)   What is Yom Kippur Katan all about and how is it related to Rosh Chodesh?

(3)   How do we understand the Midrash of החדש הזה לכם, which implies that Moshe had difficulty with the concept of the new

moon and certain other concepts, none of which seem to be uniquely difficult?

(4)   Why were women rewarded with Rosh Chodesh as a special holiday?

(5)   Why do we seemingly undermine our celebration at the Pesach Seder by stating that in every generation our enemies try to destroy us?

(6)   Why are the laws of Rosh Chodesh referred to in our *tefillos* as *chukim*?

(7)   Why do we say *Hallel* on Rosh Chodesh, why is it only a *minhag*, and why only half-*Hallel*?

(8)   Why do we need a lunar calendar at all since the timing of our Yomim Tovim is based upon the seasons, which are governed by the sun?

These questions will not really be answered until the end of this *d'var*, when it hopefully all comes together.

❧ MIDRASHIM AND HALACHOS REGARDING ROSH CHODESH

I would like to now review several *midrashim* and *halachos* which will provide a very intriguing overview of the deep significance of the mitzvah of Rosh Chodesh.

MIDRASHIM

The Gemara (*Sanhedrin* 42a) gives us two very strong statements which highlight the special importance of Rosh Chodesh:

אמר ר' יוחנן, כל המברך על החדש בזמנו כאילו מקבל פני שכינה.

Rav Yochanan stated, "Whoever blesses the new moon in a timely way, it is as if such person has greeted the Shechina."

Very few *mitzvos* have such a dramatic description describing the performance of the mitzvah. The Gemara then continues with an even more powerful statement regarding Rosh Chodesh, one which is incorporated into the *tefillah* of *Kiddush Levana*:

תנא דבי רבי ישמעאל אילמלא לא זכו ישראל אלא להקביל פני אביהן
שבשמים כל חדש וחדש דיים.

Rebbe Yishmael taught the following: "If Bnei Yisrael did nothing more than greet their Father in Heaven once a month, this would be sufficient."

Rashi, commenting on the word דיים, offers this astonishing explanation of the Gemara:

אילו לא זכו למצוה אחרת אלא לזו.

It would be sufficient if we had no mitzvah other than this one.

Even with the *mitzvos* of *Talmud Torah* and *yishuv Eretz Yisrael*, which the Gemara tells us are each equivalent to all of the other *mitzvos*, we are not told that it would be sufficient if we had no other mitzvah. Why is Rosh Chodesh so special?

HALACHOS OF ROSH CHODESH

Aside from the *midrashim* we just learnt, the *halachos* and *minhagim* of Rosh Chodesh also reflect the special character of this mitzvah. One of the most astounding of these *halachos* is that, in the times of the Beis HaMikdosh (when the new moon was established through witnesses), witnesses who saw the new moon on Shabbos were permitted to violate Shabbos in order to reach Beis Din in a timely manner (Rambam *Hilchos Kiddush HaChodesh* 3:2). The significance of this halacha is highlighted all the more when we realize that there is no assurance that the testimony of these witnesses would have even been accepted or necessary (in which case their violation of Shabbos would have been for naught), firstly because, after questioning by Beis Din, their testimony may have been rejected, and secondly, because of the possibility that other witnesses may have preceded them.

And the Ramoh, in an amazing statement which is rarely focused upon, states in a halacha to which we will return later in more detail (*Hilchos Rosh Chodesh* 426:2):

עושין שמחות וריקודין בקידוש החדש דוגמת שמחת נשואין.

We organize *simchas* and dancing during *Kiddush Ha-Chodesh* just like we do at a wedding reception.

Rabbi Abraham Chill, in his *sefer* on *minhagim*,[1] in discussing the reasons behind various *mitzvos*, quotes the Vilna Gaon for the *minhag* that the clothes worn on Rosh Chodesh should be more festive than those worn on regular weekdays. The source for this *minhag* is given as the *pasuk* in Bamidbar (10:10):

וביום שמחתכם ובמועדיכם ובראשי חדשכם.
On your joyful days, holidays, and Rosh Chodesh.

In this important *pasuk*, we see that Rosh Chodesh, by juxtaposition, is compared to the other Yomim Tovim, although we have not yet explained why this should be so.

In ספר מנהג ישראל תורה, a compendium by Rav Yosef HaLevi of *halachos*, *minhagim*, and responsa, the author notes that the Vilna Gaon wore his Shabbos hat on Rosh Chodesh.

The Kitzur Shulchan Aruch (97:2) notes the following halacha:

מצוה להרבות בסעודה בראש חדש ואם חל בשבת יעשה תבשיל אחד יותר מבשאר שבתות.

It is a mitzvah to increase the number of one's meals on Rosh Chodesh, and if Rosh Chodesh falls on Shabbos [when we already have our full quota of meals], it is a mitzvah to prepare one cooked food over and above what a person would normally eat on Shabbos.

And Rav Yosef HaLevi states in the second part of his *sefer* (para. 419) that, although there is no obligation to eat bread on Rosh Chodesh, it is nevertheless a mitzvah to do so and he quotes one *posek* who goes so far as to say that a person should eat the Rosh Chodesh meal with a *lechem mishneh* (419:1), in order to give the meal greater significance than a regular weekday meal, and that it should also be eaten with particular respect, as on Shabbos and Yom Tov. He also quotes another Rav who states that it is appropriate to glorify the Rosh Chodesh meal with meat and fish (419:1). The author then refers to a *minhag* in one country where they would light candles the night of Rosh Chodesh, just like on Shabbos (419:3).

---

1. Rabbi Abraham Chill, *The Minhagim: The Customs and Ceremonies of Judaism, Their Origins, and Rationale* (Sepher Hermon: 1978), 470.

And, as we know, Rosh Chodesh is marked by *Yaaleh V'yavo*, *Hallel*, and *Musaf*.

So we see from the *midrashim* and *halachos* we have just reviewed, that Rosh Chodesh has a very unique and special status. I would now like to begin our analysis of this mitzvah.

✺ GEMARA IN CHULLIN

In order to help us understand the special character of Rosh Chodesh, I would like to analyze an incredibly fascinating, and very symbolic, Gemara (*Chullin* 60b), which discusses the creation of the sun and the moon. The *pasuk* on which this Gemara is based, reads as follows (Bereishis 1:16):

> ויעש אלקים את־שני המאורות הגדולים את־המאור הגדול לממשלת
> היום ואת המאור הקטן לממשלת הלילה, ואת הכוכבים.
> And Hashem made the two great luminaries, the great
> luminary to rule during the day and the small luminary
> to rule at night, and the stars.

The Gemara has the following intriguing and well-known discussion of this *pasuk*:

> רבי שמעון בן פזי רמי . . . כתיב את־שני המאורות הגדלים וכתיב את־
> המאור הגדל ואת המאור הקטן אמר ירח לפני הקב״ה, רבש״ע, וכי אפשר
> לשני מלכים שישתמשו בכתר אחד אמרה לה, לכי ומעטי את עצמך.
> Rebbe Shimon ben Pazi asks, "It states: 'the *two great* lu-
> minaries' and then the *pasuk* refers to 'the great luminary
> and the small luminary.'"

In other words, there is an obvious contradiction between the beginning and the end of the *pasuk* – is it "two great luminaries" or is it "the great luminary and the small luminary"?

Rebbe Shimon ben Pazi then explains the contradiction:

> רבש״ע, וכי אפשר לשני מלכים שישתמשו בכתר אחד?
> The moon approached Hashem and said, "Ribbono Shel

Olam, is it possible for two kings to rule under the same crown?"

Whereupon Hashem said to the moon:

לכי ומעטי את עצמך.
Go and make yourself smaller.

Now, as a noteworthy aside, it is very puzzling to note that many have interpreted this Midrash as a lesson regarding the evils of arrogance. A common line of interpretation is that the moon was arrogant for not accepting its equal status with the sun and that Hashem symbolically taught the moon a lesson by making the moon smaller.

Respectfully, it seems almost inconceivable that this Gemara has anything to do with the notion of arrogance. First of all, this explanation is completely inconsistent with the Gemara's recitation, cited below, of Hashem's solicitous attempts to console the moon. Secondly, if the moon were truly a symbol of arrogance – a character trait analogous in our tradition to worshiping *avoda zara* – it would make no sense for us to sanctify the moon each month, in very special ceremonies spanning a number of days.

So, if the issue is not arrogance, what is the symbolism in this Midrash? Let's get back to the Gemara. We were at the point where Hashem tells the moon:

לכי ומעטי את עצמך.
Go and make yourself smaller.

The Gemara continues:

אמרה לפניו רשב"ע הואיל ואמרתי לפניך דבר הגון, אמעיט את עצמי.
The moon responded, "Ribbono Shel Olam, just because I said something appropriate, should I now go and *'mima'et'* myself?"

אמר לה, לכי ומשול ביום ובלילה.
So Hashem said, "Go rule during both the day and at night."

אמרה ליה, מאי רבותיה דשרגא בטיהרא מאי אהני.
The moon responded [to the suggestion that the moon also shine during the day], "What use is a candle when there is lots of light?"

In other words, the moon's light makes no impact when it shines during the day.

A couple of lines later, the Gemara continues:

זיל ליקרו צדיקי בשמיך, יעקב הקטן, שמואל הקטן, דוד הקטן.

So, Hashem said, "Go and have the Tzaddikim called in your name, as it says, יעקוב הקטן, שמואל הקטן, דוד הקטן."

[This is a reference to the advice to the moon to make itself smaller.]

חזייה דלא קא מיתבא דעתה.

Hashem saw [after several attempts] that the moon was not appeased.

אמר הקב"ה הביאו כפרה עלי שמיעטתי את הירח.

So Hashem said, "Bring a *korban* as atonement for Me for being '*mima'et*' the moon."

Now, to understand the last part of this Gemara, we have to understand that a שעיר (male goat) is brought on each Yom Tov as atonement for Bnei Yisrael. As the Torah, in Parshas Pinchas, describes its purpose: לכפר עליכם (to act as atonement for you). However, in the case of Rosh Chodesh, the words לכפר עליכם are not used. Instead, the Torah tells us, almost unbelievably, that the שעיר of Rosh Chodesh is intended as a חטאת לד' (Bamidbar 28:16), which means, as the Gemara explains it, an atonement for Hashem. And so the Gemara concludes:

והיינו דאמר ר"ש בן לקיש מה נשתנה שעיר של ראש חדש, שנאמר בו לד', אמר הקב"ה, שעיר זה יהא כפרה על שמיעטתי את הירח.

And this is what Rebbe Shimon ben Lakish said, "How is the *korban* of Rosh Chodesh different, since it says חטאת לד', a sin-offering for G-d, and the answer is that Hashem said that 'this *korban* will constitute atonement for Me, in that I was *mima'et* the moon.'"

This idea, namely that we bring a *korban* on Rosh Chodesh as atonement for Hashem is (aside from utterly dispelling the notion that the moon was punished on account of its "arrogance"), I believe, one of the most astounding statements that any of us have seen in the Talmud. In fact, this Gemara is so mysterious that Rash Lakish's statement, namely that the *korban* of Rosh Chodesh constitutes an atonement for Hashem, is addressed in a footnote (#15) in the Schottenstein Gemara, with the following comment:

> This puzzling statement is addressed by many commentators. What can "bringing an atonement for G-d" possibly mean?

THE NEW MOON AS A SYMBOL OF OUR REDEMPTION

Before we attempt to further analyze this Gemara, we should mention that there are a number of *midrashim* and *halachos* which portray the moon as symbolic of Bnei Yisrael, with the new moon heralding our ultimate redemption (analogously, the sun would represent the nations of the world). To illustrate, I would now like to turn back to two sources we touched on earlier:

We discussed Rebbe Yochanan's statement in *Sanhedrin*, that:

כל המברך על החדש בזמנו כאילו מקבל פני שכינה.

> Whoever blesses the new moon in a timely way, it is as if such person has greeted the Shechina.

The Maharsha elaborates on Rebbe Yochanan's statement with the following words:

וי"ל לפי שישראל בגלותן אין זוכין לראות פני שכינה ורחוקה מקבלתה אבל חידוש הלבנה הוא סימן לישראל שהם עתידין להתחדש כמותה לפאר ליוצרם בקיבול פני שכינה כמו שיורה על זה נוסח ברכת הלבנה ולזה כשאנו מברכין על החדש בזמנו שהוא סימן שאנו עתידין להתחדש כמותה והרי אנו כאילו מקבלין פני השכינה.

Rav Yochanan intends the following: Bnei Yisrael, in their exile, are far removed from the privilege of receiving the Shechina. However, the renewal of the moon is a sign to Bnei Yisrael that they will be renewed just as the moon, and they will be glorified in the greeting of the Shechina, just as is taught in the blessing of the new moon. And it is for this reason that blessing the new moon is likened to greeting of the Shechina.

And in a similar vein, it is worth quoting in full the striking statement of
the Ramoh (we earlier quoted the very last portion), likening the celebratory joy of *Kiddush Levana* to a wedding reception. The Ramoh states,
regarding the *tefillah* of *Kiddush Levana* (*Hilchos Rosh Chodesh* 426:2):

ונוהגין לומר דוד מלך ישראל חי וקיים, שמלכותו נמשל ללבנה, ועתיד
להתחדש כמותה, וכנסת ישראל תחזור להתדבק בבעלה, שהוא הקב"ה,
דוגמת הלבנה המתחדשת עם החמה . . . . , ולכן עושין שמחות ורקודין
בקידוש החדש דוגמת שמחת נשואין.

And our *minhag,* in *Kiddush Levana,* is to say דוד מלך ישראל
חי וקיים, because his kingdom [alluding to David HaMelech being the forefather of Moshiach] is compared to the
moon and will be renewed just like the moon. And Bnei
Yisrael will then once again be wedded to their Master,
and this is why we organize *simchas* and dancing during
Kiddush HaChodesh, just like we do at a wedding reception.

And so we see from these two great commentators, the Maharsha and
the Ramoh, that the blessing of the new moon is a very significant ceremony, likened to a wedding reception, because it marks the eventual
reunion between our people and our Creator.

In fact, there are very good reasons for the new moon to be a particularly appropriate symbol of our redemption. On Rosh Chodesh,
we see only a sliver of the new moon, and a person who has only
seen this sliver might have a difficult time visualizing the glorious
appearance of the full moon. Similarly for us as a people. For example,
as we know all too well from recent experience, as the Palestinian
rockets, bullets, and bombs are flying, we surely feel as if we can only
see the sliver of the new moon and, although we feel in our hearts
that our full moon of final redemption is inevitable, we have great
difficulty visualizing it.

✍ GEMARA IN CHULLIN (CONTINUATION OF ANALYSIS)

It is in this context that I would like to now turn back to the Gemara
in *Chullin* and offer the following interpretation:

Hashem originally created the sun and the moon of equal size, symbolizing that Bnei Yisrael and the other nations were intended to be equally dominant in this world. However, the moon (representing Bnei Yisrael) then approached Hashem and said: "How is it possible for two kings to serve under the same crown?"

I believe that this question (far from signifying, in any way, the moon's arrogance) is in fact a reference to the fundamental inconsistency between the values of the Torah and the values by which the other nations live. We all know the very famous Midrash about Hashem offering the Torah to each of the other nations of the world and that each rejected it because of some commandment in the Torah (such as not stealing or not committing adultery or not speaking *lashon hara*) which that particular nation felt was inconsistent with its character and would be impossible for it to abide by. Only Bnei Yisrael accepted the moral imperative of the Torah in its entirety.

So, perhaps, when the moon said that two kings cannot rule under the same crown, the moon's point was that if this world would be governed by the crown of Torah, then it could not possibly be ruled at the same time by the crown of the other nations of this world.

So Hashem said to the moon (meaning Bnei Yisrael), in response, לכי ומעטי עצמך (which means, literally, "Go and make yourself smaller"). What does this mean in the context of our discussion?

In order to better understand the concept of לכי ומעטי עצמך, we need to examine a *pasuk* (Devarim 7:7), which gives us a great deal of insight into the meaning of the word *mima'et* (literally, making something "small" or "few"), as this word is applied to Bnei Yisrael. In this *pasuk*, Hashem is speaking to Bnei Yisrael through Moshe and says:

לא מרבכם מכל־העמים חשק ד' בכם ויבחר בכם כי אתם המעט מכל־
העמים.

The literal translation is as follows:

> It is not because you were the largest of the nations that Hashem desired you and chose you, but because you were the smallest of the nations.

It is clear, however, that the literal translation of this *pasuk*, namely that Hashem prefers Bnei Yisrael because we are the fewest in number, is very problematic. First of all, it is far from certain that the Jews are the fewest in number – there are many other small nations and probably some that are smaller than we are. And, in any event, what if a nation is few in number but has an inferior, deficient character – will Hashem favor that nation just because it is small in numbers? And thirdly, if only numbers count, what about a nation that is not the smallest but the second smallest – isn't it also entitled to Hashem's favors?

Rashi, clearly recognizing that the word *mima'et* in this *pasuk* almost demands a non-literal meaning, offers a different and much more meaningful analysis of the word. Rashi explains the word *mima'et* as follows:

המממעטין עצמכם, כגון אברהם שאמר אנכי עפר ואפר, וכגון משה ואהרן שאמרו ואנחנו מה.²

A nation which minimizes its own importance, like Avraham Avinu, who said, "I am dust and ashes" and like Moshe and Aharon, who said "what are we."

So now we see that when Hashem told the moon, and symbolically to Bnei Yisrael, לכי ומעטי עצמך (go and make yourself smaller), He did not mean "make yourself smaller in size, or fewer in numbers," but rather "make yourself modest or humble."

Now, this leads us to ask several additional questions as to the meaning of the Gemara. First of all, why would Hashem's suggestion to become humble, which seems like a worthwhile suggestion as well as a meritorious characteristic to strive for, engender so much protest by the moon (i.e., Bnei Yisrael)? Secondly, why would this suggestion, for our nation to become humble, lead Hashem to be trying so hard, כביכול, to appease the moon, as we see in the Gemara? And why is the ultimate outcome of this dialogue that Hashem declares that the *sa'ir korban* of Rosh Chodesh would serve as an atonement for Hashem for making Bnei Yisrael become humble? And finally, what is the process by which Bnei Yisrael become humble?

In response, I would like to suggest the following thoughts: Homiletically, it was Hashem's initial intention to make the sun and the

---

2. Note the striking similarity of Rashi's words to Hashem's direction to the moon, represented by the words לכי ומעטי עצמך.

moon of equal size. This means that Bnei Yisrael and the nations of the world would each rule in this world. The moon, representing Bnei Yisrael, correctly argued that this was an impossibility, since the rule of Torah was by definition antithetical to the rule of the value systems practiced by the nations of the world. Hashem then said to the moon, OK, you will rule in the Messianic Era. However, this grand prize is not handed out for free but must be earned through a refinement of the national character of Bnei Yisrael. In other words, Bnei Yisrael must first be *mima'et* themselves, or become humble.

How does this happen? We all know, and many *midrashim* tell us, that, both on an individual and on a national level, prosperity and comfort breed haughtiness – the very antithesis of humility. As the Torah tells us (Devarim 32:15):

וישמן ישורון ויבעט.
Bnei Yisrael became comfortable (literally, fat) and rebelled.

And there are many other *pesukim* and *midrashim* to the same effect.

Accordingly, the unfortunate implication of what we just said is that the way to become humble is through the very opposite of success and comfort, namely oppression and suffering, which Bnei Yisrael have endured throughout history.

And this of course explains why the moon was so upset by Hashem's suggestion and why Hashem tried so hard to appease the moon.

And we can also now understand why none of Hashem's attempts at appeasing the moon worked because, after all, how is it possible to appease Bnei Yisrael for the suffering we have incurred through the ages, beginning with the slavery of Mitzrayim and right through to Nazi Germany, *yemach shemom*, and the Arabs today.

So in the end, when Hashem saw that no appeasement worked, He said:

שעיר זה יהא כפרה על שמיעטתי את הירח.

I suggest, homiletically, that this means that Bnei Yisrael have a legitimate complaint, so to speak, to Hashem and it goes as follows. "G-d, why did You have to create us in a way such that our national

character could only be refined through oppression and suffering –
You could have created us in such a manner that we would appreciate
Your Torah, and maintain our refined character, even in the midst of
success and prosperity."

So Hashem said to Bnei Yisrael: "I understand your dismay and
your being totally perplexed at My purpose in creating you in a way
which, on account of your limited understanding, appears deficient
and which will cause you enormous suffering down through the
ages." Therefore, Hashem said: "On the very day which symbolizes
your faith in your ultimate redemption, namely Rosh Chodesh, you
will bring a *korban* as symbolic atonement for Me for making the moon
smaller, meaning that you were forced to endure such terribly painful
experiences throughout history in order to refine your character and
earn the right to the ultimate redemption and the right to rule when
it really counts – in *yemos HaMoshiach*."

And perhaps that is why even Avraham Avinu, although he
overcame the idol worship of his family to recognize Hashem and to
become the father of our people, and who seemingly earned Hashem's
favors, nevertheless was put through so many severe tests and deprivation, including famine, exile from his homeland, war, and (as a
precursor to modern Israel's constant fight for survival) the possible
sacrifice of his only son. This, I believe, is a classic example of מעשה
אבות סימן לבנים and represents the very process by which Bnei Yisrael
become humble or, as the Gemara states, are *mima'et* themselves.

Accordingly, when we say, in the Haggadah, שבכל דור ודור עומדים
עלינו לכלותינו, we are attesting to the fact that our being constantly in
the line of attack by the nations of the world, causes us to be forever
looking to Hashem for help and, through the resulting refinement
of our national character, we merit the ultimate redemption. It is not
through prosperity but only through deprivation and persecution that
the character of Bnei Yisrael (one of modesty and self-effacement) is
formed. This represents the concept of *mi'ut*.

THE SIGNIFICANCE OF THE FIFTEENTH DAY
   OF THE LUNAR MONTH

As we have seen, the new moon appears to be a symbol of approaching redemption and, by logical extension, the full moon symbolizes

redemption itself. In an effort to demonstrate that this concept of the full moon as representing our redemption is deeply embedded in our tradition, I would now like to focus on the remarkable significance of the fifteenth day of the lunar month – the day on which the moon reaches its full illumination.

Most people probably do not appreciate (as I certainly did not until my preparation for this *d'var*) that, in six out of twelve of our lunar months, a yom tov or other important day falls on the fifteenth day of the month. Moreover, each of these six days has, as a central theme of the day, redemption in some form. To illustrate:

PESACH AND SUKKOS

Pesach and Sukkos, representing *Yetzias Mitzrayim* (our very first, and extremely significant, redemption), begin on the fifteenth day of Nisan and Tishrei respectively.

PURIM

Purim, which represents our redemption from Amalek, the arch-enemy of Bnei Yisrael through the ages, and which also represents a renewed acceptance by Bnei Yisrael of the Torah – קימו וקבלו – is generally observed on the fourteenth day of the month. However, in Shushan itself, where the miracle actually occurred, the Mishna Berura explains (688:1, end of note 1) that we read the Megilla on the fifteenth day of Adar. And Yerushalayim, of course, being a walled city, also observes Purim on the fifteenth.

So far, that's three holidays on the fifteenth.

TU B'AV

Another very important day which occurs on the fifteenth is Tu B'Av. Although this day does not directly involve redemption, its central theme is forgiveness of Bnei Yisrael, which is logically a pre-requisite to a *geula shleima*. Let us read, from Rabbi Eliyahu Kitov, a short quote about this day. Kitov, among other things, compares Tu B'Av, on account of its aspect of forgiveness, to Yom Kippur:[3]

---

3. Rabbi Eliyahu Kitov, *The Book of Our Heritage*, Vol. 3, transl. by Rabbi Nachman Bulman (NY: Feldheim, 1973), 303, 307.

In times past, this day was observed as a full festival . . .
The joy with which Israel invested the fifteenth of Av in
earlier generations was motivated by the attainment of
forgiveness from sin, similar to . . . Yom Kippur. . . . The
fifteenth of Av was likewise a day of forgiveness for the
דור המדבר (the generation of the Wilderness) for the sin of
the *meraglim*.

TU B'SHVAT

Another holiday (the fifth in our series) to occur on the fifteenth day
of the month is Tu B'Shvat. On this day, the theme of redemption is
represented by renewal of the land of Eretz Yisrael. *Tachanun* is not
said in *Shacharis* or the preceding *Mincha* and it is customary to eat
a fruit which comes from Eretz Yisrael, and to eat a new fruit, over
which one says *Shehechiyanu*. Here again, let us read an excerpt from
Kitov.[4]

> The reason for the festive mood of Tu B'Shvat . . . is that
> [the day] speaks the praise of the Land of Israel, for on
> this day the strength of the soil of the land is renewed. . . .
> When the soil of Eretz Yisrael renews its strength, to give
> forth its riches, the people of Israel who love the Land
> and yearn for it, also rejoice.

PESACH SHENI

A most compelling illustration of the deep significance, in our tradition, of the fifteenth day of the lunar month, and the relationship
of this day to the concept of redemption, can be seen in the Torah's
account of Pesach Sheni (the sixth and last in our enumeration of
Yomim Tovim or other special days occurring on the fifteenth day of
the lunar month).

Like so many other precious jewels in the Torah, this message
lies hidden and requires some analysis to reveal. The *pesukim* read
(Bamidbar 9:6–8):

---

4. Kitov, *The Book of Our Heritage*, Vol. 1, 347, 348.

ויהי אנשים אשר היו טמאים לנפש אדם ולא יכלו לעשות הפסח ביום
ההוא. ויקרבו לפני משה ולפני אהרן ביום ההוא. ויאמרו האנשים ההמה
אליו אנחנו טמאים לנפש אדם למה נגרע לבלתי הקריב את קרבן ד׳
במעדו בתוך בני ישראל. ויאמר אלהם משה עמדו ואשמעה מה יצוה ד׳
לכם.

And there were certain people who were impure and,
as a result, were unable to bring the *korban Pesach* (the
Pesach sacrificial offering) on that day [referring to the
korban which was eaten on the evening of the fifteenth
and sacrificed the prior afternoon] and they approached
Moshe and Aharon and said, "Why should we be worse
off than others so as not to be able to sacrifice the *korban
Pesach* in its proper time." Moshe replied, "Wait and you
will hear what Hashem has to say."

Hashem responded to Moshe that, if a person were impure or too
distant to bring the *korban Pesach* in time for it to be eaten on the
fifteenth day of Nisan, then that person's *korban* should be brought
the following month, on the fourteenth day of Iyar, so that it may
be eaten on the evening of the fifteenth day of Iyar. The *pasuk* states
(Bamidbar 9:11):

בחדש השני בארבעה עשר יום בין הערבים יעשו אותו על מצות ומרורים
יאכלהו.

In the month following Nisan, on the fourteenth day
of the month, in the evening, the *korban Pesach* shall be
brought and shall be eaten with *matzo* and *maror* [mean-
ing on the evening of the fifteenth of Iyar].[5]

We have by now taken for granted that the date established by
Hashem for the observance of Pesach Sheni is the fifteenth day of
Iyar, one month after the fifteenth of Nisan, and we probably do not
appreciate the fact that this postponement appears to be inconsistent
with every *halachic* principle with which we are familiar. Normally,
when a mitzvah cannot be performed in a timely manner, there are

---

5. See http://www.jewishpress.com/judaism/torah/q-a-pesach-sheni/2003/06
/13/ for reference to eating the *korban Pesach* on the night of the fifteenth. Thank
you to my good friend Jacob Nefoussi for this reference.

two possible *halachic* principles which apply: either (1) the mitzvah is totally forfeited because its time has passed; for example, one cannot fulfill the mitzvah of shofar the day after Rosh Hashana, or (2) it is deferred to the next available weekday time, such as a *bris*. Where a child is too ill to have a *bris* on the eighth day, then his *bris* takes place as soon as he is healthy enough – certainly not one month later. We have no *halachic* principle which justifies postponement beyond the next available opportunity.

Why is Pesach Sheni the only mitzvah which involves such an anomalous deferral? To reinforce this question, we note that the Gemara infers from the words ביום ההוא that these impure or distant persons were only in such condition for that one day (on the fifteenth of Nisan) הא למחר יכולין לעשות (*Sukkah* 25b). Accordingly, the Torah seems to be going out of its way to tell us that these people could have eaten the *korban Pesach* one day later, on the sixteenth of Nisan, still on the holiday itself, and yet we require them to postpone the *korban* for a full month.

I believe that the one month postponement of Pesach Sheni, to the fifteenth day of Iyar (i.e., to the very next fifteenth day of the month), reinforces the very notion we have developed in this *d'var*, namely the enormous significance in our tradition of the fifteenth day of the month – the day on which the full moon appears – as a symbol of our redemption.

And, in addition, I would like to note the Torah's use of the words ביום ההוא in the expression ולא יכלו לעשות הפסח ביום ההוא. I believe that the Torah's use of the very words ביום ההוא, rather than specifying the actual day of the month, are very significant. Just as, in the account of the *meraglim*, where the *pasuk* says ויבכו העם בלילה ההוא ("and the nation cried on that night"), we are taught that the words בלילה ההוא symbolize a day of mourning, darkness, and tragedy for the generations, so too, I believe, do the words ביום ההוא signify joy and redemption for our people, the Aleinu *tefillah* being just one example.

Moreover, Rebbe Yehoshua states that the fifteenth of Nisan is a day which was designated, at the time of the Creation of the world, for redemption, and that the final *geula* will occur on the fifteenth day of Nisan (*Rosh Hashana* 11b).

And so it is apparent, from the dates on which we observe Pesach, Sukkos, Purim (in Shushan and Yerushalayim), Tu B'Av, Tu B'Shvat and Pesach Sheni – all on the fifteenth day of the lunar month – and from the majestic use of the words ביום ההוא in the Torah, and indeed from the date of the final *geula*, that this fifteenth day of the month was not randomly selected for our holidays, but (in confirmation of the hope and faith in our ultimate *geula* which we demonstrate each Rosh Chodesh) the six holidays which we celebrate on the fifteenth day of the month stand as powerful reminders to us – six times a year, every year – that our redemption is uppermost on Hashem's agenda.

✦ MIDRASH – החדש הזה לכם ראש חדשים

At the outset, we referred to the *pasuk* of החדש הזה לכם ראש חדשים ("This month shall be for you the head of the months") and the Gemara which commented that the word הזה signified that Moshe literally had difficulty understanding the new moon's configuration, as well as details of the Menorah and the *shemona shratzim* (eight rodents). So Hashem had to point out these items to Moshe with Hashem's אצבע. We then asked several questions which pointed out the difficulties with the literal interpretation of this Gemara.

I would now like to suggest a different interpretation of this Gemara – one which is consistent with the theme of this *d'var*.

In fact, it is quite logical that Moshe had absolutely no more difficulty conceptualizing the appearance of the new moon or of the Menorah than he did any other mitzvah. Moshe was consistently at the top of his class and needed no special tutoring. Rather, what Moshe Rabbeinu had difficulty visualizing was not the shape of the new moon but rather the ultimate redemption of Bnei Yisrael, as represented by the new moon. Let us remember that the nation Moshe led out of Mitzrayim had witnessed miracles unparalleled in our history and rebelled nevertheless, to the point where they were not even permitted to enter Eretz Yisrael. And it is for this very reason, I believe, that Moshe Rabbeinu could not begin to imagine how such a people would ever be redeemed (see also Shemos 2:14, Rashi on וַיִּירָא מֹשֶׁה).

Accordingly, when the Midrash states that Hashem showed Moshe the new moon with Hashem's אצבע, it does *not* mean that Hashem showed Moshe the shape of the new moon, but rather that Hashem showed Moshe the אצבע אלקים through which Bnei Yisrael would eventually be redeemed. The words אצבע אלקים are used only twice in the

Torah, once by Pharoah's sorcerers when they recognized that they had no dominion over an object as small as the plague of lice, and again to describe the *luchos* which, although the words were cut completely through the stone, appeared the same way from either side.

And so we see that אצבע אלקים is used to describe a phenomenon which is beyond the boundaries of human understanding. Accordingly, when the Midrash states that Hashem used His אצבע to show Moshe the new moon, I believe the meaning to be that Hashem showed Moshe Rabbeinu the אצבע אלקים working through history, which would eventually culminate in the final redemption of Bnei Yisrael – a conclusion which Moshe, using his logic, had difficulty visualizing.

And the reference to the Menorah similarly alludes to redemption. Specifically, I would suggest that part of Hashem's demonstration to Moshe of the historical process which would lead to the *geula* of Bnei Yisrael, as symbolized by the new moon, included Hashem's showing to Moshe the modern State of Israel, the *atchalta d'geula*, whose official symbol is the Menorah.[6] So, when the Midrash states that Moshe had difficulty understanding the Menorah, it means that Moshe had trouble visualizing how we, as a people, would ever reach the threshold of our final redemption, as represented today by the Menorah as the proud symbol of Medinat Yisrael.

And finally, the *shemona shratzim* represent, I believe, the evil tyrants which have oppressed Bnei Yisrael down through the ages. Just as all of us react to rodents in a manner as if to say: "What possible reason could G-d have had to create these obnoxious and loathsome creatures?" so too do we react that way to the evil oppressors of Bnei Yisrael. Similarly, Moshe did not understand why we as a people would be forced to regularly endure such bitter and powerful enemies throughout the generations.

So, once again, Hashem showed Moshe that even these evil rulers are part of the אצבע אלקים and that their existence is a necessary part of the historical process leading to the *geula shleima* (although the reason for it is beyond human comprehension).

---

6. The establishment of the Menorah as the symbol of the modern State of Israel is discussed by Rabbi Prof. Daniel Sperber in an entire chapter of his *Minhagei Yisrael*, Vol. 5 (Jerusalem: Mosad HaRav Kook, 1995).

✺ CONCLUSION

In the final portion of this *d'var*, I would like to answer some of the questions with which we began. The only question I will not specifically answer is why we need a lunar calendar because, after we have concluded, the answer will be "all of the above."

We asked why Rosh Chodesh was given to Bnei Yisrael just as they were about to leave Mitzrayim, rather than a short two months later at Matan Torah. We have seen, however, that, Rosh Chodesh represents our complete faith in our *geula*, and it therefore makes a great deal of sense that Bnei Yisrael were given the mitzvah of Rosh Chodesh just prior to their being redeemed from the slavery of Mitzrayim, on Rosh Chodesh Nisan of that very month. Thus, was it ingrained in our national fiber that Rosh Chodesh would forever represent to Bnei Yisrael our hope of the approaching full moon of redemption.

We also wondered, in view of the Haggadah's statement of

יכול מראש חדש, תלמוד לומר ביום ההוא.

why we would have thought that the Haggadah should be recited on Rosh Chodesh. Now that we have seen that Rosh Chodesh is our everlasting symbol of redemption,[7] we can better understand the reason for יכול מראש חדש.

As for the connection between Rosh Chodesh and the women not participating in *chet ha'egel*, I believe that each represents similar acts of faith. Just as when we first see the new moon, we believe in the full moon of redemption even though we cannot (on account of the travails of our exile) visualize it, so too did the women of the דור המדבר have faith in the eventual return of Moshe even though they did not understand why he had not yet appeared. The special significance to women of Rosh Chodesh represents the *midda k'neged midda* of having faith in a *yeshua* which cannot easily be visualized.

We hopefully now better understand why the *halachos* and *minhagim* related to Rosh Chodesh treat this mitzvah of Rosh Chodesh with such reverence, virtually tantamount to a regular Yom Tov,

---

7. Note that the Gematria of החדש הזה לכם is 424, which is the same as the Gematria of משיח בן דוד.

even, some say, with *lechem mishneh*, candles, Shabbos clothes, and special meals. Just as the other Yomim Tovim represent the great miracles of redemption which Hashem performed for us in the past, so does Rosh Chodesh represent the great miracles of our future redemption.

I would suggest that the *minhag* of *Hallel* may have developed on Rosh Chodesh as advance recognition and praise by Bnei Yisrael of the great miracles of our future redemption. However, because this redemption and these miracles have not yet occurred, it stands to reason that the *Hallel* of Rosh Chodesh is, for now, only a *minhag* and that we only say half-*Hallel* on Rosh Chodesh.

And perhaps we can also appreciate Rebbe Yishmael's statement that it would be sufficient if we had no mitzvah other than Rosh Chodesh. To the extent that *geula* is our ultimate objective, and since Rosh Chodesh symbolizes *geula*, it is symbolically true that we need no other mitzvah.

We have already explained why the Torah states that the *korban* of Rosh Chodesh would act as an atonement to Hashem for creating us in such a way that Bnei Yisrael could only earn their ultimate reward by first going through a refinement process which entailed a great deal of suffering and oppression.

And this also helps explain why we state in the Haggadah:

שבכל דור ודור עומדים עלינו לכלותינו.
In each generation they attempt to destroy us.

This declaration describes the difficult process through which Bnei Yisrael is *mima'et* itself, as symbolized by the moon, and through which we are inculcated with deep faith in Hashem and earn for ourselves the final redemption.

And perhaps we refer to the laws of Rosh Chodesh as חוקי ראשי חדשים because, as an exquisite irony, Hashem hid from us the true meaning of the day. In the same way that Rosh Chodesh represents the process of *geula* which is very difficult for us to comprehend, and is concealed from us, so too did Hashem keep the true meaning of Rosh Chodesh somewhat hidden.

We asked why the concept of Yom Kippur Katan is related to Rosh Chodesh. Referring to Yom Kippur Katan, the Aruch Hashulchan states as follows (*Hilchos Rosh Chodesh* 417:11):

יש אנשי מעשה שנהגו להתענות ער"ח משום מיעוט הירח ועניינים
גדולים תלויים בזה נוגע למצבינו ולעתיד תתחדש הירח כמו אנחנו, כמו
שאומרים בברכת קידוש לבנה ולכן יש מהמקובלים שהתענו עד המולד.
There were persons of very high character who had the
custom of fasting Erev Rosh Chodesh on account of the
mi'ut of the moon and very significant principles are
involved in this custom. And in the future, the moon
will be restored to its former glory, just as Bnei Yisrael
will be so restored, as we affirm in *Kiddush Levana*. And
that is why there are experts in Kabbalah who would fast
until the *molad* (meaning the point where the new moon
is poised to reappear).

This, of course, is the custom of Yom Kippur Katan, to which we
alluded earlier. I would like to suggest a reason for this custom which
is consistent with our discussion. If the sliver of the new moon represents our hope in the ultimate full moon of our redemption, perhaps
the blackout period immediately preceding the new moon represents
a brief period of despair, of *hester panim*, of those darkest moments in
our history where we virtually lost hope.

It is therefore appropriate that, even when Hashem's presence is
least apparent to us, we clearly demonstrate our hope and faith in the
אצבע אלקים being just around the corner, by fasting and saying special
tefillos. The fact that the *mekubolim* would fast precisely until the onset
of the *molad*, when Hashem's presence is symbolically again apparent,
is an absolutely beautiful concept.

I would also like to note a very touching, and almost unnoticed,
Rashi at the beginning of Bereishis (1:16), in the *pasuk* which tells us
about Hashem's creation of the moon and the stars. Rashi comments:

על ידי שמיעט את הלבנה הרבה צבאיה להפיס דעתה.
Because Hashem was *mima'et* the moon, He created
many stars to appease the moon.

We all know from Hashem's dialogue with Avraham Avinu that Bnei
Yisrael are compared to the stars. Perhaps Rashi is alluding to the
fact that, although the *mi'ut* of the moon symbolizes the exile and
suffering of Bnei Yisrael, each one of us, through our conduct, has the
power to console the moon, by becoming our own shining star in the

darkness of the exile of our people, and this will surely give the moon comfort. By perfecting our *middos,* each of us has the power to bring closer the day that the moon is renewed to its former glory.

And finally, we note that the Aruch Hashulchan (*Hilchos Rosh Chodesh* 426:1) sets forth very eloquently the enormous significance of the mitzvah of *Kiddush Levana*:

קידוש הלבנה הוא ענין גדול ונורא כקבלת פני השכינה, ובודאי יש בזה
סודות גדולות ונוראות כאשר האריכו חכמי הקבלה.

Kiddush Levana represents a great and awesome concept, similar to the greeting of the Shechina, and this mitzvah certainly embodies great and wondrous secrets, as elaborated upon at length by the experts of Kabbalah.

I sincerely hope that our somewhat elaborate attempt to explain the enormous significance of the mitzvah of Kiddush HaChodesh has helped shed some light on the "great and wondrous secrets" of the mitzvah, as noted by the Aruch Hashulchan, and will make the mitzvah more meaningful for all of us. May our sincere and heartfelt performance of the mitzvah of Rosh Chodesh, in all its magnificent aspects, inspire each of us to do our utmost to hasten the *geula shleima*.

"YOM TOV": WHAT'S IN A NAME?

WHY DO WE CALL THE HOLIDAY "YOM TOV"?

For this *d'var*, I have tried to come up with some thoughts which are original in the sense that I did not see them in any *sefer* and I hope that you will find them interesting and worthwhile.

On each of the Yomim Tovim, we wish each other a "good Yom Tov." Aside from the fact that this greeting seems grammatically incorrect (since it literally appears to mean "have a good, good day"), there is a more fundamental question underlying this greeting – namely, why do we call the day Yom Tov in the first place? On the surface, this seems like a trivial question, but I would like to suggest an answer which can provide us with a deeper insight into the meaning of these holidays.

Now, the words *Yom Tov* are not found in the Torah, which refers to a holiday as *chag, mo'ed, regel,* and *mikra kodesh*; the Mishnah, on the other hand, uses the words *Yom Tov* to refer to our holidays, as in ביצה שנולדה ביום טוב.

The Rambam states (*Hilchos Yom Tov* 1:1):

ששת ימים האלו שאסרן הכתוב בעשיית מלאכה, שהן ראשון ושביעי של פסח, וראשון ושמיני של חג הסוכות, וביום חג השבועות, ובאחד לחדש השביעי, הן הנקראין ימים טובים.

The six days on which the Torah imposed a *melacha* prohibition – namely, the first and last days of Pesach, the first and last days of Sukkos, Shavuos, and the first day of Rosh Hashana, constitute days: וש]הן הנקראים ימים

טובים – which people call *Yom Tov*.

Two questions come to mind upon reading this Rambam. First of all, the Rambam's choice of words is unusual – after all, the Rambam does not say about Shabbos: שהן נקראים שבת – that people call it Shabbos. Clearly, Yom Tov is different in that it is a name which did not originate in the Torah and evolved over time. Secondly, why are only the days on which there is an *issur melacha* called *Yom Tov* – why not *chol hamo'ed* as well?

It is also interesting that Megillas Esther uses the words Yom Tov at least twice in the context of Purim (9:19, 9:22):

על כן היהודים הפרזים הישבים בערי הפרזות עושים את יום ארבעה

עשר לחדש אדר שמחה ומשתה ויום טוב ומשלוח מנות איש לרעהו.

So, when we look in Tanach, we find that the days which we refer to as *Yom Tov* are not referred to as such. Purim, on the other hand – a day which we do not commonly refer to as *Yom Tov* – has the name Yom Tov associated with it by Megillas Esther.

✺ USE OF THE WORD TOV IN THE TORAH AND IN MEGILLAS ESTHER

MAASEH BEREISHIS

In order to obtain some insight into the meaning of the name Yom Tov, it might be helpful to explore the meaning of the word *tov* as it is used in the Torah and in Megillas Esther. Now, on a superficial level, this analysis seems to have no purpose. After all, *tov* is a simple three-letter word which means "good." What else could it possibly mean? However, we will see that a careful study of even the simplest of words, as used in the Torah, will demonstrate that nothing can be taken for granted and that Hashem, in His infinite wisdom, can inject even seemingly very simple words with a much deeper meaning than their common, everyday translation would indicate.

We find the word *tov* used very early on in Bereishis. For example, at the end of each day of Creation (except for the second day's activity, which was completed on the third day), the Torah uses the word *tov,* as in ‫ויֹרא אלקים את האור כי טוב‬. Why is the word *tov* used in this context? What did Hashem feel was *good* about light specifically and His creations generally in order to warrant repeated use of the word *tov* in describing them?

Clearly, Hashem had a purpose in creating the world, and the word *tov* must reflect the fact that this purpose was accomplished by Creation of our world. What was Hashem's purpose? The ArtScroll commentary in Parshas Shelach suggests an answer. After the story of the *meraglim*, Moshe pleads for Bnei Yisrael. Moshe uses the argument that, if Hashem were to destroy the Jews on account of the great sin of the *meraglim*, the nations of the world would believe that Hashem did not have the power to take the Jews out of Mitzrayim.

Now, when you think about it, Moshe's reliance, when asking Hashem to forgive Bnei Yisrael, upon the preservation of Hashem's reputation, seems a bit strange, since Hashem's reputation apparently has nothing whatsoever to do with whether or not Bnei Yisrael deserved to be punished for the sin of the *meraglim*. The ArtScroll comments that: "The purpose of Creation is to bring glory to G-d" – in other words, the importance of Hashem's reputation is so fundamental that a potential punishment of Bnei Yisrael may be set aside when Hashem's reputation might be adversely affected by such punishment. ArtScroll, in support, quotes a *pasuk* in Isaiah (43:7):

‫כל הנקרא בשמי ולכבודי בראתיו יצרתיו אף עשיתיו.‬
I created everything for My Glory.

The above *pasuk*, not surprisingly, appears in the first *haftora* in the Torah, in Parshas Bereishis.

Rambam on Ahavas Hashem

If, in fact, the purpose of Creation is to bring glory to Hashem, then the repeated use of the word *tov* in *Maaseh Bereishis* must indicate that the nature of Hashem's creations promoted this objective. How is this so? The Rambam helps us to understand this. The Rambam states (*Hilchos Yesodei HaTorah* 2:2):

‫והיאך היא הדרך לאהבתו ויראתו. בשעה שיתבונן האדם במעשיו‬
‫וברואיו הגדולים ויראה הן חכמתו שאין לה ערך ולא קץ מיד הוא אוהב‬
‫ומשבח ומפאר ומתאוה תאוה גדולה לידע השם הגדול.‬

What is the path to love and fear Hashem? As a person contemplates Hashem's wondrous creations, and appreciates the unparalleled and infinite wisdom embodied in these creations, a person will love, praise, and have a very strong desire to know and better understand the *Shem HaGadol*.

The Rambam clearly felt that study of G-d's creations would bring us closer to Hashem. Physicians or scientists probably experience this concept regularly. Some of the rest of us experience this concept by observing the incredible intricacy of the natural world and the myriad beautiful, even breathtaking, scenes in Nature.

So we see that the use of the word *tov*, in the case of *Maaseh Bereishis*, means not only "good," but on a deeper level signifies that Hashem's creations, in and of themselves, bear testimony to Hashem's infinite power and Glory.

In fact, I believe it can be shown that the word *tov*, in the Torah and at least one of the Megillos, often has an important secondary meaning (in addition to its natural meaning of "good") which involves Hashem's revelation to us in a way which demonstrates His power and *hashgacha* over us. Although not every usage of the word *tov* has this secondary meaning, we can understand the point more easily by referring to certain specific examples. After reviewing these examples, I believe we will be able to better understand how the name Yom Tov developed.

USE OF THE WORD TOV IN CONNECTION WITH ERETZ YISRAEL

A very interesting use of the word *tov* in the Torah, and one where we very clearly see its dual dimension and deeper meaning, occurs in connection with the *meraglim*, an episode to which we referred earlier. We recall that ten of the *meraglim* painted a very threatening picture of the power of the inhabitants of Eretz Yisrael (Bamidbar 13:32–33):

ארץ אוכלת יושביה היא.
It is a Land which eats its inhabitants.

ושם ראינו את הנפילים בני ענק מן הנפילים ונהי בעינינו כחגבים וכן
היינו בעיניהם.

. . . there are giants there and we were like grasshoppers
in their eyes.

Yehoshua and Calev replied to the other ten *meraglim* as follows (14:7):

טובה הארץ מאוד מאוד.

On the surface, this means "the Land is extremely good."
However, there are problems with this literal translation.

(1)   First of all, what kind of answer is this to the other *meraglim*? If
the inhabitants of Eretz Yisrael were indeed a serious physical
threat to Bnei Yisrael, what difference does it make if the Land
is good – this does not reduce in any way the physical threat
which the Jews faced?

(2)   Secondly, why is the word *me'od* doubled up?

(3)   Thirdly, in the immediately succeeding *pasuk*, Yehoshua and
Calev explain what they mean by the words טובה הארץ מאוד
מאוד. The *pasuk* states (14:8):

אם־חפץ בנו ד' והביא אותנו אל־הארץ הזאת ונתנה לנו ארץ אשר־הוא
זבת חלב ודבש.

If Hashem desires it, He will bring us to this Land and
enable us to conquer the Land which is a Land of milk
and honey.

Now, if *tov* means "good," how are the words אם חפץ בנו ד', etc.
an elaboration of *tov*?

(4)   And finally, what is the connection between the first part of *pasuk* 14:8 above and its concluding words זבת חלב ודבש, and what
do Yehoshua and Calev mean by זבת חלב ודבש? Did Yehoshua
and Calev mean that Israel's milk and honey tastes better than
the milk and honey of other countries? This does not seem to
be a plausible response to the very serious security concerns
raised by the *meraglim*. So what is intended by the words זבת
חלב ודבש?

I believe that these questions can all be answered by reference to the secondary meaning of *tov* which we have been discussing. By the words, *tova ha'Aretz*, Yehoshua and Calev did not mean that Eretz Yisrael is "good" in the literal sense (although it certainly is), but rather that it is the Land which Hashem had revealed to Avraham would be the homeland of the Jews forever. *Tova ha'Aretz* means that the Land itself, as we will shortly elaborate, is testimony to Hashem's Glory.

Accordingly, *tova ha'Aretz* means that Hashem reveals Himself to the Jewish people, and in fact to the world at large, through the Land of Eretz Yisrael, by demonstrating that the conquest of Eretz Yisrael can overcome even the most daunting of obstacles. Consequently, Yehoshua and Calev are able to confidently state that Hashem will enable Bnei Yisrael to conquer Eretz Yisrael, no matter how powerful its inhabitants may be.

Now, our first question (how *tova ha'Aretz* could be an appropriate response to the other *meraglim*'s complaint about the overwhelming physical power of the inhabitants of the Eretz Yisrael) is answered. *Tova ha'Aretz* does not mean that Eretz Yisrael is good in a literal sense but that Hashem's *hashgacha* manifests itself through Eretz Yisrael. And this also answers our second question as to how the pasuk of אם חפץ בנו ד', is an elaboration of *tova ha'Aretz*.

As to our third question – the meaning of זבת חלב דבש – I would like to suggest a meaning which reinforces the deeper concept of *tov* which we have been discussing.

Eretz Yisrael, being in the middle of the desert, should not be a fruitful land. In fact, the *Tochacha* in Bechukosai tells us that our enemies will be astonished at how barren the Land is during the times of our exile. The fact that the Land is זבת חלב דבש – it is suddenly fertile when Bnei Yisrael settle the Land – is also a sign of G-d's power and *hashgacha* over us. Accordingly, זבת חלב דבש is another example of *tova ha'Aretz* – the Land itself is a sign of G-d's *hashgacha* over the Land and over His people.

So, now we have also answered the last of our questions with respect to these *pesukim* in the Chumash – namely why is *me'od me'od* doubled-up. It symbolizes the fact that Hashem's power and influence over us, with respect to Eretz Yisrael, is reflected in two ways: Firstly, by enabling us to conquer the Land in the face of seemingly invincible enemies and, secondly, by making an astonishingly barren land bloom as soon as our people settle it. Either way, we can perceive the deeper meaning of *tov* (or *tova ha'Aretz*, in this case), as representing G-d's Revelation to us through the medium of Eretz Yisrael.

USE OF THE WORD TOV IN CONNECTION WITH SHIDDUCHIM

Another use of the word *tov* in the Torah illustrates Hashem's Glory with respect to *shidduchim*. We all know that Hashem is the Master Shadchan. The Gemara (*Sotah* 2a) states that forty days before the creation of a child, a Heavenly voice proclaims: "The daughter of *ploni* is destined to marry the son of *ploni*." We acknowledge this Gemara by referring to our life-partner as our *bashert*.

In the context of *shidduchim*, we again see an application of the word *tov* when the Torah states: לא טוב היות האדם לבדו (Bereishis 2:18). A plain meaning of course is that it is not good for man to be alone. But I would suggest a deeper, secondary meaning is that, without the institution of marriage, we would never witness the incredible manner in which individuals find their way to the life-partner who was predestined for them. When we observe that this process was not accidental, we appreciate G-d's miraculous influence in bringing husband and wife together.

USE OF THE WORD TOV IN CONNECTION WITH DREAMS

Yet another example of the use of the word *tov* (or at least a variation of the word) occurs in the area of interpretation of dreams. The subject of dreams, as we know, is a very mystical one – as we see in the following excerpt from a *tefillah* recited in *Chutz la'Aretz* by the *tzibbur* during *Birkas Kohanim*:

חלום חלמתי ואיני יודע מה הוא.
I dreamt and I do not know what it means.

After Yosef interpreted Pharaoh's dream, and Pharaoh was clearly very pleased with Yosef's interpretation, the Torah states (Bereishis 41:37): וייטב הדבר בעיני פרעה. Pharaoh, who did not exactly walk around with G-d's name on his lips, echoed Yosef's statement that dreams are

interpreted correctly only through the direct inspiration of Hashem.
Pharaoh says about Yosef (41:38):

הנמצא כזה איש אשר רוח אלוקים בו.

Can a man such as this [i.e., so infused with G-d's spirit]
be found?

So again, we see use of the word *tov* in connection with G-d's revelation, this time to a complete heathen, albeit through the medium of
Yosef.

USE OF THE WORD TOV IN CONNECTION
WITH MOSHE

The final use of the word *tov* in the Torah which I would like to mention occurs in connection with Moshe. Of all of the personalities in
Tanach, clearly no-one approaches Moshe's role in Revelation. G-d
spoke *panim el panim*, as it were, only with Moshe, and Moshe received
the Torah and passed it on to Bnei Yisrael. Under these circumstances,
we might expect the word *tov* to be used in connection with Moshe.
When Moshe was born, the Torah tells us (Shemos 2:2):

ותהר האשה ותלד בן, ותרא אתו כי טוב הוא.

And the woman became pregnant and gave birth to a
son, and she saw that he was good.

Moshe's parents saw that Moshe was good. How was he good? Did
he sleep through the night? Was he a neat eater? Obviously, *tov* in
this pasuk means something other than "good" in the traditional
sense. Rashi comments that the entire room was lit up when Moshe
was in it. So, in line with our discussion, we can interpret *ki tov hu*
as meaning that Moshe's parents were able to discern, through a
sign from Hashem, that Moshe would be an instrument of Hashem's
revelation to His people.

MEGILLAS ESTHER

The hidden miracle of Megillas Esther began when King Achashverosh
demanded that Queen Vashti appear naked at a public banquet. The

pasuk relates the beginning of this incident with the following words (Megillas Esther 1:10):

ביום השביעי כטוב לב המלך ביין.

Seemingly, the plain meaning of the word *tov* here is not relevant at all and it is certainly peculiar at best to associate the word *tov* with a state of intoxication. However, our secondary meaning of the word *tov*, signifying G-d's revelation, fits perfectly, as we can see in the Purim story how the salvation of the Jewish people began precisely with this apparently innocuous event.

❧ RELATIONSHIP TO YOM TOV

So how does all of this relate to Yom Tov? Let us remember that Yom Tov is a word which the Jews themselves developed. The Rambam says about these days: הן הנקראים יום טוב – "they came to be called Yom Tov." This was a name which evolved. I believe that Bnei Yisrael called the *chagim* "*Yom Tov*" because of this aspect of *tov* that we have been discussing.

Tov means that something happened which, in and of itself, is an instrument of Kiddush Hashem or Revelation. As we have seen, our Scriptures use the word *tov* in a number of instances where Hashem's presence and influence are clearly demonstrated, such as Creation of the world; the making of *shidduchim*; interpretation of dreams; the designation of Eretz Yisrael as the Land set aside by Hashem for the Jewish people; the birth of Moshe Rabbeinu; and the onset of the great miracle of Purim.

Similarly, Yom Tov represents the days on which Hashem revealed Himself to His people through the awesome experiences of *Yetzias Mitzrayim* on Pesach, the many miracles which occurred in the Sinai desert, as symbolized by the *sukkos* of protection, and of course Matan Torah on Shavuos. זה היום עשה ד' נגילה ונשמחה בו. We consider these days to be *tov*, in line with the idea that Hashem's Revelation to us on these days is very apparent. Just as Hashem sometimes used the word *tov* in the Torah to denote events which bring people closer to recognition and appreciation of Hashem, so too do the tremendous miracles symbolized by our Yomim Tovim bring us closer to Hashem.

If all this is true, why did the Torah not call the days *Yom Tov*? I submit that this question can be answered by the Midrash which discusses why the Torah uses the word *Atzeres* to refer to the last days of Sukkos while the Jews generally refer to the holiday as *Sukkos*.

We refer to it as Sukkos to symbolize the fact that G-d protected us through His *sukkos*. G-d, on the other hand, refers to the last days as *Atzeres* as a term of endearment. *Atzeres* means "wait" and the name symbolizes the fact that Hashem, so to speak, does not wish Bnei Yisrael to leave Him after the many holidays in which we were so close to Him. Bnei Yisrael and Hashem each use a name which expresses appreciation for the other. Similarly, Hashem left it for *us* to develop the name Yom Tov, which represents our recognition and acknowledgment of His Revelation on these momentous days.

It is also worthwhile noting the mitzvah of *simchas Yom Tov* in this context. The Mishna Berura (*Hilchos Yom Tov* 529:11), discusses the different ways in which we demonstrate *simcha* on Yom Tov:

ובגדי יום טוב יהיו טובים משל שבת.

One should wear nicer clothes on Yom Tov than even on Shabbos.

Rabbi J.J. Schacter, in his introduction to *Siddur Nechamat Yisrael* (a *siddur* designed to be used in connection with *aveilus*), refers to an exposition of Rav J.B. Soloveitchik, *zt"l*, to the effect that *simchas Yom Tov* means something different than merely being joyful.

> [The Rav, *zt"l*] pointed to an additional dimension of *simcha* [aside from the common conception], one that transcends the physical or emotional. He noted that, very often, the word *simcha* in the Torah is juxtaposed to the phrase of *lifnei Hashem* (e.g. Devarim 12:7, 26:10, 11). As a result . . . what *simcha* really means is an awareness that whatever occurs to us, does so *lifnei Hashem* . . . Simcha, according to the Rav, *zt"l*, is not simply an emotion, but a . . . conceptual awareness that there is no such thing as chance . . . Rather, G-d himself is directly involved in all aspects of our lives – the good as well as the bad. . . .
>
> And, finally, the Torah requires us to have the awareness of *lifnei Hashem* precisely on Yom Tov when we

commemorate those great historical events in which the presence of G-d was so overt and obvious.

So, *simchas Yom Tov* means: not so much, "joy," in the common meaning of the word, but a deep sense of satisfaction and gratitude on account of what Hashem did for our people on these days of Yom Tov.

Now we see that "good Yom Tov," which literally appears to mean "have a good, good day," is not redundant. It in fact means "have a good "Yom Tov," namely a good – day on which Hashem revealed Himself to His people.

With this construct, we can perhaps understand why the Rambam states regarding the days of Yom Tov: שהן נקראים ימים טובים – they came to be called *Yom Tov*. The Jews called these days *Yom Tov* as a symbol of appreciation that these days have, as part of their essence, the Revelation of G-d to His people. In this regard, perhaps we can also understand why Purim is referred to in the Megilla as a day of *Yom Tov* (and, in fact, the name Yom Tov may have its origins in Megillas Esther). Purim was also a day on which G-d revealed Himself to us, by turning our enemies' plans around in the most spectacular, yet subtle, ways, so that another Holocaust was prevented.

We noted earlier Rambam's statement that only the days on which there is an *issur melacha* are called Yom Tov. Why is this so? I can only guess at the answer but would like to suggest the following. Throughout the ages, as difficult as it was for the Jews to stop their work as Shabbos approached, the *issur melacha* on Yom Tov has in some ways been even more problematic.

We all know how hard it is to keep our businesses and professions functioning smoothly during the *chagim*. Perhaps as a reaction to this great sacrifice, Bnei Yisrael used the name Yom Tov only in connection with those days on which there is an *issur melacha* – in other words, it was a collective acknowledgment that we were all brought closer to the Shechina on these days and that the dedication to Hashem of certain days, which dedication is symbolized, among other things, by *issur melacha*, is the least that we should do in return.

In fact, there are some remarkable declarations in our tradition which reflect the critical importance of recognizing Yom Tov as a special day of Hashem's intervention on our behalf. *The Encyclopedia Talmudit* (section on Yom Tov, column 590), quoting the Rambam and others, makes the following statement:

אותה שאמרו שהמבזה את המועדות כאלו עובד עבודה זרה. . . . . .
והמבזה אותם הוא מי שאינו מכבדם כראוי, וכן אותה ששנינו: כל
המבזה את המועדות, אף על פי שיש בידו תורה ומעשים טובים, אין לו
חלק לעולם הבא.

There are those who say that a person who demeans Yom
Tov is likened to a person who worships idols. And demeaning Yom Tov means not according Yom Tov proper
respect. And we also learnt that whoever demeans Yom
Tov, even if such person is learned and is a person of
good deeds, such person has no share in *Olam HaBo*.

And finally, when we recite the Haggadah at the Seder, it is helpful
to remind ourselves that it is Hashem's special purpose in this world
that we do our best to sanctify His Name and in so doing cause each
other to recognize Hashem and His influence on our lives. As such,
Haggadah is more than just another mitzvah – telling our children
about Hashem's wondrous acts on our behalf actually fulfills one of
the fundamental goals of Creation, the glorification of our Creator.
Any way in which we get closer to G-d, or bring other people closer,
is *tov*.

THE MEANING OF "THE LAND OF MILK AND HONEY": THE *KEDUSHA* OF ERETZ YISRAEL AND ITS PRACTICAL RELEVANCE TODAY

Rebbe Chiyya the Great and Rebbe Shimon ben Chalafta were walking through the Arbel Valley at the crack of dawn and they saw the first light come up. Rebbe Chiyya the Great said to Rebbe Shimon ben Chalafta: "Master, such will be Israel's redemption – at first, Redemption will be gradual but, as time goes on, its pace will accelerate."

(Yerushalmi *Berachos* 1a)

And why is the final redemption likened to the dawn? Because there is no greater darkness than that which immediately precedes the dawn.

(Rabbi Menachem Kasher, *Israel Passover Haggadah*)[1]

✍ INTRODUCTION

I would like to explore various *pesukim*, *halachos*, and *midrashim* regarding the supremely important mitzvah of *yishuv Eretz Yisrael*, as well as how this mitzvah relates to those of us living in *Chutz la'Aretz*. Let us begin with a few questions:

(1) Why is Eretz Yisrael called the Holy Land?
(2) Eretz Yisrael is known as ארץ זבת חלב ודבש – "the Land of milk and honey." What does this expression signify and why did Hashem not use these words when describing Eretz Yisrael to the Avos?

---

1. Rabbi Menachem Kasher, *Israel Passover Haggadah* (Shengold Publishers: 1975), p. 288 (Hebrew), p. 289 (English).

(3)   Israel is seemingly always in the forefront of international news. How is it possible that such a tiny country geographically – and which numerically represents barely more than one-tenth of one percent of the world's population – plays such a central role in world affairs, and does the Torah in effect predict this surprising phenomenon?

(4)   We have all heard the joke about how G-d took us to the only place in the Middle East which does not have oil. Is it just a coincidence that there are, so far as we know, no significant oil deposits or, for that matter, gold, silver, or diamonds in Eretz Yisrael? And again, is this fact predicted in the Torah? (We will discuss the recent major discovery of natural gas in this context.)

(5)   The Midrash tells us that the world was apportioned ten measures of beauty and that Eretz Yisrael received nine of them. Would *National Geographic* agree with this Midrash?

(6)   Why do so many of us send our children to *yeshivos* and seminaries in Israel? What is it that is so special about Torah learnt in Israel?

(7)   What should our attitude be with respect to the many non-religious political leaders and citizens of the country?

By way of introduction, we note that Eretz Yisrael is integrally tied to our formation as a people. The very first time in the Torah when Hashem speaks to Avraham, it is to tell Avraham to uproot himself and go to Eretz Yisrael. Rashi interprets the word *lecha* (for you), in *lech lecha*, as signifying something which is for Avraham's benefit, namely that Avraham would be the progenitor of a great nation only if he moved to Eretz Yisrael, but not otherwise. This is remarkable in and of itself, because it tells us that Avraham, for all of his outstanding characteristics as a man of G-d, would have been relegated to relative oblivion had he not heeded Hashem's call to relocate to Eretz Yisrael. And so we see from the very beginning of our existence as a people that Am Yisrael, the Jewish nation, is inextricably linked with Eretz Yisrael.

❧ WHAT MAKES ERETZ YISRAEL SO SPECIAL?

The one overriding statement one can make about Eretz Yisrael – a statement which sets the tone for our discussion – is that Eretz Yisrael is literally G-d's country. Long before Hashem instructed Avraham to leave his home for Eretz Yisrael, Hashem had picked Eretz Yisrael for us. The Midrash Tanchuma states (Devarim Re'eh 8):

> ... כשברא העולם, חלק הארצות לשרי האומות, ובחר בארץ ישראל
> אמר הקדוש ברוך הוא יבואו ישראל שבאו לחלקי וינחלו את הארץ.
> When Hashem created the world, He divided the world among the nations and picked Eretz Yisrael for us.... Hashem said, "Let Bnei Yisrael come and inherit My Land."

Bamidbar Rabba similarly states (23:7):

> ... אמר הקב"ה למשה, הן הארץ חביבה עלי, ... וישראל חביבין עלי,
> אני מכניס את ישראל שהן חביבים עלי לארץ שחביבה עלי.
> Hashem said to Moshe, "This Land is dear to me, and the people of Israel are dear to me. Let me bring the people who are dear to the Land which is dear."

And Hashem also called Eretz Yisrael *Artzi* (My Land), as it says in Yoel (4:2):

> ואת ארצי חלקו.
> And they [referring to Israel's enemies] divided up My Land.

And so it seems that an important element which gives Eretz Yisrael *kedusha* is the fact that Eretz Yisrael, unlike any other place on earth, is called by Hashem "My Land"; we also see that Eretz Yisrael was hand-picked, so to speak, for us by Hashem.

It is now apparent why Eretz Yisrael has always been treasured by our people. The Midrash Tanchuma, quoted earlier (Devarim Re'eh 8, referring to Devarim 3:23–25), notes that David HaMelech said, addressing G-d:

אמר דוד לפני הקב״ה, ריבונו של עולם : אפילו יש לי פרקטלין וטרקלין
בחוצה לארץ, ואין לי אלא הסף בארץ ישראל, בחרתי הסתופף.

"Master of the Universe, even if I had the choice between
palaces in *Chutz la'Aretz* and a mere doorpost in Eretz
Yisrael, I would choose Eretz Yisrael."

৩ THE LAND IS FRUITFUL ONLY FOR OUR PEOPLE

THE LAND WILL BE DESOLATE DURING OUR EXILE

A most dramatic manifestation of the fact that Hashem hand-picked
Eretz Yisrael for us is the fact that the soil of our Land has refused to
be fertile for any other nation. In the very midst of the first *tochacha*
in the Torah, we find powerful words of consolation for our people
(Vayikra 26:32):

והשמתי אני את הארץ ושממו עליה אויביכם היושבים בה.

I will make the Land desolate [during your Exile] and
your enemies who reside there will be astonished [at the
extent of the desolation].

Rashi, on the above *pasuk* (quoting Toras Kohanim), comments:

זו מידה טובה לישראל שלא ימצאו האויבים נחת רוח בארצם שתהא
שוממה מיושביה.

This is a favorable sign for our people – that, in the absence of the Jewish people from Eretz Yisrael, none of
our enemies will achieve any success in their attempts
to cultivate the Land.

The quote below, which describes Mark Twain's journey to the Holy
Land in 1867, brings the Torah's prophecy, as stated in the *tochacha*,
into very sharp focus. Note his words of astonishment, just as the
Torah predicts:

A desolate country whose soil is rich enough, but is
given over wholly to weeds . . . a silent mournful ex-
panse. . . . a desolation. . . . we never saw a human being

on the whole route. . . . hardly a tree or shrub anywhere. Even the olive tree and the cactus, those fast friends of a worthless soil, had almost deserted the country.[2]

Ramban on Vayikra 26:32:

That which is stated here, *"and your enemies that shall dwell therein shall be desolate in it,"* constitutes a good tiding, proclaiming that during all our exiles, our Land will not accept our enemies. . . . This is also a great proof and assurance to us, for in the whole inhabited part of the world, one cannot find such a good and large land which was always lived in and yet is as ruined as it is today, for since the time that we left it, it has not accepted any nation or people, and they all try to settle it, but to no avail.[3]

THE LAND MIRACULOUSLY REVIVES WHEN BNEI YISRAEL RETURN — PORTENT OF THE FINAL REDEMPTION

The Talmud (*Sanhedrin* 98a) offers numerous signs which portend the arrival of Moshiach and concludes with what the Talmud assures us is the truest sign of all that our final redemption is at hand:

ואמר רבי אבא, אין לך קץ מגולה מזה שנאמר ואתם הרי ישראל ענפכם תתנו ופריכם תשאו לעמי ישראל, כי קרבו לבוא.

Rebbe Abba said, "There can be no more manifest sign of redemption than this [i.e., Eretz Yisrael becoming fertile once again], as it is said, 'But you, O mountains of Israel, will bring forth your branches, and yield your fruit to My people Israel, for they are soon to come' (Yechezkel 36:8)."

---

2. Mark Twain, *The Innocents Abroad*, 361–362.

3. *Ramban Commentary on the Torah*, transl. by Rabbi Dr. Charles B. Chavel (NY: Shilo Publishing House, 1976), 473.

HaRav Yisachar Shlomo Teichtal was a very great *tzaddik* who wrote a *sefer* called *Eim Habanim Semeichah*. He died at the hands of the Nazis, ימח שמם. During the 1930s, Rav Teichtal was a staunch anti-Zionist. In the 1940s, while hidden in an attic in Hungary, he completely reversed course, and without the benefit of any *seforim*, writing entirely from memory, wrote this monumental *sefer* dedicated to proving the righteousness of the Zionist philosophy. The *sefer* has been translated into English and is a must-read.[4]

Rav Teichtal (p. 182) quotes the Gemara (*Megilla* 17b) in order to demonstrate that the arrangement of certain *berachos* in *Shemoneh Esrei* reflects the fact that the Ingathering of the Exiles will follow closely upon the Land becoming fruitful:

ומה ראו לומר קיבוץ גלויות לאחר ברכת השנים?
Why did the *Anshei Knesses HaGedola* see fit to place the *bracha* of תקע בשופר גדול לחרותינו immediately after the *bracha* of מברך השנים?

The Gemara responds, referring to the *pasuk* in Yechezkel (36:8) quoted above:

Because it is written, "But you, O mountains of Israel, will bring forth your branches, and yield your fruit to My people Israel, for they are soon to come."[5]

Rashi, on the above Gemara, elaborates on the prophecy contained there:

אלמא קיבוץ גלויות בעת ברכות השנים היא.
We see that the Ingathering of the Exiles will occur in the same era as the Land becoming fruitful.

---

4. HaRav Yisachar Shlomo Teichtal, *Eim Habanim Semeichah: On Eretz Yisrael, Redemption, and Unity*, transl. by Rabbi Moshe Lichtman (Mevaseret Tzion, Israel: Kol Mevaser Publishers, 2000).

5. Teichtal, *Eim Habanim Semeichah: On Eretz Yisrael, Redemption, and Unity*, 182.

Rav Teichtal comments (p. 182):

> The mountains and hills, which were desolate during the entire exile, will yield their fruits when redemption draws near. . . .
>
> This is actually happening today! Many of our Jewish brethren came to the Land and . . . transformed great expanses of disease-infested swamps into dry land and fertile, prosperous fields. They sacrificed and endangered themselves to build the Land . . . Is there even a shadow of a doubt that this is the wondrous work of Hashem, and that it is a sign that our salvation is soon to come?![6]

Taking into account that the above was written during World War II, it is all the more remarkable that Rav Teichtal, in hiding and in fear for his life, which he ultimately lost in a violent manner, was able to perceive unmistakable signs of impending salvation amidst utter chaos and indescribable despair!

✽ ISRAEL AS CENTRAL IN THE NEWS

The next subtopic I would like to briefly cover is related to the main topic only in a very general way. However, it is a subject which has entered almost everyone's mind from time to time, namely how remarkable it is that Israel is so regularly at the forefront of the world's news headlines. Why should this be so, considering Israel's miniscule size in both territory (barely visible on a globe) and in population?

In Parshas Ekev (Devarim 11:12), the following statement is made about Eretz Yisrael:

> ארץ אשר ד' אלקיך דורש אותה תמיד, עיני ד' אלקיך בה, מרשית השנה
> ועד אחרית שנה.
> A Land with which Hashem concerns Himself constantly, from the beginning of the year until the end of the year.

---

6. Teichtal, *Eim Habanim Semeichah: On Eretz Yisrael, Redemption, and Unity*, 183.

Rashi on this *pasuk* asks the obvious question:

(יב) אשר ד' אלקיך דורש אותה : והלא אף כל הארצות הוא דורש, שנאמר
להמטיר על ארץ לא איש אלא כביכול אינו דורש אלא אותה, ועל ידי
אותה דרישה שדורשה, דורש את כל הארצות עמה. תמיד עיני ד' אלקיך
בה : לראות מה היא צריכה, ולחדש בה גזרות עתים לטובה, ועתים לרעה,
כדאיתא בראש השנה,

But does Hashem not concern Himself with all lands and
not only with Eretz Yisrael? However, it only appears
as if Hashem concerns Himself exclusively with Eretz
Yisrael. How is this so? Because [referring to a Gemara
in *Rosh Hashana*] Hashem first enters into an inquiry as
to what is appropriate for Eretz Yisrael, and then brings
about His decrees affecting the rest of the world accordingly (sometimes for good and sometimes for bad).

Here we have a prediction in the Torah, as explained by Rashi, which
is so illogical as to be almost preposterous – namely that tiny Eretz Yisrael should drive the events of the world – yet we have seen this come
to pass again and again. So when we see the news headlines featuring
Eretz Yisrael so prominently, we should not be surprised because this
is what the Torah in effect predicted thousands of years ago.

✺ THE NATION OF ISRAEL AS A MAVERICK AMONG THE NATIONS

הן עם לבדד ישכן ובגוים לא יתחשב.
*It is a nation which dwells alone and is not reckoned among
the other nations* (Bamidbar 23:9).

The above prophecy in the Chumash can be entirely substantiated by
the following excerpt from the *New York Times*,[7] and needs no further
commentary:

---

7. Published: January 12, 2009

ISRAELIS UNITED ON GAZA WAR AS CENSURE RISES ABROAD
by Ethan Bronner

JERUSALEM — To Israel's critics abroad, the picture could not be clearer: Israel's war in Gaza is a wildly disproportionate response to the rockets of Hamas, causing untold human suffering and bombing an already isolated and impoverished population into the Stone Age, and it must be stopped.

Yet here in Israel very few, at least among the Jewish population, see it that way. . . .

And while tens of thousands have poured into the streets of world capitals demonstrating against the Israeli military operation, antiwar rallies here have struggled to draw 1,000 participants. The Peace Now organization has received many messages from supporters telling it to stay out of the streets on this one.

As the editorial page of *The Jerusalem Post* put it on Monday, the world must be wondering, do Israelis really believe that everybody is wrong and they alone are right?

The answer is yes.

"It is very frustrating for us not to be understood," remarked Yoel Esteron, editor of a daily business newspaper called *Calcalist*. "Almost 100 percent of Israelis feel that the world is hypocritical. Where was the world when our cities were rocketed for eight years and our soldier was kidnapped? Why should we care about the world's view now?"

☙ PHYSICAL CHARACTERISTICS OF THE LAND: WHY NO GOLD, SILVER, DIAMONDS, OR OIL?

Even though a very significant natural gas field was recently discovered in Israel, and this seems to run counter to the analysis below, the end of this section addresses this discovery in the context of our analysis.

Why indeed did G-d take us to one of the only places in the Mideast which is not rich in oil? To help us answer this question, let us refer to Devarim (8:7, 9), where the Torah focuses on the physical aspects of Eretz Yisrael, and states as follows:

פסוק ז': כי ד' אלקיך מביאך אל ארץ טובה ארץ נחלי מים עינות
ותהומות יוצאים בבקעה ובהר.

For G-d your L-rd is bringing you to a good Land, a Land of flowing streams, and underground springs gushing out in valleys and mountains.

פסוק ט׳: ארץ אשר לא במסכנות תאכל בה לחם לא תחסר כל בה, ארץ
אשר אבניה ברזל ומהרריה תחצב נחושת.

A Land in which you will not eat bread in poverty, in
which you will lack nothing. A Land whose stones are
iron and from whose mountains you will mine *copper*.[8]

If we carefully examine the words of these *pesukim*, it is apparent
that G-d seems to be signaling to us not to expect to find major oil or
precious metal deposits in Israel. The *pesukim* talk about underground
springs – but do not promise us underground oil wells. The *pesukim*
talk about mining copper from the mountains of the Land – but do
not promise us gold or silver. The *pesukim* talk about stones which
are iron – but do not promise us diamonds. The *pesukim* talk about
not eating bread in poverty – but do not promise us that we will eat
bread in wealth.

Yet, despite pointedly failing to promise us a land full of precious
metals or oil deposits, the Torah (Devarim 8:9) promises us a land in
which we will lack nothing (לא תחסר כל בה). How do we understand
this?

Leaving this question unanswered for the moment, let us examine yet another *pasuk* where the physical aspects of Eretz Yisrael are
discussed. The *pasuk* states (Devarim 11:11):

והארץ אשר אתם עוברים שמה לרשתה ארץ הרים ובקעות למטר
השמים תשתה מים.

And the Land which you are about to inherit is a Land
of hills and valleys; from the rain of Heaven shall you
drink water.

Rashi, on the immediately preceding *pasuk*, explains that Eretz
Yisrael is not like Egypt, which is dependent on the Nile for water,
and where water had to be brought, with great exertion, to farmland
which was situated on higher ground. In Eretz Yisrael, which is dependent on rain for irrigation, Rashi says that Hashem brings the rain,

---

8. The words "iron" and "copper" are emphasized to denote a remarkable
reference to iron and copper in the Ki Savo *haftora*, discussed in the final paragraph
in this section with respect to the major gas discovery off the northern coast of
Israel.

while Bnei Yisrael sleep, to water both the high and the low ground.

Rashi presents the fact that Eretz Yisrael relies on rain for irrigation as a positive feature of Eretz Yisrael. However, whereas it is true that the rain which Hashem brings serves to water the high ground, and it is therefore not necessary to schlep the water from down below, the flip side of this fact is that when there is a shortage of rain, neither the high nor the low ground has enough. In fact, the Gemara states that Eretz Yisrael starts to pray for rain earlier than Babylonia because Eretz Yisrael needs the rain more (*Taanis* 10a). So we see that this dependence on rain appears to be a mixed blessing.

Earlier, we noted the *midrashim* which state that Hashem hand-picked Eretz Yisrael for our people. But from what we understand so far of the Torah's description of the physical characteristics of the Land, we cannot help but wonder why Hashem would hand-pick for us a land which appears to have little or no oil, gold, silver, or diamonds, and which is dependent on rain (which is often absent) for irrigation. What is so special about the Torah's description of the physical features of Eretz Yisrael? Rav Shimshon Raphael Hirsch helps us answer this question.

Rav Hirsch, discussing the word *tova*, as used by G-d to describe Eretz Yisrael to Moshe for the first time (Shemos 3:8), states brilliantly that the word *tova* is not used purely as a description of the Land *per se*, but is rather a description of the Land as reflective of the actions and conduct of Bnei Yisrael (i.e., the Land reacts in a manner which is "good" when our conduct is appropriate, and vice-versa). Rav Hirsch states:

> The Land is *tova* – it is in accordance with the intended intellectual and moral development of the nation . . . A Land which, unlike Egypt, does not offer its inhabitants simply to take advantage of its natural conditions of fertility [in modern terms, oil and precious metals]. . . . When it gets water, it blossoms out luxuriously. But it only gets this water from Above. It is a Land that makes it necessary for its inhabitants to be good.

It is apparent from Rav Hirsch's interpretation that Eretz Yisrael's dependence on rain forces Bnei Yisrael to look to Hashem, because the rain is not there unless we are deserving, and that this is a positive feature of Eretz Yisrael (hence the Torah's use of the word *tova* to describe the Land). Incidentally, we note that this dependence on Hashem for rain directs our hearts towards Hashem at the beginning of the rainy season and possibly explains the solemnity and importance of *Tefillas Geshem*.

The Arabs of today present us with very powerful evidence of how enormous natural resources, far from being a blessing, can utterly destroy a nation's moral fabric. We also note from the following Gemara that this very same phenomenon was evident thousands of years ago. The Gemara states as follows (*Sanhedrin* 109a):

תנו רבנן, אנשי סדום לא נתגאו אלא בשביל טובה שהשפיע להם הקב״ה
ומה כתיב בהם . . . . מקום ספיר אבניה ועופרת זהב לו.

The Rabbis taught in a *baraisa*: The people of Sodom became arrogant only because of the bounty that Hashem lavished upon them. As it states (Job 28:6): "Its very stones yielded sapphire, its very dust was gold."

This notion may answer the question we posed, namely why there appears to be no gold, silver, diamonds, or oil in Eretz Yisrael and why the Torah does not promise us any. As Rav Hirsch notes, Hashem apparently does not wish to endow Eretz Yisrael with natural resources which serve to make us wealthy regardless of whether or not we are deserving, as this would, no doubt, have a very negative impact on our national character, as the Torah indicates more than once.[9] By contrast, being forced to look to Hashem for our sustenance helps to ensure that we will always appreciate whatever Hashem provides for us. And this is all the more true preceding the *shmitta* and *yovel* years when the Land miraculously produces sufficient food for three years. Thus, it is apparent that Hashem's *hashgacha* over the agricultural productivity of the Land is yet another feature which endows Eretz Yisrael with an extraordinary aspect of spirituality.

And this, I believe, is the key to how the Torah can tell us that we will lack nothing in a Land which seems to lack natural riches. I would suggest that the spiritual benefits of the Land are so significant that its inhabitants feel blessed even though they are not sitting on deep oil wells or gold deposits. In fact, each one of us knows one or more

---

9. E.g., Devarim 32:15: וישמן ישורון ויבעט.

people living in Eretz Yisrael who seem happy far beyond what one would expect based only upon their physical resources and assets. Eretz Yisrael is indeed a Land in which a person, if he or she extracts the Land's full measure of spiritual benefit, will lack nothing.

*

The recent huge gas discovery off the northwestern coast of Israel does not, I believe, contradict the points made here. We note that Hezbollah has already laid claim to the resource, on account of its proximity to Lebanon, and exploitation may be very problematic. More significantly, the find may constitute yet another signal that our final redemption is rapidly approaching. The *haftora* of Ki Savo includes a *pasuk* from Isaiah (60:17) which seems to state that, in the days of Moshiach, Hashem will convert the copper to gold and the iron to silver (note the very same reference to copper and iron in the *pasuk* quoted at the beginning of this section). In other words, the Land will then produce the wealth it has previously withheld.

❧ LEARNING TORAH IN ERETZ YISRAEL

אווירא דארץ ישראל מחכים.

The very air of Eretz Yisrael makes you wise.
(Bava Basra 158b)

One of the questions we asked at the outset was: What is so special about Torah learning in Eretz Yisrael? During the frequent outbursts of extraordinary terrorism in past years, many parents inevitably questioned whether there is a particular benefit in learning Torah in Eretz Yisrael rather than elsewhere. Note the following heartrending question posed to Rav Yaakov Klass some years ago:[10] "My son is enrolled in one of the major *yeshivos* in Israel. Though he is learning very well, I am extraordinarily tense at all times . . . In times of danger like today, is it proper to allow him to continue learning there? Would it not be possible for him to learn elsewhere with the same results?"

The Gemara provides us with some insight on this subject and states as follows (*Kiddushin* 49b):

---

10. *The Jewish Press*, July 12, 2002.

עשרה קבין חכמה ירדו לעולם, תשעה נטלה ארץ ישראל, ואחד כל העולם
כולו.

Ten measures of wisdom descended to the world. Eretz
Yisrael took nine, and the rest of the world took the re-
maining one.

Rashi tells us that this virtual monopoly of wisdom as possessed by
Eretz Yisrael, refers not only to Torah but to both Torah and *derech
eretz*. And Vayikra Rabba states (13:5):

אין תורה כתורת ארץ ישראל, ואין חכמה כחכמת ארץ ישראל.

There is no Torah like the Torah of Eretz Yisrael and no
wisdom like the wisdom of Eretz Yisrael.

And in Isaiah, we have the famous statement (2:3):

כי מציון תצא תורה ודבר ד' מירושלים.

The Torah shall emanate from Tzion, and the words of
Hashem from Yerushalayim.

We see that our tradition uniformly echoes the unique status of Eretz
Yisrael as a place of Torah.

Rav Yitzchak Mirsky wrote a superb two-volume *sefer* called
Hegyonei Halacha. In an essay entitled חיבת הארץ (Love of the Land),[11] he
states that he had heard from a certain *mashgiach* of Yeshivat Chevron
that when the *Chutz la'Aretz* students of the Slobodka Yeshiva were
called upon to make *aliya* to Eretz Yisrael, it was primarily the average
students who responded to the call, since the top students had strong
attachments to their Rebbes in *Chutz la'Aretz*. The *mashgiach* noted
that almost all those students who made *aliya* to Israel exceeded by
far the achievements which (based upon their prior progress) they
would have accomplished in their former locations, and were serving
in prestigious positions as Rabbis and Dayanim in Israel. Rav Mirsky
notes that this is testimony to the adage noted in a number of places
in the Gemara, namely that אוירא דארץ ישראל מחכים – the very air of Israel
makes a person wise.

---

11. Rabbi Yitzchak Mirsky, *Hegyonei Halacha*, Vol. 1 (Jerusalem: Mosad HaRav
Kook, 1989).

What is it about Eretz Yisrael which has such a phenomenal effect on the Torah learnt there? The Midrash Shocher Tov on Tehillim (105:4) relates that Rav Yosi ben Chalafta told his son Rebbe Yishmael: "Do you want to witness G-d's presence in the world? Go study Torah in Eretz Yisrael," as it says (in Tehillim 105:4):

דרשו ד' ועוזו, בקשו פניו תמיד.

Seek the L-rd amidst His strength, seek His face continuously.

What is the meaning of Rav Yosi ben Chalafta's statement that a person should learn Torah in a place where you see Hashem in His strength; why should that make a difference; and why is it that a person has the ability, when in Eretz Yisrael, much more so than elsewhere, to perceive Hashem's strength?

I believe this Midrash refers to the *emuna* which a person develops when personally witnessing the miracles and *kedusha* of Hashem which permeate Eretz Yisrael in so many ways. I asked my children, when they were studying in Eretz Yisrael for the year, their personal opinion as to what it is about Eretz Yisrael that so inspires yeshiva and seminary students there.

Their thoughts (and every student would no doubt have his or her own list) are the following: the Kotel; witnessing first-hand the sheer miracle of Israel's survival despite its being surrounded by so many implacable enemies; holy places such as Yerushalayim and Tzfas; and the phenomenon of *Klal Yisrael*, as evidenced by so many ordinary Israelis who go out of their way to show *hachnasas orchim* and perform other acts of *chesed* towards others. This is called: seeking Hashem and His strength, as stated in Tehillim, in the *pasuk* we quoted above. No wonder our children are so inspired and so motivated in Eretz Yisrael.

✺ YISHUV ERETZ YISRAEL – UNIQUE HALACHOS AND MIDRASHIM

אין השכינה שורה [אלא באי"י].

The Shechina resides [only in Eretz Yisrael].   (Mechilta Bo 1)

To briefly recap, we have noted so far that Eretz Yisrael was handpicked for us by Hashem, as evidenced in part by the fact that no other nation has succeeded in making the Land fertile; it is called "My Land" by Hashem; Hashem manipulates world events according to the needs of Eretz Yisrael, and the Torah itself seems to emanate from Eretz Yisrael, radiating outward in all directions to impact the rest of the world.

Given all these incredible features of Eretz Yisrael, it should come as no surprise that the *halachos* and *midrashim* related to *yishuv Eretz Yisrael* make it very clear that living in Eretz Yisrael, as well as supporting Eretz Yisrael in any way that we are able, is an enormously important mitzvah, almost in a category of its own. In fact, our Sages have clearly explained the overriding value of Eretz Yisrael, stating that the precept of living in Israel has equivalent weight to the aggregate of all of the other *mitzvos* of the Torah. *Yishuv Eretz Yisrael* is one of very few *mitzvos aseh* which is described this way by our tradition:

אמרו ישיבת ארץ ישראל שקולה כנגד כל המצוות שבתורה.

The mitzvah of settling Eretz Yisrael is equivalent to that of all the other *mitzvos*.[12]

Let us now briefly review some key *halachos* which dramatically illustrate the tremendous importance of the mitzvah of *yishuv Eretz Yisrael*.

SPOUSE'S DESIRE TO MOVE TO ERETZ YISRAEL

What happens if the fulfillment of the mitzvah of *yishuv Eretz Yisrael* entails a conflict with the fulfillment of other key *mitzvos*? The first halacha we will discuss seems to have the astounding result that *yishuv Eretz Yisrael* takes precedence both over the critically important notion of *shalom bayis* and the holy institution of marriage.

We all know how highly our tradition values marriage, and we are familiar with the Midrash which states that if a couple divorces, the very *mizbe'ach* weeps. Nevertheless, the Rambam (in *Hilchos Ishus* 13:20) discusses what happens if one spouse, but not the other, wishes to move to Eretz Yisrael:

אמר האיש לעלות לארץ ישראל והיא אינה רוצה, תצא בלא כתובה.
אמרה היא לעלות והוא אינו רוצה, יוציא ויתן כתובה, והוא הדין לכל

מקום מארץ ישראל עם ירושלים, שהכל מעלין לארץ ישראל, ואין הכל
מוציאין משם. הכל מעלין לירושלים ואין הכל מוציאין משם.

When a husband desires to move to Eretz Yisrael and his
wife does not desire to do so, he may divorce her without
paying her the *kesuvah*. If she desires to move to Eretz
Yisrael, and he does not desire to do so, he must divorce
her and pay her the *kesuvah*.

The Rambam also states that this halacha applies even where the
proposed move is from a "high-end" zip code in *Chutz la'Aretz* to a
less desirable neighborhood in Eretz Yisrael, or from a place in *Chutz
la'Aretz* where the majority of residents are Jewish to a place in Eretz
Yisrael where the majority of residents are not Jewish.[13]

This is a unique halacha. I do not believe we find anywhere else in
the Shulchan Aruch that if a wife wishes to perform a certain mitzvah
which cannot be performed in the place where the couple currently
resides, and the husband is unwilling to relocate, that we force the
husband to grant her a divorce so that she may relocate and perform
the mitzvah.

In sharp contrast, halacha mandates that, even for the critically
important mitzvah of *kibbud av va'em*, a wife's desire to honor her
parents is subordinated to the needs of the marriage if necessary:

אחד האיש ואחד האשה שוין בכבוד ובמורא של אב ואם אלא שהאשה
אין בידה לעשות שהיא משועבדת לבעלה, לפיכך היא פטורה מכיבוד אב
ואם בעודה נשואה.

Husband and wife have equivalent obligations of fear
and respect for parents. However, a woman's capacity

---

13. The *mitzvah* of *yishuv Eretz Yisrael* seems to override even the great importance
of living amongst neighbors who set a good example for others. The Rambam in
Hilchos Melachim (5:12), echoing the Gemara at the end of *Kesuvos*, states:

לעולם ידור אדם בארץ ישראל, אפילו בעיר שרובה עכו"ם ואל ידור בחוצה לארץ ואפילו בעיר
שרובה ישראל שכל היוצא לחוצה לארץ כאילו עובד ע"ז, שנאמר כי גרשוני היום מהסתפח בנחלת
ד' לאמר לך עבוד אלקים אחרים.

It is preferable to live in Eretz Yisrael, even in a town where a majority of the
population are not Jewish, than to live outside Eretz Yisrael, even in a town where
the majority of the residents are Jewish, because living outside Eretz Yisrael is akin
to worshipping *avoda zara*.

for this mitzvah is limited *because she is subservient to her husband and is therefore exempt while married* [in the event of a conflict between her obligations to her husband and the mitzvah of *kibbud av va'em*, emphasis added] (Yoreh De'ah *Hilchos Kibbud Av Va'em* 240:17).

In light of the above, how remarkable is it that, in the case of *yishuv Eretz Yisrael*, the wife's desire to perform the mitzvah takes precedence even over the institution of marriage.

NON-JEWISH EVED

Just as incredible is the halacha regarding a non-Jewish *eved* (slave) who wishes to move to Eretz Yisrael. Similar to the case of a spouse in the preceding halacha, we see that halacha goes out of its way to accommodate an *eved*'s desire to move to Eretz Yisrael, although halacha does not appear to do so for a non-Jewish *eved* who desires to perform any other mitzvah. The Rambam states as follows (*Hilchos Avodim* 8:9):

> עבד שאמר לעלות לארץ ישראל, כופין את רבו לעלות עמו או ימכור אותו למי שיעלוהו לשם. רצה האדון לצאת לחוצה לארץ, אינו יכול להוציא את עבדו עד שירצה ודין זה בכל זמן אפילו בזמן הזה שהארץ ביד עכו"ם.
>
> If an *eved* wants to make *aliya* (according to the Kesef Mishneh, Rambam is referring here to a non-Jewish *eved*), we force his master to accompany him to Eretz Yisrael, or we force a sale to a master who will go to, or already is in, Eretz Yisrael. This halacha applies even [as in the Rambam's era] when the Land was controlled by others.

Not only does this non-Jewish *eved*'s desire to move to Eretz Yisrael result in his master possibly being forced to cut him loose, but the Gemara indicates that his living in Eretz Yisrael merits very great reward. The Gemara makes the following remarkable statement (*Kesuvos* 111a):

> אמר ר' אבהו, אפילו שפחה כנענית שבא"י מובטח לה שהיא בת העולם הבא.
>
> Rav Avahu said, "Even a non-Jewish maidservant who

lives in Eretz Yisrael can be certain that she has a share in *Olam HaBo*."

TZEDAKA

Not surprisingly, *yishuv Eretz Yisrael* also affects *tzedaka* priorities. We find the following halacha (Yoreh De'ah 251:3):

ויושבי ארץ ישראל קודמין ליושבי חוצה לארץ.

Citizens of Eretz Yisrael have priority when it comes to charity.[14]

BURIAL

The *kedusha* of Eretz Yisrael has a halachic impact even when a person is no longer alive. Yoreh De'ah states that, although it is generally forbidden to move a body from one grave to another, a body may nevertheless be transferred to Eretz Yisrael for burial (363:1). The Rambam helps us understand the rationale behind this leniency when he states that burial in Eretz Yisrael atones for a person (*Hilchos Melachim* 5:11):

אמרו חכמים, כל השוכן בארץ ישראל עוונותיו מחולין . . . אפילו הלך בה ארבע אמות זוכה לחיי העולם הבא. וכן הקבור בה נתכפר לו. וכאילו המקום שהוא בו, מזבח כפרה שנאמר כפר ואדמתו עמו.

The Sages declared: "Whoever dwells in Eretz Yisrael, his or her sins are forgiven. And even a person who merely walks a distance of four cubits in Eretz Yisrael merits *Olam HaBo*. And similarly, one who is buried there receives atonement as though the place in which he is buried is an altar of atonement, as Devarim states (32:43): 'His Land will atone for His people.'"

Although the Gemara and the Rambam cannot literally mean that the sins of any resident of Eretz Yisrael are forgiven, the mere expression of this statement is yet another very powerful example of the great importance of *yishuv Eretz Yisrael* in our tradition.

---

14. We derive this from the *pasuk* (Devarim 16:7) כי יהיה לך אביון . . . בארצך.

PURCHASING LAND IN ISRAEL FROM A GENTILE ON SHABBOS

It is generally a Torah prohibition to ask a non-Jew to write something on Shabbos, even for the purpose of fulfilling a mitzvah. Nevertheless, the Gemara (*Gittin* 8b) concludes that it is permissible to ask a non-Jew to write a bill of sale on Shabbos in order to conclude purchase of land in Israel from a non-Jew.

PERFORMING MITZVOS IN CHUTZ LA'ARETZ

We conclude this part of the discussion with one of the most astounding Rashi's we will find anywhere. Rashi, commenting on a *pasuk* in Devarim, states as follows (referring to the Sifri, Yirmiyahu 31:20):

אַף לְאַחַר שֶׁתִּגְלוּ, הֱיוּ מְצוּיָּינִים בְּמִצְוֹת, הַנִּיחוּ תְּפִילִין, עֲשׂוּ מְזוּזוֹת, כְּדֵי
שֶׁלֹּא יִהְיוּ לָכֶם חֲדָשִׁים כְּשֶׁתַּחְזְרוּ, וְכֵן הוּא אוֹמֵר הַצִּיבִי לָךְ צִיּוּנִים.

Even after Bnei Yisrael go into exile, we should perform the *mitzvos*, putting on *tefillin* and affixing *mezuzos*, so that when we return to Eretz Yisrael, these mitzvos will not seem new to us (Devarim 11:18).

Why does Rashi have to give us this reason for performing *mitzvos* in *Chutz la'Aretz*? Why indeed do we need a reason? Rashi, incredibly, appears to be implying that the only purpose of doing *mitzvos* in *Chutz la'Aretz* is so that we do not forget how to perform them by the time we make our way to Eretz Yisrael.

Now that we have seen some examples of how *halachos* and *midrashim* treat the mitzvah of *yishuv Eretz Yisrael* with extreme deference, virtually without parallel among *mitzvos*, I would like to turn to a related and extremely important subject – how we talk to others about Eretz Yisrael.

◆ NOT SPEAKING BADLY OF ERETZ YISRAEL

Almost each one of us has returned from a visit to Eretz Yisrael at some point in our lives and voiced to others some complaint, either about a hotel we stayed at, the attitudes of certain service people, or whatever. Is there anything wrong with our having done so?

In *Kesuvos* (112a), we are told that Rebbe Chanina would remove obstacles from, and correct the unevenness of, the roads in Eretz Yisrael – ר׳ חנינא מתקן מתקליה. Rashi comments:

> משוה ומתקן מכשולי העיר מחמת חיבת הארץ שהיתה חביבה עליו,
> ומחזר שלא יצא שם רע על הדרכים.
>
> He would fix and remove public hazards out of love for the Land. He did not want any words of criticism to issue from people towards the Land and its highways.

Rashi, on this Gemara, states that Rebbe Chanina would fix any obstacles in the roads because of his love for the Land and because he wanted to make certain that no-one would utter a *"shem ra"* (a derogatory report) with regard to the roads. This is an amazing statement. Rashi almost humanizes Eretz Yisrael by declaring that one should not speak *lashon hara* even about the inanimate objects (such as the roads) of Eretz Yisrael. In fact, we see from Rebbe Chanina's filling of potholes – an apparently demeaning activity for someone of Rebbe Chanina's stature – that a person should also do everything possible to dissuade others from speaking badly even about the mere terrain of Eretz Yisrael.

In the aforementioned essay in Rav Mirsky's *Hegyonei Halacha*, the following passage appears:

> The Sages loved Eretz Yisrael, because it is after all a Holy Land enveloped in *mitzvos*. And because of their deep love for Eretz Yisrael, the Sages guarded the Land, and endeavored to correct any hazards found there. They were also vigilant not to speak in a negative or critical way about Eretz Yisrael, as noted at the very end of *Kesuvos*. The Gemara there discusses how the Sages manifested their love for Eretz Yisrael. For instance, Abaye would kiss its stones. Rav Ami and Rav Asi, when they were learning Torah during the summer, and the sun would begin to beat down upon them, would pick themselves up and move to a shady location; and during

the winter when they became chilly they would move to
a warmer location.

Rav Mirsky notes that the Gemara relates this story to emphasize the
lengths to which these great Sages would go in order to make certain
that they would not have any pretext to complain about their living
conditions in Eretz Yisrael.

Eretz Yisrael is a special gift to us from our Creator, as we have
seen, and it follows that we have an obligation to treat Eretz Yisrael
with extreme love and reverence. The Rambam states as follows
(*Hilchos Melachim* 5:10):

גדולי החכמים היו מנשקין על תחומי ארץ ישראל ומנשקין אבניה,
ומתגלגלין על עפרה, וכן הוא אומר כי רצו עבדיך את אבניה ואת עפרה
יחוננו.

Great sages would kiss the borders of Eretz Yisrael, kiss
its stones, and roll in its dust. Similarly, Tehillim (102:15)
declares: "Behold, your servants hold her stones dear
and cherish her dust."

৶ APPROPRIATE ATTITUDE TOWARDS THE NON-RELIGIOUS

Now, since it is clearly so important not to speak badly of Eretz Yisrael
or its people, what should our attitude be towards the non-religious
leaders and other citizens of Eretz Yisrael whom we as a community
have often been quick to criticize?

A frequently heard argument, made in some circles, against the
legitimacy of Medinas Yisrael is the purported non-religious make-up
of its political and military leaders. A very sad contemporary example
of this phenomenon is manifested by statements made by some to
the effect that Ilan Ramon, the fallen NASA astronaut, was not a hero
because he did not keep Shabbos properly and because no secular
Jew could be a hero to a Torah Jew. I would like to briefly address
this issue.

In *Eim Habanim Semeichah*, Rav Teichtal, addressing the issue of
the non-religious Zionist pioneers, says the following:

[The zealots] consider them [i.e., the non-religious] wicked because [the zealots] do not see them as G-d's messengers, with foundations at the height of sanctity. But I myself disagree. In my opinion, these builders are not wicked. They are genuine descendants of Avraham, Yitzchak, and Yaakov. . . . It is a mitzvah to love them and bring them near, as the Rambam writes (*Hilchos Mamrim* 3:3).

Let this be a lesson for all those who are quick to call their fellow Jews "*rasha*." G-d forbid to do such a thing. . . . Hashem will shower upon them a purifying spirit from above . . . . and He will draw them near to His service by virtue of the mitzvah of *yishuv Eretz Yisrael*, for which they sacrifice themselves. Amen, so may it be G-d's will.[15]

Rav Teichtal refers to a Gemara (*Chullin* 63a). The Gemara there states that we have a tradition that if a certain bird called a *sherakrak* sits on the ground and whistles, Moshiach will come, referring to a *pasuk* in Zecharya (10:8) which states (10:8):

אשרקה להם ואקבצם כי פדיתים.

This verse means "I will whistle to them and will gather them"; the word אשרקה refers to this *sherakrak* bird.

Rav Teichtal comments:

I was astonished when I read this statement. According to Chazal, the prophet promises us that an unclean bird [namely, the *sherakrak*] will signal the final redemption . . .

What will you say about this, my son. You can now question G-d . . . Why would He bring the tidings of the most prodigious event, the one which we await with bated breath, specifically through an unclean bird? Would it not have been more appropriate to do so

---

15. Teichtal, *Eim Habanim Semeichah: On Eretz Yisrael, Redemption, and Unity*, 193.

through kosher birds and bring good tidings through
meritorious and pure individuals? . . .

However, the truth is, as Job says: "Can you fathom
the searchings of G-d?" . . . Who can comprehend His
way? . . . Most importantly, it is self-evident that these
pioneers [referring to the non-religious Israelis] are G-d's
messengers.[16]

The Maharsha[17] derives from the Gemara that even the sinners of
Israel are as full of *mitzvos* as a pomegranate is full of seeds. And, as
stated by the editors of *The Jewish Press*[18] (in response to two letters
denigrating the Kiddush Hashem achievements of Ilan Ramon):

The [letters] are very, very sad. Did Abba Eban's lack of
religious commitment make him any less of a spokesman
for Jews everywhere when his soaring rhetoric in defense
of Israel resonated in the United Nations? Was the capture of Jerusalem in 1967 any less historic because Moshe
Dayan was a secular Jew? Was Motta Gur's cry of *"Har
HaBayit beyadenu"* (the Temple Mount is in our hands)
any less thrilling to all Jews because he was non-obser-
vant? Were thousands of non-frum Jewish soldiers who
fell in battle in 1967 and 1973 any less heroic because they
did not fulfill the *mitzvos*? Are secular members of the
IDF who today protect the Jews of Israel anything less
than valiant defenders of the Jewish people?

Moshe Dayan perhaps captured it best when, arriving
at the Western Wall immediately after its capture in the
Six-Day War, he kissed some of its stones and with obvious emotion declared: "We have returned to our holiest
of places, never to abandon them again." When a startled
reporter asked him if he had become a "born-again Jew,"
Dayan responded: "I was not religious yesterday and I

16. Teichtal, *Eim Habanim Semeichah: On Eretz Yisrael, Redemption, and Unity*,
184–185.

17. See Schottenstein, fn. 13 in *Megilla* 6a.

18. *The Jewish Press*, February 14, 2002.

may not be religious tomorrow. But at this moment, no one in Israel is more religious than I."

✒ MEANING OF THE EXPRESSION זבת חלב ודבש

The words זבת חלב ודבש are very prominent in the Torah's description of Eretz Yisrael, with approximately fifteen references in the Torah and five more in Nach. The Gemara discusses the meaning of זבת חלב ודבש and states as follows (*Kesuvos* 112a):

זבת חלב ודבש – שמנים מחלב ומתוקים מדבש.

[The fruits are] richer than milk and sweeter than honey.

What does this mean? If we take the Gemara's statement at face value, namely that the fruits of Eretz Yisrael are sweet, why would the Torah repeatedly highlight such a seemingly insignificant feature to describe Eretz Yisrael? Has anyone ever gone on vacation to a country and, upon returning, marveled to their friends about the sweet fruit? We talk about the beautiful scenery, the magnificent beaches, the quality of the hotel, but sweet fruit?

To reinforce our puzzlement at the Torah's description of Eretz Yisrael by way of reference to the sweetness of the Land's agricultural production, let us refer to yet another example – a *pasuk* in Yirmiyahu (3:19) and its interpretation in the Gemara. The *pasuk* reads:

ואתן לך ארץ חמדה נחלת צבי.

And I will give you a cherished Land, the inheritance of a deer.

The Gemara (*Kesuvos* 112a) discusses Yirmiyahu's comparison of Eretz Yisrael to a deer.

למה ארץ ישראל נמשלה לצבי? לומר לך, מה צבי זה אין עורו מחזיק בשרו, אף ארץ ישראל אינה מחזקת פירותיה.

Why is the Land of Eretz Yisrael compared to a deer? To tell you that just as it is true of the deer that its hide cannot contain its own flesh after it is skinned, so too is it true of Eretz Yisrael that its borders cannot contain the abundance of its produce.

Similarly, the Gemara provides another explanation for the *pasuk*'s comparison of Eretz Yisrael to a deer (*Kesuvos* 112a):

דבר אחר מה צבי זה קל מכל החיות, אף ארץ ישראל קלה מכל הארצות
לבשל את פירותיה.

Just as a deer is quicker than the other animals, so too is Eretz Yisrael quicker than other lands to see its fruits ripen.

But we cannot help but ask: Does this mean that Eretz Yisrael is cherished just because its fruits ripen more quickly or because it produces more fruit than it needs? There are many countries in this world which produce more food of various types than its inhabitants can consume. How does this fact alone make Eretz Yisrael unique, or cherished? Alternatively, just because the fruits of Eretz Yisrael ripen earlier than in other countries, is this really the reason why the *pasuk* states that Eretz Yisrael is ארץ חמדה – a cherished Land? Because we can eat oranges a few weeks early?

It is apparent by now that the expression זבת חלב ודבש, as well as the other references in the Gemara and *midrashim* describing Eretz Yisrael through imagery of fruit, must have a much deeper meaning. And so, in order to gain insight into the true meaning of זבת חלב ודבש, and the imagery of fruit in connection with Eretz Yisrael, let us turn our attention to a Midrash which discusses the *arba minim* of Sukkos and particularly the *esrog* – a fruit which is a key component of the celebration of the holiday.

Vayikra Rabba (Emor 30:11) suggests that the *arba minim* represent the four types of Jews. The *lulav* has taste but no smell and represents the Jew who has Torah knowledge but not good deeds. The *hadas* has smell but no taste and represents the Jew who has good deeds but not Torah knowledge. The *arava* has neither smell nor taste and represents the Jew who has neither good deeds nor Torah knowledge. The *esrog* however is in a different category:

מה אתרוג זה יש בו טעם ויש בו ריח, כך ישראל יש בהם בני אדם שיש
בהם תורה ויש בהם מעשים טובים.

> Just as the *esrog* has both taste and smell, so too are there Jews who possess both Torah knowledge and good deeds.

I believe that this Midrash regarding the *esrog* – as representing a person whose scholarship and observance are exemplary – helps us understand the symbolism of זבת חלב ודבש. We asked why, in view of the Gemara's explanation that זבת חלב ודבש meant that the fruits of Eretz Yisrael are richer than milk and sweeter than honey, the Torah would emphasize such a seemingly insignificant feature to describe Eretz Yisrael. But now that we have seen, in the case of *esrog*, that the Torah's use of the symbolism of fruit can have very strong spiritual connotations, it is apparent that זבת חלב ודבש means much more than good fruit, of the kind that a person eats.

In this context, I believe we can now understand why the Gemara interpreted the *pasuk* in Yirmiyahu, which likened the inheritance of Eretz Yisrael to a deer, to mean that *the produce of Eretz Yisrael* ripens quickly. This is far more than an agricultural comment which, in and of itself, would not be all that meaningful. Rather, I would suggest that the produce of Israel to which the Gemara refers means *the production, not of fruit, but rather of persons who represent Torah in the finest sense*, and that the deeper meaning of the Gemara's statement – that the fruits of Eretz Yisrael ripen exceedingly quickly – is exactly what very many parents have witnessed for themselves, namely the amazingly rapid progress many of our children have made while attending yeshivos or seminaries in Eretz Yisrael and how they ripen and mature at a pace we did not think was possible.

Along the same lines, the Gemara's statement that the borders of Eretz Yisrael cannot contain the abundance of its produce is symbolic, I believe, of the fact that Eretz Yisrael has such a powerful impact on scholars nurtured there, whether our children or others, that this has a profound impact on Jewish communities everywhere. Surely, just about every Jewish community in the world has benefited enormously from the influence and involvement of individuals whose Torah and *hashkafa* were transformed by their studies in Eretz Yisrael.

We can see a fascinating example of this dual (physical and spiritual) aspect of זבת חלב דבש in the episode of the *meraglim*. The Torah tells us that the *meraglim* reported back as follows (Bamidbar 13:27):

ויספרו לו ויאמרו באנו אל הארץ אשר שלחתנו וגם זבת חלב ודבש הוא
וזה פריה.

The *meraglim* stated that the Land was זבת חלב ודבש and
here is its fruit.

Rashi makes the following comment to the report of the *meraglim*
(Bamidbar 13:27):

זבת חלב ודבש הוא. כל דבר שקר שאין אומרים בו קצת אמת בתחלתו,
אין מתקיים בסופו.

The *meraglim* described Eretz Yisrael as a Land of milk
and honey. Every falsehood which does not contain a
partial truth at its beginning will not endure.

Why does Rashi state that the *meraglim* began their report with a
partial (קצת) truth? After all, the *meraglim* used Hashem's exact words
of זבת חלב ודבש in describing Eretz Yisrael! Why was this not *the whole*
truth?

I believe, however, that Rashi can be explained very nicely using
the ideas we expressed earlier. We suggested that the expression
זבת חלב ודבש has both physical and spiritual elements – the physical
element is that it represents sweet fruit, literally, and the spiritual
element is that the Land has the power to foster and produce a person
whose Torah and *mitzvos* are exemplary. The error of the *meraglim*
was in their exclusive focus on the physical element of זבת חלב ודבש,
as we see in the manner in which the *meraglim* demonstrated זבת חלב
ודבש – their evidence consisted, the *pasuk* tells us, of simply showing
Bnei Yisrael the immense fruit produced by Eretz Yisrael at that time.
This is only a partial truth, as Rashi brilliantly notes.

Of course, if זבת חלב ודבש means only material, physical things, then
we understand why the daunting physical challenge of conquering
the Seven Nations caused the *meraglim* to issue their negative report.
If the benefits of Eretz Yisrael are purely material – only sweet fruit
– we can become materially well-off almost anywhere, and since the
inhabitants of Eretz Yisrael were at that time so powerful militarily,
there was no reason for Bnei Yisrael to risk their lives to conquer the
Land.

Perhaps that is why Yehoshua and Calev responded טובה הארץ מאוד
מאוד, with a doubled-up use of the word מאוד. Yehoshua and Calev

were stating that Eretz Yisrael is good not only physically but, more significantly, spiritually as well and that it therefore did not matter that the then inhabitants of Eretz Yisrael were powerful, because there is no other place where Bnei Yisrael can attain the spiritual heights which Hashem intended for us.

Our construct of זבת חלב ודבש can also explain why Hashem did not use this expression when describing Eretz Yisrael to the Avos. Since זבת חלב ודבש is an expression which symbolizes Eretz Yisrael's unique capacity to nurture Torah learning, it stands to reason that Hashem would reserve use of this expression when addressing someone who would be entering Eretz Yisrael only after the Torah had been given.

Incidentally, this deeper meaning of זבת חלב ודבש can help us understand the Midrash which states that Eretz Yisrael was given nine out of ten measures of beauty allotted to the world – this cannot literally refer to physical beauty, as there are countless beautiful land and seascapes in this world (Grand Canyon, etc.), but clearly refers to the extraordinary spiritual achievement which Eretz Yisrael has the unique ability to nurture.

❧ CONCLUSION

We began this *d'var Torah* by referring to *midrashim* which clearly state that Eretz Yisrael is a special gift, hand-picked for us, so to speak, by Hashem and that His Shechina resides only there. This is manifested by the incredible historical fact that Eretz Yisrael has refused to be fertile for any of its many conquerors. We also noted that Hashem manipulates world events according to the needs of Eretz Yisrael.

We analyzed the deeper meaning of the words זבת חלב ודבש by reference to the symbolism of *esrog*. We suggested that זבת חלב ודבש represents not merely good fruit of the kind that we eat but, on a deeper level, signifies the spiritual fruitfulness which Eretz Yisrael uniquely has the ability to nurture.

And we reviewed *halachos* and *midrashim* which clearly show the uniqueness of *yishuv Eretz Yisrael* – a mitzvah which takes precedence even when its performance conflicts with the extremely important notions of *shalom* and marriage (as when one spouse wants to move to Eretz Yisrael and the other does not).

We have seen that the mitzvah of *yishuv Eretz Yisrael* finds very great favor with Hashem. As the Gemara says: "Whoever walks four *amos* in Eretz Yisrael, merits *Olam HaBo*" and, in fact, the very earth of Eretz Yisrael appears to have the power to forgive the sins of one who is buried there. Rashi seems to go so far as to say that performing *mitzvos* in *Chutz la'Aretz* is mere practice for our eventual *aliya* to Eretz Yisrael.

What does all this mean for us living in *Chutz la'Aretz*? Aside from the fact that halacha makes certain allowances for those who live outside of Eretz Yisrael for reasons of *parnasa*, I believe that there are many significant ways in which we are able to assist, to our very great merit, in the fulfillment of the mitzvah of *yishuv Eretz Yisrael*, even as we reside in *galus*.

In this regard, we noted how halacha goes out of its way to accommodate the desire of a lowly *eved*, not even Jewish, to settle in Eretz Yisrael. In fact, according to the Gemara, this *eved* is assured of a share in *Olam HaBo*. Why should this be so? Why would a non-Jewish *eved*, who may be doing nothing more significant than making beds or cleaning house, be elevated to such an exalted status?

As we indicated earlier, I believe that the halachos regarding an *eved* make it clear that the mitzvah of *yishuv Eretz Yisrael* is of such overriding significance that even if someone is performing the most menial tasks associated with *yishuv Eretz Yisrael*, such person merits very great reward. Surely, therefore, we cannot help but conclude that every single activity which assists Eretz Yisrael and in which we engage, whether or not we actually reside there, has enormous merit and is precious in the eyes of Hashem.

Moreover, there are *meforshim* who indicate that activities such as planting a tree or buying an apartment in Eretz Yisrael rise to the level of *yishuv Eretz Yisrael*.[19] Accordingly, it may very well be the case that we, to some degree, fulfill the great mitzvah of *yishuv Eretz Yisrael* by visiting Eretz Yisrael, sending our children to learn there, lobbying on behalf of Eretz Yisrael, participating in *chesed* programs and organizations directed at residents and institutions in Eretz Yisrael, purchasing Israeli products, etc.

Whatever we have done on behalf of Eretz Yisrael in the past,

---

19. See Rambam (*Hilchos Melachim* 5:11) which states, following the Gemara in *Kesuvos* 111a, that even walking four *amos* in Eretz Yisrael assures a person of *Olam HaBo*. See also *Encyclopedia Talmudit*, "Eretz Yisrael," p. 223, fn. 22.

surely we will do so with all that much more determination, diligence, and enthusiasm if we understand and appreciate the monumental importance of this mitzvah, which we are told by the Midrash has the weight of all of the other *mitzvos* of the Torah.

We have also noted how the *chachamim* manifested their love for Eretz Yisrael and how they went to great lengths to make certain that no-one would speak badly of the Land or its inhabitants. Amazingly, it was apparently not beneath the dignity of the great Rebbe Chanina to fix potholes just so that others would not speak negatively of Eretz Yisrael. This is a critically important concept with respect to which almost all of have inadvertently stumbled. If we bear in mind that Eretz Yisrael is Hashem's special gift to us, we would surely do everything in our power to speak well of Eretz Yisrael and to make sure that others do the same. There is a passage in Tehillim which states (102:14–15):

אתה תקום תרחם ציון כי עת לחננה כי בא מועד. כי רצו עבדיך את אבניה
ואת עפרה יחננו.

And now rise and have mercy on Zion, for it is time to give her favor, the time has come. For your servants have cherished her stones and favored her dust.

The Kuzari explains that Jerusalem will be rebuilt only when the Jewish people long for it so much that they will crave even its stones and its dust (*Sefer HaKuzari*, at the end). Just as our great Sages kissed the stones of Eretz Yisrael and rolled in its dust, all of which clearly reflected their belief that every nook and cranny of Eretz Yisrael has great *kedusha*, so too should we demonstrate, by our special efforts on behalf of the Land and its inhabitants, that we regard Eretz Yisrael with the greatest of reverence and respect.

And an important part of this respect consists of our attitude towards the many non-religious pioneers in Eretz Yisrael who, as Rav Teichtal points out, are clearly G-d's messengers. Rav Teichtal, in the passage we quoted earlier, wondered why Hashem would bring about our redemption through so many non-religious pioneers. Perhaps this is a test, to determine whether we would treat our non-religious brethren with true *ahavas Yisrael*. Unfortunately, not only have we, all too often, failed this crucial test, but we have severely compounded our error by speaking *lashon hara* about Eretz Yisrael through our bitter criticism of these people.

Rav Teichtal says about those who engage in such criticism:

> These zealots spread hatred . . . against the group which devoted itself to building up our Land to its former glory.[20]

Using very strong language, and implying that baseless hatred of the non-religious pioneers was at least partially to blame for the Holocaust, Rav Teichtal compares the critics of the non-religious pioneers to the *meraglim*, and states:

> Today's "spies" [referring to critics of the non-religious pioneers] . . . having added sorrow onto sorrow, [have brought] us to our present situation in which we see horror after horror and weeping after weeping in the House of Israel.[21]

Let us make up for past errors by redoubling our *ahavas Yisrael* and our efforts to speak kindly of Eretz Yisrael and all of its people.

The Gemara, at the end of *Kesuvos* (112b), after predicting the decimation of the Jews which it said would occur in the era in which Moshiach comes, apparently wants to end on a hopeful note, and states:

> עתידין כל אילני סרק שבארץ ישראל שיטענו פירות.
>
> At that time all the barren trees in Eretz Yisrael will bear fruit.

We suggested earlier that trees and fruit, in connection with Eretz Yisrael, appear to have a symbolism beyond the literal and may signify Torah and *mitzvos*. I believe that the Gemara in *Kesuvos* is telling us that, at the end of days, even those Jews in Eretz Yisrael who are "barren," meaning those who do not have a religious upbringing, will come to appreciate Torah and *mitzvos* or, to use the Gemara's expres-

---

20. Teichtal, *Eim Habanim Semeichah: On Eretz Yisrael, Redemption, and Unity*, 27.

21. Teichtal, *Eim Habanim Semeichah: On Eretz Yisrael, Redemption, and Unity*, 27.

sion, they will bear fruit. We witnessed this, in a magnificent way, in the case of Ilan Ramon who, despite his secular background, did so many things to create a *Kiddush Hashem* across the world and for all time. Ilan, once "a barren tree," produced the most beautiful fruit, in fulfillment of the prediction made by the Gemara in *Kesuvos*. What a coincidence (or perhaps not), in light of the Gemara's statement, that his name was Ilan (and also Ramon, a pomegranate, the seeds of which are likened to the 613 *mitzvos*).

And finally, we conclude with a quote from the great Rav Avraham Yitzchak Hakohen Kook, *zt"l*, who said:

> יסוד הגלות והשפלות הנמשך בעולם, בא רק ממה שאין מודיעים את
> ארץ־ישראל, את ערכה וחכמתה, ואין מתקנים את חטא המרגלים
> שהוציאו דבה על הארץ.

> The root cause of the exile and depression which exist in this world lies in our not acknowledging Eretz Yisrael, its value, and wisdom, and in our failing to remedy the sin of the *meraglim* in uttering slanderous statements regarding the Land.[22]

Let us take serious note of Rav Kook's statement and acknowledge, by our actions, that we appreciate the incredible gift which Hashem gave us in the form of Eretz Yisrael. Let us understand that this is the Land where Hashem's Shechina resides and that it is only in Eretz Yisrael where we as a people can fulfill our highest spiritual goals. Let us show our true love for Eretz Yisrael and all of its people, by doing everything in our power to help Eretz Yisrael in every way, and by determining to always speak well of Eretz Yisrael and its inhabitants, particularly those whom we view as non-religious, and to do everything in our power to make certain that others do so as well. In this merit, may Hashem help us to bring about a *geula shleima, bimheira beyameinu*.

---

22. אגרות הראי״ה, אגרת צ״ו

BILAAM: IMPACT OF A *BRACHA* AND *KELALA* UPON AN INDIVIDUAL AND A NATION, AND APPLICATION TO ISRAEL'S EPIC BATTLE WITH ITS CURRENT ENEMIES

INTRODUCTION

Although Parshas Balak seems superficially to be an anachronistic tale of black magic, curses, and a talking donkey, the *parsha* has, I believe, extraordinary relevance to the epic battle being waged today between the Jews and their Arab enemies and indeed may hold the key to our achieving victory in this battle. In fact, as we shall see, it could be argued that Balak is one of the most underestimated *parshios* in the Torah. The Zohar declares:[1]

> Whoever thinks the stories in this passage (referring to Parshas Balak) relate only to that period is an ignorant person.

In order to understand the Zohar's statement that the events of Parshas Balak have significance beyond that era, it might be helpful to frame our discussion with the following questions:

- What does it mean to curse a people? Does cursing involve black magic or does it mean something else entirely?
- If the *parsha* is about sorcery, what is the role of the *korbanos* which Bilaam repeatedly asks Balak to bring, and why does Bilaam regularly invoke Hashem's Name and state that he is strictly beholden to G-d's instructions?
- What does the Gemara mean when it states that G-d becomes

---

1. As quoted in Rabbi Elie Munk, *Call of the Torah, Bamidbar* (NY: ArtScroll), 262.

angry at one particular moment during the day and that Bilaam knew when that moment occurs? Does Hashem really have a moment of weakness, when He is vulnerable?

- If in fact Bilaam knew the secret moment that he could "get to" Hashem, so to speak, why were his efforts unsuccessful?
- The Gemara tells us that Bilaam would normally have used a horse for transportation but that day was riding a donkey because he had put his horses out to graze. What a strange explanation this is! There is clearly significance in Bilaam's riding a donkey on that particular day. We also wonder why he was riding a female donkey.
- We know that Hashem operates *midda k'neged midda* – measure for measure. If so, why did the donkey crush Bilaam's leg against the wall when Bilaam was sinning with his mouth?
- Why is the *Ma Tovu tefillah*, uttered by Bilaam, a non-Jewish prophet, placed at the very forefront of our *Shacharis tefillos*, ahead of the many eloquent prayers composed by the *Anshei Knesses HaGedola*?
- Why does this *parsha*, alone among all the others in the Torah, contain specific Messianic allusions?

We will propose, and hopefully demonstrate, that Parshas Balak contains remarkable parallels with the epic battle being waged between the Jews and Arabs today. Before launching into our presentation, it is worth noting a very striking example of this parallel. Just as Bnei Yisrael are today battling countries (such as Iran and Syria) which use stateless terrorists as proxies (such as Hezbollah, the Palestinians, Hamas, and others), so too did Midian retain Bilaam, who was so named, according to the Gemara (*Sanhedrin* 105a), because he was not part of any people, as shown by the manner in which the Gemara parses his name: בלא עם.

◦§ BACKGROUND

At the end of the prior *parsha* of Chukas, we are told that Bnei Yisrael had just destroyed the powerful armies of Bashan and Emor. The Jews were a ragtag group of erstwhile slaves and were not supposed to be accomplished militarily. Yet, in a stunning reversal of roles reminiscent of the modern State of Israel throughout most of its existence, Bnei Yisrael was not only winning the war of brute force but was steamrollering its enemies militarily. This very notion seems to have been a source of great discouragement to Moav. The *pasuk* tells us (Bamidbar 22:3):

ויקץ מואב מפני בני ישראל.

Moav was disgusted in the face of Bnei Yisrael.

On the word ויקץ, Rashi comments "קצו בחייהם" – Moav was disgusted with their very lives.

Balak, the King of Moav, having seen how easily Bnei Yisrael conquered the armies of Bashan and Emor, was terrified that the Jews would easily overcome the other nations living in the Land – just like an ox eats through the grass in the field (כלחוך השור את ירק השדה). Balak urgently sends for Bilaam to curse the Jews so that Balak can drive the Jews out of Israel. Bilaam was a non-Jewish prophet who communicated with G-d and was reputed to have extraordinary powers. Rashi tells us that Bilaam had, on a prior occasion, successfully applied his cursing skills on behalf of Sichon in a battle against Moav (Bamidbar 22:6).

What induced Moav to hire Bilaam to do battle against the Jews? To answer this question, we begin with the observation that Balak (the King of Moav), in a desperate state following Bnei Yisrael's devastating military victories, went so far as to seek advice from his country's traditional enemy, Midian. Rashi (22:4) quotes the following very significant Midrash Tanchuma to explain why Moav approached Midian, of all nations, for advice:

ומה ראה מואב ליטול עצה ממדין? כיון שראו את ישראל נוצחים שלא כמנהג העולם, אמרו מנהיגם של אלו במדין נתגדל, נשאל מהם מה מידתו. אמרו להם, אין כוחו אלא בפיו. אמרו אף אנו נביא עליהם אדם שכוחו בפיו.

What did Moav see in order to warrant its seeking advice from Midian? Moav perceived Bnei Yisrael being victorious in a supernatural manner. Moav noted that the leader of Bnei Yisrael [Moshe] grew up in Midian and decided to ask the King of Midian wherein lay the special strength of Bnei Yisrael. The response was that

> Bnei Yisrael's unique strength was through its mouth,
> and thereupon Moav resolved to attack Bnei Yisrael with
> a man [Bilaam] whose unique power was through his
> mouth.

I believe that if we closely analyze this Midrash, we will see that it can
help us unlock one of the great secrets of this *parsha*. What did Midian
mean in stating that the power of Bnei Yisrael was through its mouth?
Surely, Midian never saw Bnei Yisrael using incantations or other
forms of verbal sorcery. On the contrary, it seems that the wonders
performed on behalf of Bnei Yisrael in Mitzrayim were viewed by the
Egyptians, and presumably by Midian as well, as the Yad Hashem,
and not the result of some sort of black magic.

For example, during the ten plagues, when the sorcerers of Mitzrayim were unable to replicate the lice, they responded: אצבע אלקים
היא – it is the Finger of G-d (Shemos 8:15). And during *kriyas Yam Suf*,
the Egyptians said: כי ד׳ נלחם להם במצרים – Hashem is fighting the Jews'
battle in Mitzrayim (14:25).

Therefore, when Midian informed Moav that the source of Bnei
Yisrael's strength was through its mouth, Midian must have been
referring to *tefillah* and not sorcery. Accordingly, when Moav hired
Bilaam to turn this weapon of the mouth against Bnei Yisrael, the
intent must have been for Bilaam to apply not black magic but rather
the power of prayer (and we will see considerable additional evidence
of this). After all, since the objective of Moav's inquiry to Midian was
to ascertain the secret strength of Bnei Yisrael, and to then use this
strength against Bnei Yisrael, it would not make a lot of sense for
Moav to use sorcery as a weapon when Bnei Yisrael's strength was in
tefillah and not sorcery.

In support of this idea, and constituting one of the many veiled
allusions to the fact that Balak focuses on the power of *tefillah* rather
than on black magic, Moav (no doubt without fully appreciating the
import of this statement) makes a very uncommon, but meaningful,
reference to Bnei Yisrael at the beginning of the *parsha*. The *pasuk*
states (Bamidbar 22:4):

> ויאמר מואב אל זקני מדין, עתה ילחכו הקהל את כל סביבתינו.
> And Moav said to the elders of Midian: this *congregation*
> will chew up our entire surroundings.

The word *kahal* is a very unusual word in the Torah to describe Bnei Yisrael and is used mostly in connection with *korbanos* which, as we know, are today represented by *tefillah b'tzibbur*. Even today, when we refer to a congregation of a *shul*, we talk about a *kehila*. And so the Torah informs us that it is Bnei Yisrael, acting specifically as a *kahal*, which threatened to conquer its enemies militarily. And it therefore seems that it is the power of Bnei Yisrael's *tefillos* which so intimidated Moav and which Moav attempted to counter by hiring Bilaam.

BNEI YISRAEL'S INHERENT POWER OF TEFILLAH

And so we see that Bnei Yisrael's super-weapon, which allows it to confidently approach the battlefield even against its most formidable enemies, is *tefillah*. How and when did we acquire this weapon? It is in fact built into our very character, as Rashi explains in a dramatic and revolutionary explanation of one of the most well-known incidents in *sefer* Bereishis.

We know that Yaakov attempted to wrest the *bracha* of the *bechor* from Esav. A superficial, or *p'shat*, reading of the relevant passage indicates that Yaakov attempted to trick his father into giving Yaakov the *bracha* which rightfully belonged to Esav. In the process, Yaakov, in responding to one of Yitzchak's questions, invoked Hashem's Name, and Yitzchak, apparently mystified that Esav would use such deferential language, responded הקול קול יעקב – the voice is the voice of Yaakov. This statement is traditionally interpreted to mean that Yitzchak became suspicious as to which son was in fact standing before him.

However, according to a remarkable Rashi (Bamidbar 20:16), quoting the Midrash Tanchuma, the words הקול קול יעקב, far from being words of Yitzchak's puzzlement and suspicion, in fact constituted a deliberate and purposeful *bracha* that Yaakov's descendants would possess the enormous power of the קול of *tefillah*.

The *pasuk* in Parshas Chukas states: ונצעק אל ד' וישמע קולנו – and, when we were enslaved in Mitzrayim, we cried out to Hashem, Who heard our voice. Rashi comments on the words: וישמע קולנו:

בברכה שברכנו אבינו הקול קול יעקב שאנו צועקים ונענים.

Hashem heard our voice of prayer, our קול, in Mitzrayim, as a result of the *bracha* of הקול קול יעקב with which

> Yitzchak blessed our people, through which our cries are
> heard by Hashem and answered.

This is the blessing of the power of *tefillah*, which was apparently
intended to overcome Esav's *bracha* of military might – והידים ידי עשו.
And it is this very *bracha* which we find playing such a prominent role
at the very outset of Parshas Balak, first through the meaningful use of
the word קהל (עתה ילחכו הקהל את כל סביבתינו) and immediately thereafter
in our learning that Balak, the King of Moav, set out to co-opt and
trump this great power of *tefillah* by retaining Bilaam to use this very
weapon against Bnei Yisrael (we will discuss in some detail just how
he went about doing so).

Before we further analyze the *parsha*, however, it is useful to briefly
summarize some of the *parsha*'s other developments.

❧ SUMMARY OF THE PARSHA

After Bilaam is summoned by Moav to curse Bnei Yisrael, G-d appears
to Bilaam, who informs G-d that Balak wants him to curse the Jews.
G-d tells him not to bother because the Jews are blessed – לא תאור
את העם כי ברוך הוא (Bamidbar 22:12) – and not to accompany Balak's
messengers. Bilaam is persistent, however, and G-d finally gives him
permission to go on his mission, but on condition that Bilaam may
only say what G-d permits him to say. Despite G-d's clear instructions, Bilaam proceeds with the wrong intentions – he apparently
thinks that he will be able to change G-d's mind. The Midrash tells
us that, although Bilaam believed in G-d, he thought that G-d had
vulnerabilities.

Bilaam continues his efforts to obtain G-d's permission to curse
the Jewish people. Bilaam offers numerous sacrifices to G-d but this
doesn't work either. Finally, in his last attempt, Bilaam observes Bnei
Yisrael from a distance, hoping to spot some negative characteristic
which he can then present to G-d as evidence that the Jews deserve
to be cursed.

This approach not only does not work; it backfires when Bilaam
observes the positive characteristics of the Jewish people. For example,
Bilaam notices that Bnei Yisrael pitched their tents in such a manner
that the opening of each person's tent faced away from the opening

of his neighbor's tent. Bilaam admires this display of modesty and privacy and gives up for good his attempt to curse the Jews and in fact blesses them instead.

Bilaam then offers a series of sacrifices, in a final effort to curse the Jews, but each time blesses them instead, culminating with a prediction of Israel's final victory באחרית הימים (in the end of days) over its oppressors (24:14–24 and Rashi). As part of his blessing, Bilaam speaks the very famous words of מה טובו אוהליך יעקב – how good are your dwellings – the *tefillah* with which we begin our morning prayers every day.

✌ WHAT DOES IT MEAN TO CURSE A PEOPLE AND HOW IS THIS ACCOMPLISHED?

A BRACHA IS A PRAYER SAID OUT OF LOVE

We turn now to the first of our opening questions – what does a curse mean and how does one go about cursing a people. We might be able to gain a better understanding of this if we examine the opposite of a curse – namely, a blessing. What does it mean when we bless somebody? I believe we can demonstrate that a blessing is in fact a prayer for good things to happen to a person and is said out of love for the person whom we are trying to bless.

BIRKAS KOHANIM

The classic example is *Birkas Kohanim*. We know that the *bracha* which the Kohanim recite when they bless their fellow Jews, ends with the word *b'ahava* – out of love. Why does this mitzvah of blessing other Jews need to be done *b'ahava*, out of love? Presumably, only if the Kohanim truly love their fellow Jews, will their prayers for others be deemed heartfelt and only then will Hashem listen to their prayers and bless the people.

In the passage of the Torah dealing with *Birkas Kohanim*, Hashem says "*v'ani avoracheim*" – "I will bless them." The Kohanim themselves do not really have the power by themselves to bless the Jewish people. However, the Kohanim do have a special power to say this particular prayer and, if it is said with good intentions and the right feelings, namely love for their fellow Jews, G-d will listen and bless the nation.

So we see that the blessing of *Birkas Kohanim* is really a prayer which has to be said with love in order to be effective.

BLESSING OF THE BECHOR GIVEN BY YITZCHAK

Another example of a blessing given with love is the blessing of the *bechor* given by Yitzchak to Yaakov, where the Torah seems to go out of its way to connect the concepts of love and *bracha*. When the Torah tells us that Yitzchak wished to bless Esav, it notes that Yitzchak loved Esav (ויאהב יצחק את עשו) because Esav was a hunter and always brought Yitzchak food. However, the Torah also tells us that Rivka loved Yaakov (ורבקה אוהבת את יעקב) (Bereishis 25:28) and so she redirected Yitzchak's *bracha* from Esav to Yaakov. So we see from the Chumash itself that love of another seems to be a prerequisite for the granting of a *bracha* to such person.

FATHER'S BLESSING OF CHILDREN

Another example with which we are all familiar is when a father blesses his children at the onset of Shabbos. Such *bracha* is also given out of an abundance of love and so we see once again that a blessing is a prayer said with love.

THE CONVERSION OF BILAAM'S CURSE TO A BRACHA ON ACCOUNT OF G-D'S LOVE FOR HIS PEOPLE

The Torah, with reference to Bilaam, provides a fascinating illustration of the very close connection between love and a blessing. The Gemara tells us that the Jews did not deserve at that time to be saved from the devastating effect of Bilaam's curses (*Berachos* 7a and discussion herein). Nevertheless, Hashem's abiding love for His people prevented Bilaam's curses from having their intended effect. We find the following passage in Devarim (23:6):

ולא אבה ד' אלקיך לשמוע אל בלעם ויהפך ד' אלקיך לך את־הקללה
לברכה כי אהבך ד' אלקיך.

And Hashem your G-d was unwilling to heed Bilaam's prayer, and Hashem converted Bilaam's curse to a blessing because Hashem loves you [referring to Bnei Yisrael].

The Torah tells us that Bilaam's efforts backfired because Hashem loved the Jews and would not countenance their being cursed.

❧ A CURSE IS A PRAYER FOR BAD, SAID OUT OF HATE

Now that we better understand that a blessing is a prayer founded upon love, it becomes apparent that a curse is just the opposite of a blessing, and is in fact a prayer said out of dislike or hatred. The person delivering the curse is in effect praying that G-d do harm to a specific person or group of persons. This explains why Bilaam seems to be discussing his plans with G-d in advance and why he brought so many *korbanos*, and also helps us understand the many other allusions to *tefillah* in the *parsha*, as explained below. This *parsha* is not about black magic but rather about prayer.

But now we need to ask ourselves a very obvious and powerful question. Whereas we can easily understand how a prayer for the welfare of another, said with love for that person, can have a positive outcome, the reverse is far from clear. Why indeed should a prayer said out of hate have any effect at all on G-d? Indeed, we will now discuss several examples which demonstrate that, remarkably, a prayer for bad, otherwise known as a curse, may resonate in Shomayim.

As an aside, it is not immediately apparent why this should be so, but perhaps, since each of us has certain vulnerabilities, and each has some merits, it is possible that Hashem may simultaneously recognize the merits of the person uttering the curse (i.e., praying for bad things to happen to someone) as well as the demerits of the person who is being cursed, and grant the supplicant's request even though it is a prayer said with a negative and destructive objective.

The following are some examples where we see that a prayer for bad or, in the terminology of Parshas Balak, a curse, can be effective.

UNWARRANTED SUSPICION

The Gemara (*Berachos* 31b) discusses a person who suspects his fellow unjustifiably of committing a transgression. The Gemara states the following:

אמר רבי אלעזר, מכאן לחושד את חברו בדבר שאין בו, שצריך לפייסו
ולא עוד אלא שצריך לברכו.

Rebbe Elazar said: A person who suspects his fellow unjustifiably, that person is obligated not only to appease
his fellow, but must also give that person a *bracha*.

Superficially, it is not at all clear why the person doing the suspecting
has to give a *bracha* to the person he or she suspected. It seems, however, that the *bracha* is an antidote to the improper suspicion, which
may be a form of a subconscious curse. I believe we can discern here
a very important idea, namely that the mere act of suspecting another
person of acting improperly serves in effect as a prayer that the suspected person should be punished for his wrongdoing. And this can
have a negative effect in Shomayim on the person being suspected,
even though such person did not commit the act of which he or she
was suspected. Therefore, the antidote for this silent prayer for bad
is to give the person a *bracha*, which is a prayer that good things will
happen to the person.

RIBBONO SHEL OLAM TEFILLAH IN BIRKAS KOHANIM

Another example of the possible effectiveness of a prayer for bad
things to happen to someone is found in the *tefillah* of *Ribbono Shel
Olam*, which we say in the midst of *Birkas Kohanim*. This *tefillah* contains
a dramatic illustration of the fact that even subconscious thoughts, if
negative, can adversely affect another person. In the *Ribbono Shel
Olam*, we pray that our dreams about another be reinforced if they
were dreams for good things to happen, and should be cured if they
were dreams for bad. What is the significance of this prayer? Why
should mere dreams have an effect on another person, good or bad?
Here again, we see that mere thoughts about other people, *even if
subconscious as with dreams*, can act as a prayer for good, or G-d forbid,
the opposite.

CITIES OF REFUGE

A third example of the potential effectiveness of prayers for bad things
to happen to another is found in *Makkos* (11a). The Mishnah states:

לפיכך אימותיהן של כהנים מספקות להן מחיה וכסות כדי שלא יתפללו
על בניהם שימותו.

[Because the persons who were exiled to the Cities of
Refuge could go free when the Kohen Gadol died, there
was an incentive for those in exile to pray for the death of
the Kohen Gadol,] and so the mothers of these Kohanim
would bring food and clothing to the exiles so that they
would not pray for their sons to die.

Here again we see that a prayer can have an effect even if its objective
is improper. This example is dramatic because not only has the Kohen
Gadol done nothing manifestly wrong, he has a very important and
distinguished position in *Klal Yisrael*. Yet there is concern that a prayer
for his premature death may be effective.

CURSE OF A TALMID CHACHAM AND OF AN
ORDINARY PERSON

The Talmud concisely summarizes the gist of our discussion when it
states (*Makkos* 11a):

קללת חכם אפילו בחינם היא באה.

The curse of a Talmid Chacham, even if undeserved, will
come to pass.

Moreover, the Gemara states that even the curse of an ordinary person
can have an effect (*Megilla* 15a).

AYIN HARA — THE EVIL EYE

To most people, the ultimate curse, or prayer for bad, is found in the
case of *ayin hara*. Here, it is jealousy which arouses the bad thoughts
and, even if this jealousy does not take the form of an explicit curse
(the person may not be thinking beyond his or her jealousy), the
impact has all the characteristics of a very powerful curse. The Schottenstein edition of the Bavli expresses this notion very well when it
states, in an explanatory footnote:[2]

---

2. *Berachos* 20a, fn 20.

> Maharal understands the "evil eye" to be a destructive
> force . . . which is engendered by jealous attention. . . .
> The blessings bestowed by G-d upon an individual
> should not serve as a source of anguish to others. If one
> allows his blessings to cause pain to others less fortunate
> – and certainly if one flaunts his blessings – one arouses
> a Divine judgment against himself . . .

Since *ayin hara* is the ultimate and most common form of a curse, or
a prayer for bad, it is therefore no surprise that *Pirkei Avos,* in highlighting the darkest characteristics of Bilaam, states that he had an *ayin
ra'a,* or evil eye, which sounds like an allusion to Bilaam's ability, and
desire, to curse others through jealousy and hatred.

Let us now try to understand more specifically just how Bilaam
went about his business of cursing Bnei Yisrael. Specifically, we need
to understand the content and timing of Bilaam's curses and just
what it is that gave him the maximum chance to succeed in his efforts.

✄ HOW BILAAM WAS INTENDING TO
ACCOMPLISH THE CURSE

The Gemara tells us the following about Bilaam (*Berachos* 7a):

שהיה יודע לכוין אותה שעה שהקב"ה כועס בה.

Bilaam was able to determine that exact moment when
Hashem gets angry.

The Gemara (*Berachos* 7a) goes on to say:

ואימת רתח בהנך תלת שעי קמייתא.

When does Hashem become angry? At some moment
during the first three hours of the day.

These Gemaras bring us back to certain of the questions we asked
at the outset. Is it possible that Hashem really has a weak moment,
when He is angry and can be more easily influenced? We also were
puzzled by the Gemara's statement that this anger occurs during the

first three hours of the day. In order to help us solve these mysteries, let us examine a Gemara which discusses certain circumstances under which Hashem's Presence is manifest.

The Gemara (*Berachos* 6a) derives from certain *pesukim* that Hashem's presence dwells even with one person who studies Torah by himself; to a greater degree when two people study Torah together, and when three people sit in judgment. The Gemara then states that there is a *pasuk* which teaches us that Hashem's presence is found when a *minyan* of people are praying together, as it states (Tehillim 82:1): אלקים נצב בעדת א'ל – G-d dwells among an *"eidah"* [which we know from the *meraglim* signifies a *minyan*].

The Gemara then asks why we need a *pasuk* to tell us that Hashem's presence resides with a *minyan*, since we could infer this fact from the statement that Hashem dwells among three who sit in judgment. The Gemara responds that, with a *minyan*, we need a special *pasuk* because when a *minyan* is involved, there is a unique dimension to Hashem's Shechina:

עשרה קדמה שכינה ואתיא.
Hashem gets there ahead of time and waits for the *minyan* to form.

We see that a *minyan* has such overriding significance that the Shechina of Hashem manifests itself even before the *minyan* is formed.

In this regard, it is worth noting the following halacha (Orach Chaim, *Hilchos Tefillah*, 90:14):

ישכים אדם לבהכ"ן כדי שימנה היו"יד הראשונים.
A person should arrive early enough to *shul* so that he may be counted among the first ten.

The Gemara (*Berachos* 47b) states that the first ten to arrive receive the same reward as all of the later arrivals combined, even if one hundred people come to daven after the first ten have arrived. The Maharsha explains that the first ten receive such a great reward because the formation of the *minyan* is the very reason that Hashem's Shechina appeared at the *shul* in the first place. Once the *minyan* has formed, the later arrivals are, in a way, just extras.

However, the great importance of *minyan*, for all of its tremendous benefits, carries with it a serious consequence to its breach. We see this in the Gemara, which states as follows (*Berachos* 6b):

אמר רב יוחנן, בשעה שהקב״ה בא בבית הכנסת, ולא מצא בה עשרה,
מיד הוא כועס.

Rav Yochanan said: When our Creator arrives at *shul*, and does not find ten people there, He immediately becomes angry.

In order to understand the connection between this anger and the first three hours of the day in which such anger occurs, we refer to yet another Gemara (*Berachos* 10b) regarding *z'man Kriyas Shema*. This Gemara tells us that *Shema Yisrael* may be recited until the end of the third hour of the day. Moreover, the Mishna Berura (*Hilchos Kriyas Shema* 58:1, 5) holds that (except for Shabbos which has a separate rationale), it is a halachic violation to delay the starting time of a *minyan* such that the *tzibbur* will not reach *Kriyas Shema* prior to expiration of the three-hour deadline.

We see from the above Gemaras that Hashem waits for a *minyan* to form and, כביכול, gets upset when this does not happen. The fact that Hashem gets angry, *albeit* for a brief moment, during the first three hours of the day, indicates, I would suggest, that Hashem gets angry within the three-hour limitation for reciting *Kriyas Shema* if our *minyan*im have not yet formed in time to say *Kriyas Shema* in a timely manner.

I would also suggest that Bilaam, by observing Bnei Yisrael, presumably through his extraordinary power of prophecy, knew just the moment when there was no longer any hope on a particular day that their *minyanim* would form in a timely manner, such that *Kriyas Shema* would be recited before the end of the third hour of the day. Consequently, Hashem, who preceded the *minyanim* and waited for them to form, was left in the lurch, so to speak. Bilaam knew that this was a time when Bnei Yisrael would be particularly vulnerable to Bilaam's prayers in the form of a curse.

And so we see an interesting twist to the notion that Bilaam knew just when Hashem got angry, which on the surface appears deceptively to signify that Hashem has a moment when He can be more easily influenced. In fact, Bilaam knew just the moment when *Bnei*

Yisrael deserved Hashem's anger – this was all about Bnei Yisrael's, and not G-d's, vulnerability. In this regard, it is very instructive to note the following statement (*Berachos* 7a):

אמר רבי אלעזר, אמר להם הקב״ה לישראל דעו כמה צדקות עשיתי עמכם, שלא כעסתי בימי בלעם הרשע, שאלמלא כעסתי לא נשתייר משונאיהם של ישראל שריד ופליט, והיינו דקאמר ליה בלעם לבלק מה אקב לא קבה א׳ל, ומה אזעם לא זעם ד׳.

Rebbe Elazar stated, "Hashem said to Bnei Yisrael, 'Look what great favors I did for you, that I did not allow My-self to become angry in the days of the wicked Bilaam because, had I done so, no remnants of Bnei Yisrael would have remained.'"

This Gemara speaks volumes about the critically important power of *tefillah b'tzibbur*. We clearly see from this Gemara that our culpability is greatly magnified, even to the point of being vulnerable to the de-structive curse of a terrible *rasha* such as Bilaam, if we are delinquent in this great mitzvah. All the more so if our *minyanim* fail to form in a sufficiently timely manner so as to take into account *z'man Kriyas Shema*.

BILAAM'S ATTEMPTS TO COUNTER BNEI YISRAEL'S POWER OF TEFILLAH THROUGH HIS OWN DILIGENCE IN TEFILLAH – SYMBOLS OF BILAAM'S TEFILLAH IN THE PARSHA

At the outset, we noted that Bilaam was hired by Balak for the spe-cific purpose of countering Bnei Yisrael's primary source of military power, which we have seen to be *tefillah*. Bilaam used the power of *tefillah* in a very potent two-pronged attack against Bnei Yisrael. Not only did Bilaam highlight Bnei Yisrael's glaring shortcomings in the realm of *tefillah*, and particularly (as we have suggested) in *tefillah b'tzibbur* and its timely performance, Bilaam compounded the impact of his advocacy to Hashem by showing himself, as well as Balak, to be extraordinarily diligent in *tefillah* (as then represented by *kor-banos*), as evidenced by a number of *pesukim* in the *parsha*. For example (Bamidbar 23:4):

ויקר אלקים אל בלעם ויאמר אליו את שבעת המזבחות ערכתי ואעל פר
ואיל במזבח.

Hashem appeared to Bilaam, and Bilaam said to Hashem:
"I have prepared the seven altars and brought up a bull
and a ram on each altar."

Rashi on the above *pasuk* states:

אבותיהם של אלו בנו לפניך שבעה מזבחות ואני ערכתי כנגד כולן, אברהם
בנה ארבעה . . . ויצחק בנה אחד . . . ויעקב בנה שניים . . .

The forefathers [of Bnei Yisrael] built before You seven
altars, and I [Bilaam] prepared altars corresponding to
them all. Avraham built four altars; Yitzchak built one
altar, and Yaakov built two altars.

The Gemara tells us that each of our three daily *tefillos* were established
by one of the Avos (*Berachos* 26b). Accordingly, in order for Bilaam to
offer a prayer which would undermine Bnei Yisrael, he would need
to upstage the prayer offerings of the Avos. The Rashi we quoted
explains that Bilaam went about doing so by boasting that he and
Balak brought the same number of *korbanos* as the Avos combined.

From this Rashi, we see very clearly that Bilaam was not primarily
engaged in black magic, but was trying to replicate, and even supercede, the *tefillah* of the Avos. We suggested earlier that Parshas Balak
speaks directly to our *matzav* today – we know that *tefillos* are the
post-*churban* version of *korbanos* and, indeed, the fact that the Arabs
pray five times a day, compared with our three times, shows that
the Arabs, just like Bilaam, are using the power of prayer against us
by trying to be more diligent than are we with a critically important
mitzvah which is supposed to be our strength.

The incredible power of *tefillah, even when used for a nefarious purpose,* is dramatically illustrated by a Gemara in *Sanhedrin* (105b). We
know from the *parsha* that Balak, inspired by Bilaam, brought many
korbanos in an unsuccessful effort to pray to Hashem that Bnei Yisrael
should be harmed. Under these circumstances, one would think that
Balak would receive no reward for *korbanos* and *tefillos* offered in such
disreputable circumstances. Remarkably, the Gemara in *Sanhedrin*
(105b) tells us otherwise:

אמר רב יהודה אמר רב, לעולם יעסוק אדם בתורה ובמצוות אפילו שלא
לשמה, שמתוך שלא לשמה בא לשמה, שבשכר ארבעים ושתים קרבנות
שהקריב בלק, זכה ויצאה ממנו רות. אמר רבי יוסי בר הונא רות בתו של
עגלון, בן בנו של בלק מלך מואב היתה.

Rav Yehuda said in the name of Rav: "A person should
always be involved in Torah and *mitzvos*, even if such
person is doing so out of ulterior motives, because this
will lead to performance of Torah and *mitzvos* for pure
motives. It is because of the forty-two sacrifices which
Balak brought in an effort to curse Bnei Yisrael, that
Balak deserved that Ruth would descend from him." R.
Yosi bar Huna said: "Ruth was the daughter of Eglon,
the grandson of Balak, the king of Moav." [And Ruth
was the progenitor of King David, as we are told at the
end of Megillas Rus.]

THE PARADIGM OF YONAH AND NINVEH

Another very powerful weapon in the Arab arsenal, also reminiscent
of Parshas Balak, is the Arabs' belief in the true G-d. It is probably
no coincidence that Bilaam then, and our Arab enemies today, are
perhaps the only enemies of Bnei Yisrael over the millennia who can
be said to be both believers in the true G-d and also very strong in
their *tefillos*.

To quote just one of a number of *pesukim* which demonstrate belief
by Bilaam in the true G-d, we refer to a passage in Bamidbar (22:18):

ויען בלעם ויאמר אל־עבדי בלק, אם יתן־לי בלק מלוא ביתו כסף וזהב לא
אוכל לעבור את־פי ד׳ אלקי לעשות קטנה או גדולה.

And Bilaam responded to the emissaries of Balak: "If
Balak were to give me his entire storehouse of gold and
silver, this would not enable me to violate the word of
Hashem, my G-d, whether for a minor or a significant
matter."

In a vivid demonstration of just how powerful *tefillos* can be if
emanating from a person or nation which believes in the true G-d,
reminiscent of our Arab enemies today, we discussed the Gemara in
Berachos which makes the point that it was only Hashem's love for us

as a people which saved us from total annihilation through Bilaam's curses. To further reinforce this point, we refer to Rav Yitzchak Mirsky who, in *Hegyonei Halacha*[3] in an essay on *sefer* Yonah, discusses Yonah's strong reluctance to go on his appointed mission to inspire the non-Jewish inhabitants of the metropolis of Ninveh to do *teshuva*, and quotes the Mechilta:

ואם ישובו אנשי נינוה בתשובה, יצא מכאן קטרוג על ישראל שאינם ממהרים לשוב.

If the people of Ninveh would repent, this would create a mark of condemnation on Bnei Yisrael who are not so quick to do *teshuva*.

Rav Mirsky then quotes the Ibn Ezra (Yonah 1:2), who claims that the reason G-d was so determined to send a *navi* to Ninveh was because the inhabitants of that city did not worship *avoda zara*, as evidenced by the fact that when Ninveh did *teshuva*, there is no mention about destruction of idols. It is perhaps this fact which concerned Yonah all the more, i.e., since the people of Ninveh were already believers in G-d, their *teshuva* would make Bnei Yisrael look particularly bad in comparison because Hashem could then look down with a certain amount of affection towards a city which not only believed in Him, but also did *teshuva*.

As a result, Yonah was justifiably concerned about what possible excuse Bnei Yisrael, undistracted by idol worship, could have for not doing *teshuva*. So too with the Arabs today, who combine belief in the true G-d with a very serious approach towards their *tefillos*. Accordingly, Bnei Yisrael could easily be seriously tarnished by comparison.

⊷ BILAAM AND THE TALKING DONKEY

Fortunately for us, Parshas Balak goes much further than merely teaching us a valuable lesson about how formidable an enemy the Arabs can be. The *parsha* concludes with Messianic references and poetic descriptions of how the Jews will ultimately prevail at the end

---

3. Rabbi Yitzchak Mirsky, *Hegyonei Halacha*, Vol. 2 (Jerusalem: Mosad HaRav Kook, 1989).

of days. I would suggest that the *parsha* contains a very definite blue-print as to how we can achieve final victory and that this will become evident as we focus on probably the most well-known incident in Parshas Balak, that of the talking donkey (actually an אתון – a female donkey).

The incident of Bilaam and the donkey is exceedingly rich with symbolism and mystery. To set the stage for our discussion, we refer to a Gemara, which states as follows (*Sanhedrin* 105b):

> דאמרי ליה, מאי טעמא לא רכבת סוסיא? אמר להו, שדאי להו ברטיבא.
> Moav's messengers said to Bilaam, "Why are you not riding on a horse?" Bilaam responded that he normally rides a horse but that day he was riding a donkey be-cause he had put his horses out to graze.

Let us begin with a few questions about this Gemara and with regard to the donkey incident in general:

(1) Why would the Gemara even raise the issue about Bilaam's method of transportation that day? What difference does it make what animal Bilaam was riding?

(2) The Gemara's answer [that Bilaam had put his horses out to graze] seems very forced. If Bilaam needed a horse that day, there was just no logical reason for his having all his horses out to graze at the same time. In modern terms, no-one takes all their cars to the shop on the same day if they can help it. Apparently, the Gemara is trying to convey to us that the Torah placed the donkey in this scenario for a specific reason. But what is the message and why a donkey?

(3) If the donkey was placed in the story to teach us a specific message, why a female and not a male donkey, presumably a preferable method of transportation?

(4) Why would the Torah set up an incident where an animal is talking? Each time in the Chumash that a law of nature is bro-ken, such as the splitting of the Sea, the earth swallowing Kor-ach, and all of the miracles such as the *manna* which protected and sustained the Jews in the desert, it is in conjunction with a very major event such as *Yetzias Mitzrayim*, or quashing of a rebellion against Moshe's authority. Clearly, the Torah would

not set up a supernatural incident involving a talking donkey simply so that we can have a cute diversion in the *parsha*.

(5) Why are the words *shalosh regalim* mentioned three times in this brief incident?

(6) As we asked at the outset, why was Bilaam's leg crushed despite the fact that he was sinning with his mouth?

(7) When the Torah first describes the pathway in which the donkey was traveling, it states that there was a *gader* (a fence) on either side but in the very next *pasuk* it is described as a *kir* (a wall). Why the change in terminology?

If we are correct in our proposition that this *parsha* is a precursor to our modern battle with the Arabs, Bilaam would represent the Arabs and the donkey would represent Bnei Yisrael. While it is not too difficult to perceive how Bilaam, with his dedication to *tefillah* and his belief in the true G-d, is the paradigm of our current Arab enemy, it is less obvious why a donkey could be symbolic of Bnei Yisrael.

However, Wikipedia states that, "Donkeys have a reputation for stubbornness" and we know that the principal adjective used by the Torah in connection with Bnei Yisrael is עם קשה ערף. Furthermore, Wikipedia goes on to discuss a donkey's "highly-developed sense of self-preservation," a very apt description of our people. Wikipedia also describes a donkey as "intelligent, friendly, eager to learn, a willing and companionable partner and very dependable in work," each of which adjectives are appropriate descriptions of our people and nation. For more traditional sources for this analogy, see Vayechi (Bereishis 49:14) – יששכר חמור גרם, and Rashi on Bo (Shemos 13:13) – וכל פטר חמור.

Now that we have analogized Bilaam to the Arabs and and the donkey to the Jews, let us see how this works into Bilaam's confrontation with his donkey. Bamidbar states (22:27–28):

ויך את־האתון במקל. ויפתח ד' את־פי האתון.

Bilaam beat the donkey with his staff, whereupon Hashem opened the donkey's mouth.

Bilaam beat the donkey, just as the Arabs mercilessly torment the Jews today. Rashi at this point quotes the Midrash which notes the great irony in the fact that Bilaam, who passed himself off as a person who could accomplish great things with his mouth through prayer, had to resort to physical beating of the donkey. So too with the Arabs of today, who continually refer to Allah as guiding them to victory but who carry out their vicious schemes with terror and the worst violence.

Now we can appreciate the deep symbolism inherent in the words:

ויפתח ד׳ את־פי האתון.

and also see how incredibly apt are these words in describing our current *matzav*. The fact that Hashem opened the donkey's mouth only after Bilaam beat her takes on an entirely new meaning in light of the following astute observation by Rabbi Yissachar Frand:[4]

> The *Pirkei D'Rav Eliezer* [an early Midrash composed about 100 CE] asks why Yishmael's name is constructed in the future tense [Yishma-El: G-d will hear], rather than in the past tense? The Midrash suggests that the future tense implies that the cries of G-d's people who are suffering at the hand of Yishmael will be heard by G-d. "Yishmael," means that the prayers of the Jews will be heard and will be answered.

And so it seems that, just as the mouth of Bilaam's donkey was miraculously opened by Hashem after the donkey was beaten by Bilaam, so too is the Torah signaling to us that the terrible suffering which the Arabs are inflicting upon us today causes the mouths of the Jews to open in prayer.[5] Hashem will then listen to our *tefillos* and bring about the final *geula*.

---

4. National Jewish Outreach Program, www.njop.org. Copyright 2006. Based on פרקי דרבי אליעזר (היגר) חורב פרק ל״א ד״ה ששה נקראו.

5. In June 2014, terrorists kidnapped three Israeli youths on their way home from yeshiva. During eighteen days of uncertainty, until their bodies were found, waves of prayer by our people reverberated around the world, as has been the case on other occasions of great crisis and tragedy in Israel. One of the touching stories which surfaced during the search for the kidnapped boys was that of Israel Finance Minister, Yair Lapid, who, after visiting the families of the abducted youths, disclosed that he searched for and found a long-unused *siddur* and prayed for the first time in many years.

Indeed, the very fact that *shalosh regalim* is mentioned three times in this very brief episode of Bilaam and his donkey seems to be referring to the three times each year when the Jews are *oleh regel* to Yerushalayim, again a very powerful allusion to the importance of *tefillah*.

We suggested that the Bilaam-donkey confrontation is replete with pre-Messianic allusions, and we know that the *navi* Zecharya tells us that Moshiach will arrive on a donkey, so it is therefore very tempting to connect the two. The immediate difficulty with this analogy, however, is that the donkey in the Bilaam story is an אתון, or female donkey, whereas Moshiach will arrive on a male donkey, or חמור. However, the *pasuk* in Zecharya (9:9), which discusses Moshiach's arrival, bridges the חמור–אתון gap with a truly remarkable statement. The *pasuk* talks about Moshiach in the following terms:

עני ורכב על חמור ועל עיר בן אתונות.

[Moshiach] will arrive poor and riding on a donkey which is an offspring of female donkeys.

Why would the *navi* go out of his way to relate the self-evident fact that Moshiach's חמור will be an offspring of a female donkey – an אתון – the very animal used by Bilaam! What could be more obvious? And why an offspring of female *donkeys*, in the plural?

Indeed, I would like to now suggest that the *pasuk* in Zecharya ties in so beautifully to Parshas Balak. Bilaam's beating of the אתון is analogous to the modern Arabs' acts of terror against the Jews. And just as the mouth of the אתון was opened as soon as it was beaten by Bilaam, so too, each incident of Arab terror opens our nation's mouth in *tefillah*. The cumulative process of all our *tefillos* helps give birth to the חמור of Moshiach. And it is precisely because the *navi* Zecharya knew there would be so many incidents of Arab terror, each of which would arouse our *tefillos* and ultimately bring about Moshiach, that Zecharya refers to אתונות (in the plural) as the *navi*'s shorthand symbol of countless incidents of Arab terror – collectively constituting the mothers of Moshiach's חמור.

BILAAM UP AGAINST THE WALL

Let us now explore some of the other wonderful symbolism embedded in Bilaam's confrontation with the אתון (Bamidbar 22:25):

> ותלחץ אל־הקיר ותלחץ את רגל בלעם אל־הקיר.
> And the donkey pressed herself against the wall and crushed Bilaam's leg.

We suggested that the donkey ridden by Bilaam refers to Bnei Yisrael, and that the major theme of the *parsha* is *tefillah*. Accordingly, when the *pasuk* states that the donkey pressed herself against the wall, we can easily conjure up perhaps the most evocative image in modern times of our heartfelt *tefillos*, namely that of the Jew fervently pressed up against the Kotel.

Parenthetically, what clues do we have in the *pasuk* that the wall against which the donkey pressed itself is referring to the Kotel? We asked earlier why the Torah refers to the structure at the side of the path of the אתון as both a גדר and as a קיר. Originally, when the Angel of Hashem obstructs the donkey's path, the *pasuk* states that there was a גדר (literally, a fence) on either side. Rashi explains that when the word גדר appears in Tanach, without further elaboration, it means a גדר of stones (22:24). But in the very next *pasuk*, the wall is referred to as a קיר, which Onkelos translates as a כתלא, letters reminiscent of the Kotel. And so, the juxtaposition of the word גדר (which signifies that it was built from stones) with the word קיר (כתלא in Aramaic) seems to be directing us to the symbolism of the Kotel.

The *pasuk* tells us about the donkey: ותלחץ אל־הקיר – the donkey pressed herself against the wall – which we suggested symbolizes Bnei Yisrael pressing themselves up against the Kotel in fervent prayer. What is the consequence of doing so? The leg of the Arab is crushed. The leg is specifically the limb with which the Arab bows down in prayer, all the while cursing us in a plea to Hashem for our destruction. In turn, the way to overcome the Arab's curse is for Bnei Yisrael to make certain that our *tefillos* are more sincere and numerous than those of our Arab enemies. It is imperative that we take back the power of *tefillah* with which we were blessed by Yitzchak.[6]

---

6.   We can derive support for this view from an incredible Rashi on ותלחץ

And now we can understand that the supernatural event of the talking donkey is not just an amusing anecdote but, just like all other supernatural events in Tanach, has enormous significance, representing as it does, our *tefillos* of anguish in reaction to incessant Arab attacks, which *tefillos* will spawn the coming of Moshiach.

🕊 TZNIUS

Before we summarize and arrive at our final conclusion, it is worth noting a very significant sub-theme in this *parsha*, namely that of *tznius* (note also the last *pasuk* of the *haftora* – הצנע לכת עם ד' אלקיך). Our Arab enemies of today, at least on the surface, purport to be much stronger than we are, not only in the realm of *tefillah* but also in the critical area of *tznius*, and it is therefore important to briefly focus on this subject.

We perceive the tremendous importance of *tznius* in many places, not the least of which in Megillas Ruth. Ruth attracted Boaz's attention, in no small measure, on account of her *tznius*. The Gemara notes: (*Shabbos* 113b) דבר צניעות ראה בה – Boaz perceived a manner of modesty about her. And it seems that our tradition wished to glorify the *midda* of *tznius* by the fact that this union of Boaz and Ruth created a descendant of David HaMelech and ultimately Moshiach.

Since the Arabs represent themselves to be so circumspect in *tznius*, it is not at all surprising that Parshas Balak, as symbolic of our current battle with the Arabs, would culminate with a very vivid demonstration of how, when all else failed, Bilaam nearly succeeded in his evil plans when he had Moav entice Bnei Yisrael into the depths of depravity, which scheme was initiated by causing Bnei Yisrael to violate the bounds of *tznius* (see details in *Sanhedrin* 106a).

את רגל בלעם – and the donkey crushed the leg of Bilaam against the wall. The subject of the donkey's "crushing" seems to be only Bilaam, yet Rashi's one-word comment on ותלחץ is "אחרים", in the plural, which means that the donkey crushed the legs of "others" in the plural. This one-word Rashi, seemingly inexplicable, is in fact consistent with our suggestion that the word ותלחץ symbolically refers to our Arab enemies collectively.

✒ CONCLUSION

We have shown how Parshas Balak holds the key to our final defeat of the Arabs. It is therefore not at all surprising that Bilaam, who acknowledged that no words could come out of his mouth unless Hashem placed them there, ultimately launches into a poetic description of the Jews' dominance in the Messianic era. Very telling is Bilaam's uttering of the majestic praise of מה־טבו אהליך יעקב משכנתיך ישראל (Bamidbar 24:5). Rashi adduces two alternate, but complementary, interpretations of this *pasuk*, which concisely support our analysis of this *parsha*. Rashi's first interpretation is from the Gemara (*Bava Basra* 60a):

> שאין פתחי אהליהם מכוונין זה מול זה.
>
> The entrances of their tents were not aligned opposite each other [so that no person could see inside his neighbor's tent].

This is a clear allusion to the power of *tznius*. Rashi then follows with an alternate interpretation of the *Ma Tovu pasuk*, which directs us to Bnei Yisrael's overriding power of *tefillah* (previously represented by *korbanos*):

> דבר אחר, מה טובו אהליך, מה טובו אהל שילה ובית עולמים בישובן,
> שמקריבין בהן קרבנות לכפר עליהם.
>
> Another interpretation of *Ma Tovu*: How goodly are the tents of Shiloh, and [the Beis HaMikdosh]. While the Beis HaMikdosh exists, Bnei Yisrael bring therein offerings of atonement.

And so we see that *Ma Tovu* consists of lofty words of praise for the Jews' אהל and משכן, representing *tznius* and *tefillah*. As we have explained in detail, *tefillah* and *tznius*, which are supposed to be the domain of Bnei Yisrael, in fact comprise the essence of the Arabs' strength. In order to achieve victory over the Arabs and attain the final *geula*, it is essential that we regain our dominance and superiority in these critical areas. It is certainly no coincidence that Bilaam uttered the *pasuk* of *Ma Tovu* just before describing the Jews' dominance in the Messianic Era.

Since *Ma Tovu* extols the Jews' inherent virtues of *tznius* and *tefillah*, and since the rediscovery of these virtues is so essential to our mission as a people, it should not be at all surprising that *Ma Tovu* is placed at the very forefront of our morning *tefillos*, ahead of all of the other magnificent *tefillos* composed by the *Anshei Knesses HaGedola*.

*

In fact, the lessons of Parshas Balak are so fundamental to our fate as a nation, that the Sages of the Talmud contemplated incorporating the entire *parsha* into *Kriyas Shema*, but decided against doing so only because this would have made the *Shema* prayer much too lengthy (*Berachos* 12b). The Gemara there states that the intent to include Parshas Balak in *Kriyas Shema* was motivated by one specific *pasuk*[7] found in Bilaam's final soliloquy about the Messianic Era. The Maharsha interprets this *pasuk* to signify that Bnei Yisrael are diligent in rising early enough to say *Kriyas Shema* in a timely manner. As we have suggested in our presentation, this is a crucial part of the secret in how we bring about Moshiach.

And so, we must internalize our opening *tefillah* of *Ma Tovu*, and thus inspire ourselves to overcome the Arabs' current strengths in the areas of *tefillah* and *tznius*, which strengths they so effectively use against us. In Parshas Matos, we are told that Bnei Yisrael killed the kings of Midian and certain others, without stating how they were killed. Although nothing is stated about how the kings were killed, the *pasuk* ends by telling us that Bnei Yisrael killed Bilaam with a sword. The manner of Bilaam's death is perhaps a signal in the Torah that the Arabs' attempt to use the power of *tefillah* against us is also doomed to failure. Rashi explains why the Torah took pains to specify the method by which Bilaam was slain (Bamidbar 31:8):

> הוא בא על ישראל והחליף אומנותו באומנותם, שאין נוצחים אלא
> בפיהם ע"י תפילה ובקשה, ובא הוא ותפס אומנתם לקללם בפיו, אף הם
> באו עליו והחליפו אומנתם באומנות האומות שבאין בחרב, שנאמר ועל
> חרבך תחיה.

Bilaam rose up against Bnei Yisrael, and exchanged his specialty for theirs, because Bnei Yisrael are victorious only through *tefillah*, and Bilaam tried to seize

---

7. כרע שכב כארי וכלביא מי יקימנו (Bamidbar 24:9).

this initiative by cursing Bnei Yisrael with his mouth. Bnei Yisrael similarly turned the tables on Bilaam by using the weapon of the nations of the world, namely the sword, against Bilaam [the weapon of the sword is Esav's weapon], as it says (Bereishis 27:40), "Through your sword you shall live."

May it be the will of Hashem that we too will turn the tables on the Arabs and react to the repeated Arab violence and terror by reaching new heights in our dedication to *tefillah* and *tznius*. Parshas Balak clearly signals to us that the incessant Arab terror will inevitably cause us to repeatedly open our mouths in fervent *tefillos* which Hashem will hear and that this will in turn give birth to the חמור of Moshiach, just as predicted by the *navi* Zecharya. May we accelerate and intensify our *tefillos* and be circumspect in our attention to *tznius* and, in so doing, be privileged to see the *geula shleima bimheira beyameinu*.

CONTEMPORARY RELEVANCE
OF THE MITZVAH
OF REMEMBERING AMALEK ✌

Despite the recent diminishing in the frequency and severity of terrorist attacks, Eretz Yisrael is still in very great danger. There are continued suicide bombings and countless attempts which are foiled by the grace of Hashem.[1] Hezbollah, Iran, and Syria, among others, remain as serious and powerful threats, developing nuclear, biological, and increasingly powerful conventional and unconventional weapons.

In the potentially calamitous situation in which Bnei Yisrael finds itself today, everyone has an opinion and a strategy but few are confident that their approach is the right one under the circumstances. We desperately search for the next military or political leader who will have a magical solution, but we find none.

To gain some insights from a Torah perspective into this major crisis for our people, I would like to study and analyze together with you the mitzvah of *zechiras Amalek*, remembering Amalek, a mitzvah so fundamental that we are obligated to hear each word of the relevant Torah reading (on Shabbos Zachor), a requirement which does not apply to any other *Kriyas HaTorah*, not even the *Aseres HaDibros*. Now, what does Amalek have to do with the Arabs/Muslims? Since Amalek descended from Esav, one might be tempted to argue that the radical Muslims of today cannot possibly be considered to be Amalek. However, the *Me'am Loez* on Parshas Ki Tetzeh states as follows:

---

1. This *d'var Torah* was written in 2002, but the message remains timely, although the level of distress and violence thankfully ebbs in some years.

אבל עליכם לדעת שבכל דור ודור שעומדים עלינו לכלותינו הכל הוא
מעמלק שמתלבש בכל פעם באומה אחרת.

You should know that the statement [which we find in
the Haggadah], that in each generation they try to destroy us, this refers to Amalek, which each time appears
in the guise of a different nation.

In the same vein, in a lecture given on March 4, 1974, Rav Joseph B.
Soloveitchik, *zt"l*, stated as follows:[2]

> So who is Amalek? . . . It is not a race, a specific group, or
> a nationality . . . It is man who incarnates total evil . . . It
> is man as Demon . . . I once heard from my father, in the
> name of my grandfather, that Amalek is any people or
> group who are committed to one purpose: the destruc-
> tion of the Jewish people.

The Arabs of today – or at least those Arabs who are trying so hard
to destroy us – certainly fit the above descriptions. In addition, there
are certain striking similarities between the Torah's account of our
encounter with Amalek, and the despicable acts of our Arab enemies
of today.

Firstly, the Torah tells us, in passages which we will shortly review
in greater detail, that Amalek attacked כל הנחשלים אחריך – the weak
stragglers. So too, do our Arab enemies delight in attacking defense-
less citizens on buses and pizza shops and babies in strollers. The
Torah also tells us that Bnei Yisrael, at the time of Amalek's attacks,
were עיף ויגע – tired and utterly weary. So too do we now find ourselves
exhausted and weary from the unceasing barrage of murder and
mayhem.

And finally, the Torah tells us, regarding Amalek, ולא ירא אלקים –
and they did not fear Hashem.[3] Despite the fact that all of the other
nations were awestruck by the enormous miracles performed for Bnei
Yisrael as part of *Yetzias Mitzrayim*, and consequently these nations
were afraid to attack Bnei Yisrael, Amalek did not have any such fear.

---

2. Rabbi Aaron Rakeffet-Rothkoff, *The Rav: The World of Rabbi Joseph B.
Soloveitchik*, Vol. 2 (NY: Ktav, 1999), 152.

3. Rashi states that the expression ולא ירא אלקים applies to Amalek.

Similarly, the radical Muslims of today have witnessed the major miracles of the creation of the State of Israel; they have witnessed *kibbutz goluyos* from the four corners of the world, as forecast by our tradition; they have seen the blossoming of the Land to welcome its people back (the Torah and the Midrash tell us that the Land of Eretz Yisrael will blossom and be fruitful only for our people); and the Arabs have witnessed miraculous military accomplishments such as the Six-Day War, Entebbe, and the destruction of the Iraqi and Syrian nuclear reactors. Nevertheless, just as Amalek at the time of *Yetzias Mitzrayim* did not develop any fear of Hashem, despite the great miracles which He performed on our behalf, so too the radical Muslims of today appear to be not at all moved or impressed by Hashem's modern miracles on behalf of His people.

So we see these significant similarities between Amalek and those Arabs of today who are bent upon our destruction. Accordingly, I believe that study and analysis of our tradition's approach towards Amalek can teach us some valuable lessons as to how properly to approach the current *matzav*.

Before continuing with our analysis of the concept of Amalek, let us frame our discussion with a few questions:

(1) Why do we have two Amalek passages in the Torah, one in Beshalach and one in Ki Tetzeh?

(2) Why do we read the Ki Tetzeh, rather than the Beshalach, passage on Shabbos Zachor?

(3) In the Beshalach episode, Bnei Yisrael had killed all the warriors of Amalek and could have destroyed Amalek at that time. Why did they refrain from doing so?

(4) Why is Purim viewed as a victory over Amalek, whom we are commanded to eradicate, when there is no indication in the Megilla as to the number of Amalekites who were killed by the Jews at that time or even whether a significant portion of Amalekites were killed?

(5) Since the Torah tells us that the battle against Amalek is an eternal battle, how do we fight this battle today?

I would like to begin our analysis by reviewing the two main passages in the Torah dealing with Amalek, found at the end of *parshios* Beshalach and Ki Tetzeh. In the case of both passages, the immediately preceding *pesukim* are, as is so often the case in the Torah, quite relevant[4] and I will briefly review them as well. In the process, we will ask some questions and make some observations, although the various comments will remain loose ends until they are tied together at the end of this *d'var*.

✺ AMALEK PESUKIM – BESHALACH

Just before the first Amalek passage, in Parshas Beshalach (Shemos 17:8–16), the Torah tells us that Bnei Yisrael camped in Refidim. Rav Yehoshua (*Sanhedrin* 106a) says that the place was called Refidim because ריפו ידיהם מן התורה – meaning that Bnei Yisrael had weakened their links to Torah. In Refidim, there was insufficient water for the people's needs (this was one of the ten tests in the desert, *Arachin* 15a). And so Bnei Yisrael fought with Moshe, who severely rebuked them. The *pasuk* then says (Shemos 17:4): 'ויצעק משה אל ד – "and Moshe cried out to Hashem," perhaps the only time in the Torah that the word ויצעק is used in connection with Moshe, so we can appreciate how aggravating Bnei Yisrael must have been. Moshe exclaimed (17:4):

מה אעשה לעם הזה עוד מעט וסקלוני.
"What shall I do with these people, they are on the verge of stoning me?"

Whereupon Hashem instructs Moshe to extract water from the rock and we are told that the place was called Masa U'meriva on account of the disputes. In Refidim, Bnei Yisrael demonstrated their displeasure with the words היש ד' בקרבנו אם אין – "Is G-d amongst us or not?" (17:7), which was quite an amazing statement in view of the enormous miracles our people had just witnessed. Immediately thereafter, the *pasuk* says ויבא עמלק – "and Amalek attacked." The attack, not surprisingly, took place in Refidim.

---

4. We know that Hashem did not randomly place the Amalek passages in the Torah and that there must be a reason (as we will see by examining the preceding *pesukim*) why these Amalek passages were placed next to these *pesukim*. We will also explore why the Torah gave us two Amalek passages, rather than consolidating them into one.

Rashi connects the attack of Amalek with the immediately preceding words of היש ד׳ בקרבנו אם אין – "Is G-d amongst us or not." Rashi comments as follows (17:8):

> The passages are connected in order to teach us that I [Hashem] am always with you, ready to meet all of your needs. And yet you say היש ד׳ בקרבנו אם אין – "Is Hashem amongst us or not" – so I will cause the dog of Amalek to come and bite you and then you will know where I am.

Rashi gives the example of a father who is walking along with his child sitting on his shoulders. Periodically, the child asks his father for a certain object and the father gladly obliges. Then, the father meets an acquaintance and the son turns to the acquaintance and asks, "Have you seen my father?" Whereupon, the father angrily flings the child upon the ground where the child is attacked by a dog and then finds out the hard way where his father was all along. Clearly, the analogy is intended to emphasize how much Bnei Yisrael then, and perhaps today as well, took Hashem's protection and guidance for granted.

Amalek came and fought Bnei Yisrael in Refidim, and Moshe said to Yehoshua: "Go pick *anashim* in order to do battle with Amalek." Rashi comments that these *anashim* had to be both strong warriors and G-d-fearing people so that their merits would assist them in the battle. On the following day, Moshe, Aharon, and Chur went to the top of the hill. Rashi tells us that all three were fasting.

The Torah then tells us that (17:11):

> והיה כאשר ירים משה ידו וגבר ישראל וכאשר יניח ידו וגבר עמלק.
> When Moshe lifted his hands, Bnei Yisrael were victorious and when Moshe lowered his hands, our enemies prevailed.

The Mishnah, with which many are familiar, and referenced in Rashi, states as follows (*Rosh Hashana* 29a):

> וכי ידיו של משה עושות מלחמה או שוברות מלחמה אלא לומר לך כל זמן שהיו ישראל מסתכלין כלפי מעלה ומשעבדין את לבם לאביהם שבשמים, היו מתגברים, ואם לאו היו נופלים.
> Is it possible that Moshe's hands can wage war? Rather,

this comes to teach us that when Bnei Yisrael direct their hearts towards their Father in Heaven, they are victorious against Amalek and, if not, then they are defeated.

WHY AMALEK WAS NOT ERADICATED BY MOSHE AND YEHOSHUA

The Torah (Shemos 17:13) then goes on to tell us that:

ויחלש יהושע את עמלק ואת עמו לפי חרב.
Yehoshua weakened Amalek and his nation in battle.

Rashi comments, referring to the Mechilta:

חתך ראשי גבוריו ולא השאיר אלא חלשים שבהם ולא הרגם כולם מכאן
אנו למדים שעשו ע״פ הדיבור של שכינה.
They killed all of the strong ones and only the weak were left standing. They did not kill them all – we derive from this that the failure to kill them all was the directive of Hashem.

It is quite clear from the words of Rashi that, in a military sense at least, Amalek could have been destroyed there and then, since their warriors had all been killed and only the weak remained. However, Rashi asserts that Hashem did not permit Amalek to be eradicated at that time. This Rashi is worth noting for its tremendous importance in understanding our involvement with Amalek, as we shall see.

Why would Rashi say that it was Hashem's command that Amalek not be eradicated at that time? This statement of Rashi is all the more remarkable since, in the very next *pasuk*, the Torah in effect tells us that Hashem takes on the battle with Amalek as virtually His personal battle. Hashem declares (Shemos 17:14):

כי מחה אמחה את זכר עמלק מתחת השמים.
I [G-d] will surely eradicate the memory of Amalek from beneath the heavens.

And in the *pasuk* after that, we are told that:

כי יד על כס יˉה מלחמה לדˈ בעמלק מדור דור.

The Hand on Hashem's throne battles Amalek in each generation.

In fact, as Rashi tells us in his commentary to this latter *pasuk*, Amalek represents such an antithesis to the Shechina in this world, that the Torah, in the *pasuk* we just read, uses the Name יˉה rather than _ _ יˉה (for Hashem's Name), and כס, rather than כסא (for Hashem's throne), to symbolize the fact that Hashem's very name and His throne are incomplete so long as Amalek continues to exist. This observation reinforces our question, namely, how can Rashi declare, only two *pesukim* earlier, that it was Hashem's decree that Amalek not be wiped out at that time?

In this regard, we note that the Gemara (*Sanhedrin* 20b) lists three *mitzvos* which are to be performed when the Jews enter Eretz Yisrael (all three are to be performed only upon the orders of a *navi*). These *mitzvos* are: the appointment of a King, the destruction of Amalek, and the building of the Beis HaMikdosh. Two of these *mitzvos* were in fact performed but Amalek was never destroyed. Why not?

In our conclusion, I hope to explain, among other things, why Moshe and Yehoshua were not permitted to eradicate Amalek at that time, and why Amalek has endured to this day, despite the fact that Hashem adopted the battle against Amalek as His very own.

ی AMALEK PESUKIM – KI TETZEH

The next Amalek passage in the Torah is the one we read each year, just before Purim, in order to fulfill the mitzvah of *zechiras Amalek*. It begins (Devarim 25:17):

זכור את אשר עשה לך עמלק בדרך בצאתכם ממצרים.

Remember what Amalek did to you on your way out of Mitzrayim.

Once again, it is very instructive to review the immediately preceding *pesukim*, which, in this case, very powerfully admonish us against possessing false weights and measures. The *pesukim* state (25:15, 16):

. . . אבן שלימה וצדק יהיה לך . . . למען יאריכו ימיך על האדמה אשר ד'
אלקיך נתן לך כי תועבת ד' אלקיך כל עשה אלה.

You should possess accurate weights and measures so
that you will enjoy long life on the earth which Hashem
your G-d gave to you, and because false weights and
measures are an abomination to Hashem your G-d.

It is clear, as we will explain, that the Torah wants us to take this
prohibition very seriously. Firstly, the prohibition of false weights
and measures is unusual in that it applies not only to the use of false
weights and measures but also to *mere possession*. Secondly, the Torah
prescribes long life as a reward for adhering to this mitzvah – the
reward which many people believe is reserved only for *kibbud av va'em*
and *shiluach ha'ken*. And finally, the Torah uses the expression תועבת ד'
to describe the practice of possessing false weights and measures. The
very strong word of תועבה is sparingly used in the Torah to describe *is-
surim* and is, I believe, reserved for the prohibitions of homosexuality,
idol worship, and the eating of certain non-kosher food.

Rashi (25:17) notes the significance of the proximate placement in
the Torah of the laws of false weights and measures to the immediately ensuing recitation of the attack of Amalek. Rashi says:

אם שקרת במדות ומשקלות הוי דואג מגרוי האויב.

If you falsify weights and measures, then you have good
reason to be apprehensive about an attack from your
archenemy.

Once again we see a relevance and connection between the *pesukim*
which precede the Amalek passage and the retribution of Amalek. In
Beshalach, it was, among other things, the statement by Bnei Yisrael
of היש ד' בקרבנו אם אין, "Is G-d amongst us or not?" which triggered
Amalek's attack, and in Parshas Ki Tetzeh it is the use, and even the
mere possession, of false weights and measures.

And, significantly, this could well explain why the Torah took
the trouble to give us two separate Amalek passages. The first one,
through the preceding *pesukim*, teaches us that Amalek will attack us
if we violate the fundamental commandments of בין אדם למקום – *emuna*
in Hashem – which failure of *emuna* is represented by Bnei Yisrael's
expression of היש ד' בקרבנו אם אין.

The second Amalek passage, through *its* preceding *pesukim*, teaches us that Amalek will attack us if we violate the fundamental commandments of בין אדם לחברו – such as false weights and measures. And, incidentally, I suggest that this also explains why the Torah placed the *pasuk* of זכור את אשר עשה לך עמלק בדרך בצאתכם ממצרים in Ki Tetzeh and obligated us to read this passage (rather than the passage in Beshalach) on Shabbos Zachor. Since the Ki Tetzeh passage is preceded by a fundamental commandment of בין אדם לחברו, and since Hashem considers *mitzvos* of בין אדם לחברו more important, in certain respects, than *mitzvos* of בין אדם למקום (e.g., our tradition's view of Yom Kippur as a day of *kapara*, which *kapara* is conditional on putting our personal relationships in good order), we read the Amalek passage of Ki Tetzeh on Shabbos Zachor.

❧ THE MITZVAH AND PURPOSE TO REMEMBER AMALEK

Now that we have reviewed the two Amalek passages in the Torah, let us analyze the mitzvah of *zechiras Amalek* itself in the context of other required *zechiros*. The source for the mitzvah *mi'd'oraisa* to remember Amalek is the *pasuk* we quoted earlier. The Torah tells us (Devarim 25:17):

זכור את אשר עשה לך עמלק בדרך בצאתכם ממצרים.

Remember what Amalek did to you on your way out of Mitzrayim.

There are a total of six things which the Torah obligates us to remember through the use of the word *zachor*. It is worth noting that, in an important respect, *zechiras Amalek* seems to be out of place in the group of six *zechiros*, since the other five *zechiros* all deal with very fundamental *mitzvos* or significant aspects of our tradition such as Shabbos, *lashon hara* (referring to the mitzvah to remember what happened to Miriam), *Yetzias Mitzrayim, Maamad Har Sinai,* and *chet ha'egel,* whereas *zechiras Amalek,* apparently at least, does not ask us to remember any specific mitzvah but simply urges us to recall what Amalek did to us when we left Mitzrayim. So, another one of the questions we will explore, and which will also be answered in the conclusion of this *d'var*, is how and why does *zechiras Amalek* fit into this group of six *zechiros*.

I would now like to focus on the purpose of the mitzvah of *zechiras Amalek* and, in so doing, hopefully elucidate the valuable and practical lessons which this mitzvah teaches us.

RAMBAM'S APPARENT FOCUS ON THE EVIL OF AMALEK

The Rambam, elaborating upon the mitzvah of *zechiras Amalek*, states as follows (*Hilchos Melachim* 5:5):

ומצוות עשה לזכור תמיד מעשיו הרעים . . . כדי לעורר איבתו.
It is a positive commandment to always remember the evil deeds of Amalek so that our hatred of Amalek will be stimulated.

What appears to be underlying the Rambam's elaboration of this mitzvah is that Amalek represents pure evil and consequently does terrible things to us without provocation. The Torah then commands us to remember these terrible things so that we will be sure to destroy Amalek.

It is important to note that the Rambam appears to focus exclusively on the evil nature of Amalek and the commandment to utterly destroy and root out this people. In fact, if we read the Rambam literally, and attempt to infer, from the Rambam's words, whose fault it is that Amalek attacks Bnei Yisrael, it appears that it is all Amalek's fault. Upon first impression, as we will discuss in a moment, the Rambam's apparent exclusive focus on the evil of Amalek is very perplexing.

FOCUS ON THE FAULT OF BNEI YISRAEL

In contrast to Rambam's apparent exclusive focus on the evil of Amalek, Rashi, as we have seen, both in Beshalach and in Ki Tetzeh, makes a direct connection between the gross misdeeds of Bnei Yisrael and the immediately ensuing attack of Amalek – in one case, Rashi explains, Amalek's attacks were caused by Bnei Yisrael's attitude of היש ד' בקרבנו אם אין, and in the other case they were caused by our use, and indeed mere possession, of false weights and measures.

Of course, it is not only Rashi who makes this connection between the faulty behavior of Bnei Yisrael and the retribution of Amalek. We also see the same idea in a variety of other ways, including:

(1) Refidim: We have already discussed how, immediately preceding the attack of Amalek, the Jews rebelled in Refidim (whose very name is derived from an expression which means "weakened their links to the Torah"). It can be inferred, from the proximity of this account in the Torah to the attack of Amalek, and the fact that Amalek's attack took place in Refidim, that the two are closely related events.

(2) Moshe's hands raised in battle: As we also noted, the raising of Moshe's hands, in the battle against Amalek, was symbolic of the fact that, as stated in the Mishnah in *Rosh Hashana*, Bnei Yisrael prevail in the battle against Amalek when we subjugate our hearts and minds to our Father in Heaven and when, G-d forbid, the opposite is true, we render ourselves vulnerable to Amalek. Here, the Mishnah makes it very clear that the battle against Amalek is not merely a physical battle which Bnei Yisrael is forced to wage against a merciless enemy, but is also very much a spiritual battle whose outcome is to a great degree dependent upon our own faith and deeds.

(3) Randomness: We also mentioned that the word קָרְךָ (which alludes to happenstance) indicates that the seemingly random attack of Amalek is payback for our thinking that the events of this world are not Hashem's doing but rather random occurrences.[5]

So, if it is indeed Bnei Yisrael's rebellion and transgression which causes Amalek to attack us, why does the Rambam, when discussing the mitzvah of *zechiras Amalek*, seem to emphasize exclusively the evil nature of Amalek? Why is there not so much as a hint in the Rambam's discussion of the mitzvah of *zechiras Amalek* that the conduct of Bnei Yisrael is very much to blame for Amalek's attacks? We will shortly offer a possible rationale for the Rambam's approach.

---

5. There are numerous good reasons to make this connection, as I discuss in detail in "Megillas Esther and *Pirsumei Nisa*: The Obligation to Publicize Hashem's Miracles."

IMPORTANT LESSONS LEARNED FROM YISRO

Let us continue our analysis by examining Yisro's perspective on the events of *Yetzias Mitzrayim,* including the encounter of Bnei Yisrael with Amalek. Shortly after the beginning of Parshas Yisro, we read the following declaration of Yisro (Shemos 18:11):

עתה ידעתי כי גדול ד' מכל אלוהים כי בדבר אשר זדו עליהם.
Now I understand that Hashem is greater than all of the other gods, כי בדבר אשר זדו עליהם.

כי בדבר אשר זדו עליהם – because Hashem responds to a person's, or a nation's, actions *"midda k'neged midda,"* which means measure for measure. (*Sotah* 11a)

What I believe Yisro was saying, in effect, is that when a person observes, consistently, that reward or punishment is meted out *midda k'neged midda,* then that is irrefutable evidence that the events in question are not random and that a superior force caused the reward or punishment to occur.[6]

What was it that Yisro saw which caused him to notice Hashem's trait of rewarding and punishing *midda k'neged midda*? To assist us in answering this question, we turn to the first *pasuk* in Yisro, which reads as follows (Shemos 18:1):

וישמע יתרו כהן מדין חתן משה את כל אשר עשה אלקים למשה
ולישראל.
Yisro heard about everything which Hashem did for Moshe and his people during *Yetzias Mitzrayim.*

Rashi, on the words וישמע יתרו, tells us that Yisro heard about the splitting of the Sea and the encounter with Amalek. Now, we can easily understand the *midda k'neged midda* of the splitting of the Sea – the Egyptians acted to drown the Jewish male babies in the sea and, consequently, the Egyptians themselves were drowned there. But how do we see *midda k'neged midda* in the context of Amalek? I believe that the answer to this question lies in Rashi's interpretations of the word

---

6. See also the Torah Temima's explanation of the words כי בדבר אשר זדו עליהם (Shemos 18:11).

קרך, in אשר קרך בדרך [Devarim 25:18]. Rashi provides two alternative interpretations of the word קרך, and underlying each of these interpretations is a different illustration of how Amalek's attacks represent *midda k'neged midda*.

Rashi's first interpretation of the word קרך, based on the Sifri, is "*lashon mikreh,*" or happenstance. We have already discussed the apparent randomness of Amalek's attacks as constituting *midda k'neged midda* payback for our thinking that the events of this world are not caused by G-d's *hashgacha* but instead consist of a series of random occurrences. This is the Amalek attack in Beshalach, following Bnei Yisrael's expression of היש ד' בקרבנו אם אין.

Another interpretation of the word קרך is "cooled off," from the root קר. Rashi states that Amalek made it acceptable for the nations of the world to attack Bnei Yisrael. Initially, these nations were afraid to do so because they had heard about all of Hashem's wondrous miracles. But when Amalek showed the way, the other nations had less fear. Rashi offers the example of a scalding hot bath, which everyone is afraid to enter. But as soon as the first person enters, he cools it off for everyone else. So too did Amalek make it easier for the other nations to attack us. Now, we might ask, how did the fact that Amalek was the first nation which dared to attack Bnei Yisrael enable Yisro to discern Hashem's characteristic of *midda k'neged midda*?

In order to understand this, let us refer again to the prohibition of false weights and measures which immediately precedes the command in Ki Tetzeh to remember Amalek. We know that the non-Jews are commanded not to steal. What happens, however, when the non-Jews observe not only that some Jews steal but that some of the so-called religious ones amongst us sometimes lead the way in gross violations of business dishonesty? When this happens, instead of Bnei Yisrael being a ממלכת כהנים וגוי קדוש, and instead of our acting as a light unto the nations, we accomplish the very opposite.

When the non-Jews observe that even some of the so-called "religious" among us use false weights and measures, by cheating in business and otherwise conducting themselves dishonestly, this cannot help but greatly diminish the respect of non-Jews for the law against stealing. So, by acting dishonestly, we, in effect, "cool off" the non-Jew from his fear of G-d and His commandments.

And so we understand, as Yisro did, that the attack of Amalek, which cooled off the other nations' fear of G-d and their reluctance to attack Bnei Yisrael, despite the great miracles which the nations had just witnessed as part of *Yetzias Mitzrayim*, represents *midda k'neged midda* for our misdeeds.

Without a doubt, the Rambam was well aware of all of the clear links between our misconduct and Amalek's attacks. Yet it is not entirely clear why the Rambam failed to explicitly highlight any such links in his setting forth the commandment for us to remember Amalek. Perhaps the Rambam felt that, if we focus on the relentless and merciless evil of Amalek, and if we are aware that everything happens for a reason, we will ultimately realize that we must have provoked Hashem very greatly to have Him bring all of this suffering upon us – by our cheating in business, or by acting as if we question Hashem's very presence, or in other ways. Tragically, it is too often the case that, only by observing Hashem's punishment of our misdeeds, can we achieve a proper understanding of what we did wrong in the first place.

To summarize, I would like to suggest that the purpose of *zechiras Amalek*, which superficially appears to be merely a commandment to destroy a cruel, implacable enemy, is in reality (as we have seen indicated in the Midrash and other commentaries) a commandment to destroy all that is deficient within ourselves. So long as any vestige of Amalek remains, it signifies that the character of Bnei Yisrael requires major repair. In other words, the commandment to remember Amalek and its evil deeds is, in important respects, a reminder to us that it is of critical importance for us, along with despising Amalek and the sheer evil which Amalek represents, to intensely focus upon that very behavior in ourselves which brings about Hashem's retribution through the medium of Amalek.

The Sefer HaCharedim makes this point explicitly (Chapter 2, *Mitzvos HaTeluyos BaAretz*):

שנזכור שבשביל שרפו ידיהם של ישראל מן המצוות בא עמלק.

The mitzvah to remember Amalek means to keep in mind that it was because Bnei Yisrael let their links to Torah be weakened that Amalek came to attack us.

✌ ANSWERING SOME OF OUR QUESTIONS

Building upon these thoughts, I believe we can answer a number of our questions, as well as derive certain extremely important lessons in the process.

For example, we asked why Moshe and Yehoshua, apparently heeding G-d's edict, did not eradicate Amalek despite the fact that they had destroyed all of Amalek's warriors. As we have seen, Amalek remains at all times poised to attack Bnei Yisrael when we demonstrate ourselves not to be worthy of Hashem's protection and, in fact, it may well be that the sole purpose of Amalek's existence in this world is as an instrument of retribution against our people. Accordingly, we can infer that, despite the fact that we have a positive commandment to destroy the memory of Amalek, Hashem will not allow us to eradicate Amalek until the end of days. As Rav Soloveitchik stated, in the lecture we quoted earlier:

> Amalek will only be defeated at the commencement of
> the Messianic era. No one will be able to defeat Amalek.

[Nevertheless, as we have seen in Parshas Beshalach, and again in Megillas Esther, Amalek can be significantly weakened and even temporarily neutralized.]

Similar to Rav Soloveitchik's statement, which we just quoted, that "Amalek will only be defeated at the commencement of the Messianic era," Rav Shimshon Raphael Hirsch states in his commentary to Parshas Beshalach (Shemos 17:13):

> ... Yehoshua only weakened Amalek. His [Amalek's]
> final defeat remains for the distant future. Israel itself is
> not yet mature. Until Israel attains maturity, the existence
> of Amalek as a contrast is necessary for the development
> of Israel's education.

Rav Hirsch's statement that "the existence of Amalek as a contrast is necessary for the development of Israel's education" is quite remarkable, considering the unmitigated cruelty of Amalek. To extrapolate Rav Hirsch's statement to today's context, Rav Hirsch would say that the existence of the Arabs, despite their terrible barbarism, is necessary for the development of our education.

In any event, we now understand why, as Rashi explains, Hashem did not permit Amalek to be destroyed by Moshe and Yehoshua, even though Amalek was then completely vulnerable, with all of its warriors having been killed. Bnei Yisrael failed all of the ten tests which Hashem placed upon them in the *midbar* and clearly did not demonstrate that they deserved to have Amalek eradicated. The battle for Amalek symbolizes the battle of the good in us against our own collective *yetzer hara*, and Amalek cannot and will not be destroyed until we win this battle.[7]

The nature of this eternal battle against Amalek can be seen in what otherwise appears to be a very mysterious Rashi in the first Amalek passage. When Moshe urges Yehoshua, צא הלחם בעמלק, "Go and do battle with Amalek," Rashi comments on the word צא, with the following words (17:9):

צא מן הענן – Go out from the cloud.

As we know, the clouds in the *midbar*, the ענני הכבוד, represented Hashem's protection and guidance, which served Bnei Yisrael throughout the forty years in the *midbar* despite the fact that Bnei Yisrael were clearly not deserving of this protection. The clouds represent Hashem's unconditional protection. The battle against Amalek is otherwise – it is not unconditional. Just the opposite. We do not win the battle against Amalek if we are found wanting. And this, I believe, explains Rashi's interpretation of צא – go out from the cloud. The battle against Amalek cannot be won without good deeds and *teshuva*. The outcome is not guaranteed.[8]

Accordingly, we can determine from our discussion that, in order to meet the challenge of Amalek, it is absolutely critical to focus on improving our own collective national character. And so we conclude

---

7. Although Saul was punished for not killing the remnant of Amalek represented by Agag, I believe that Saul would not have succeeded in any event if he had attempted to kill Agag and eradicate Amalek. He was punished, however, I would respectfully submit, for deciding, on his own, not to make the attempt.

8. This helps explain why we are obligated to focus so closely on each word of the Torah reading of Parshas Zachor – the spiritual battle against Amalek requires our utmost vigilance and concentration.

that the underlying theme of the mitzvah to remember Amalek is the objective of eradicating that which is deficient in our conduct. In other words, we must focus on the spiritual battle within ourselves and not only on the physical battle with Amalek.

And this notion enables us to answer our earlier question as to how and why *zechiras Amalek* fits into the group of six *zechiros*, since it does not appear to involve remembrance of any of the fundamental *mitzvos* represented by the other *zechiros*. Since, however, remembering Amalek entails intense introspection focusing on our performance of *all mitzvos*, it is apparent why *zechiras Amalek* was included among the six *zechiros*.

An excellent illustration of the point we have been making – about the spiritual battle underlying the mitzvah of *zechiras Amalek* – can be found in connection with Purim. We celebrate Purim as our classic victory over Amalek. Yet, if we construe the mitzvah of remembering Amalek as being fulfilled only by *physically destroying* Amalek, then how do we explain the fact that there is no evidence at all that the Jews of the Megilla did so, even though Achashverosh gave them virtually a free hand?

Although the Megilla tells us that, in addition to Haman and his sons, the Jews in various countries killed over 75,000 people, we have no indication that these people were all, or even mostly, from the nation of Amalek. And even if the ones killed were all from Amalek, we have no indication that these people constituted a significant portion of the nation of Amalek as it was then. So, if the Jews of the Megilla's time left much of Amalek standing, as may very well have been the case, what is the basis for our celebrating Purim as a great victory over Amalek?

The answer, I believe, is found in our discussion. Since the battle against Amalek is very much a battle between the good and the evil in our own hearts and minds, the victory against Amalek is symbolized more by *mishloach manos* and *matanos le'evyonim* than the killing of even 75,000 of our enemies. It was only after Bnei Yisrael fasted and did *teshuva* and dealt with each other kindly, as evidenced by their celebratory performance of *mishloach manos* and *matanos le'evyonim*, that Haman's evil decree was reversed. Purim represents a dramatic renewal of our faith and commitment to our Creator – קימו וקבלו. And, I submit, this is the essence of how and why we celebrate Purim as our victory over the evil forces of Amalek.

We also see this notion towards the end of Megillas Esther. We are told that Mordechai sent a letter to the Jews in all of Achashverosh's 127 provinces, which letter was intended to confirm the celebration of Purim in subsequent years. Although the letter no doubt discussed all of the miraculous events which had transpired, it is very noteworthy that the Megilla, in referring to the contents of this letter, does not mention the hanging of Haman or his sons, nor does it mention the more than 75,000 enemies the Jews killed. Rather, the Megilla summarizes the contents of Mordechai's letter by stating, simply, that it contained the following words (Esther 9:30):

דברי שלום ואמת – words of peace and truth,

and also (9:31):

דברי הצומות וזעקתם – words of their [Bnei Yisrael's] fasting and crying out.

It should also be noted that Rav Yitzchak Mirsky in *Hegyonei Halacha*[9] discusses the purpose of the mitzvah of *mishloach manos*. He notes that Mordechai instituted three *mitzvos* related to Purim. The first is *seuda*, whose purpose he says is very understandable – as a commemoration and celebration of the miracle of Purim. The next mitzvah is *matanos le'evyonim*, which, Rav Mirsky notes, is in line with a common custom among Bnei Yisrael to ensure that everyone has sufficient means to properly celebrate each holiday. But then Rav Mirsky asks: what is the reason for *mishloach manos*?

After referring to a number of commentaries, Rav Mirsky concludes that:

משלוח מנות משמשת אמצעי לקרב את ישראל זה לזה ולאחדם.
The intrinsic purpose of *mishloach manos* is to bring Bnei Yisrael closer to each other.

Rav Mirsky then quotes the Sfas Emes, who takes this notion one step further in elaborating upon the overriding importance of unity among *Klal Yisrael*. Rav Mirsky summarizes the Sfas Emes's view as follows:

---

9. Rabbi Yitzchak Mirsky, *Hegyonei Halacha*, Vol. 1, essay 41 (Jerusalem: Mosad HaRav Kook, 1989).

לדעתו יש באחדות בפני עצמה כח מגן לישראל לעמוד בפני הפורענות,
שאין היא יכולה לשלוט בהם בעת התאחדותם.

According to the Sfas Emes, unity among our people, in and of itself, has the power to protect us from punishment and suffering, since punishment and suffering have no power to dominate and control us at any time that we are united.

Rav Mirsky states that the entire *hatzala* of Bnei Yisrael from Haman's decree came about on account of unity, as symbolized by Esther's call to Mordechai (Esther 4:15):

לך כנוס את כל היהודים – Go and assemble all of the Jews.

Rav Mirsky concludes that Mordechai instituted the mitzvah of *mishloach manos* because it would stand as a classic symbol of the critical importance of unity among our people.

❧ CONCLUSION

Hopefully, we have now achieved a much better appreciation of the purpose and importance of the mitzvah of *zechiras Amalek*, and the fact that performance of this mitzvah is predicated upon our understanding that Amalek attacks us not only because of the sheer evil of Amalek but, to a significant degree because, as noted by the Sefer HaCharedim, we allowed our links to Torah and *mitzvos* to be weakened and not because we chose the wrong political leaders, or because we need to improve our military tactics or strategy. We must realize, immediately, that the war against Amalek has a very significant spiritual component.

It is a great tragedy of the current situation that we continue to search hard for political and military solutions but seemingly refrain, much of the time, from searching the one place which counts the most. The Rambam (*Hilchos Taaniyos* 1:2–3), makes the following seminal observation, which has great relevance to the situation in which we find ourselves today:

And this matter is the path of *teshuva*, that in the time when great troubles come upon us and we cry out in anguish, we should know that all these troubles are the direct result of our misdeeds, and if we correct our improper behavior, then the troubles will dissipate. However, if we do not cry out to Hashem and if we believe that our troubles are just one of those unfortunate events which occur in this world from time to time, then this is a despicable mindset which will cause us to fail to correct our misguided and evil behavior, and our troubles will then multiply and increase in variety, as it says in the *tochacha* in Bechukosai, "when you walk with Me with *keri*," which connotes the feeling that events are random, then Hashem will react with "*chamas keri* – the anger of *keri*" – meaning even greater retribution than before.

Is there hope? Do we have the power and ability to make a difference so that we can prevail in this battle? I would suggest that we certainly can. If, when we perform the mitzvah to remember Amalek, we bear in mind not only the Amalek passages in the Torah, but also the *pesukim* which preceded them, *pesukim* which convey fundamental principles of *bein adam laMakom* and *bein adam l'chaveiro*, we will prevail.

If we also remember that our victory over Haman was a spiritual, and not a military, victory, we will prevail.

If we discern the *hashgacha* of Hashem in everyday events, both large and small, and if we are scrupulously honest in our business dealings, and take great care not to possess (let alone use) any device, such as false weights and measures, which may lead to dishonest practices, we will prevail.

If our actions reflect the spirit of *mishloach manos* and *matanos le'evyonim, shalom, emes*, unity, and קימו וקבלו, as reflected in Megillas Esther, we will prevail.

And, in addition to the major impact we can each have as individuals, it is important to note that this impact is magnified dramatically when we act as a unified group and with a common purpose. In this respect, it is very instructive that we derive the requirement that a *minyan* must have at least ten men from a chain of *gezeiros shavos* whose ultimate source is the episode of the *meraglim*. Now, it is natural to ask: why would the Torah have us derive the *kedusha* of ten people forming a *minyan* from the shameful acts of the *meraglim*?

The answer, I believe, is that the Torah wants us to fully comprehend that, in the case of the *meraglim,* it took only ten persons acting in unison to turn the Ninth of Av into a day of everlasting mourning for the Jewish people. The unstated implication, which is essential for us to appreciate, is that ten people united for a righteous cause have enormous power to make a substantial positive impact for our people.

Let us make certain that the barbaric acts of our enemies unite us in a common effort, using the special power of *minyan,* to battle the scourge of Amalek with our collective good deeds. If we do so, we shall certainly prevail.

And as we offer up our *tefillos* on behalf of Eretz Yisrael, as we regularly do, let us be cognizant of the fact that Hashem is much more receptive to our *tefillos* when the character of the person or *kehila* offering the *tefillos* reflects a full and sincere dedication to Torah and *mitzvos.*[10]

In conclusion, we say: Yes, let us perform the mitzvah of *zechiras Amalek* by focusing on Amalek's repulsive, despicable conduct towards us and the fact that the eradication of this terrible evil (a battle in which we are joined, כביכול, by Hashem) is a very important objective, but let us also begin immediately to learn, from the nature of Amalek's actions towards us, and from the Rambam's statement, in *Hilchos Taaniyos,* "that all these troubles are the direct result of our misdeeds," what we must do to immediately remedy the situation.

At the beginning of Bechukosai, just before the *tochacha,* the Torah tells us that a reward for our walking in Hashem's ways will be that no hostile weapons will traverse our Land. At a time when there are in fact hostile weapons in every corner of Eretz Yisrael, and Amalek is all over us, let us strive with all our abilities to merit Hashem's intervention on our behalf and turn the tide of *midda k'neged midda* in our favor. Let us make a special effort, individually and as a community, to perfect our *emuna* and performance of *mitzvos.* If we do so, we can be confident that this will lead to the final eradication of Amalek and to a *geula shleima, bimheira beyameinu.*

---

10. *Tefillos* are a substitute for *korbanos.* The *Nevi'im* have taught us more than once that Hashem much prefers *korbanos* when the ethics of the person offering such *korbanos* reflect the Torah's standards.

SHEVET LEVI'S EXEMPLARY CHARACTER: WHY DO WE NEED BOTH KOHANIM AND LEVI'IM? WHY INDEED DID MOSHE RESIST G-D'S MISSION?

℘ INTRODUCTION

It is axiomatic that *Yetzias Mitzrayim* is a very significant event in our history. We are commanded to remember this event twice each day; it is mentioned in Friday night *Kiddush*, in *Az Yashir*, when we put on our *tefillin*, and is the central theme in the Haggadah. Is it just a coincidence that the central characters in *Yetzias Mitzrayim* – Moshe, Aharon, Miriam, and Amram – are all members of Shevet Levi?

In the first part of this *d'var Torah*, I would like to explore with you why Shevet Levi played such an important role in *Yetzias Mitzrayim*, as well as the related question as to why members of Shevet Levi have, as we will see, a very privileged status in halacha.

In the second part of the *d'var Torah*, I would like to analyze why it is that the Torah found it necessary to do with Shevet Levi what the Torah did not do with any other *shevet*, namely create subclasses. Shevet Levi is broken down into the categories of Kohen and Levi. Why was this categorization necessary and what important lesson does this teach us about the character of Shevet Levi?

Our analysis, aside from providing what I hope will be some new and fascinating insights into otherwise familiar passages in the Torah and into the special character of Shevet Levi, will also enable us to learn some valuable lessons as to how we can bring about the future *geula*.

Let us begin by examining the status of Shevet Levi in halacha. Most of us are probably not fully aware of the fact that halacha in-stitutionalizes a great deal of respect towards descendants of Shevet Levi. We all know that there are laws of *teruma* and *maaser* which the

Torah instituted in order to make sure that Kohanim and Levi'im were supported properly. What we do not always focus on is that Kohanim and Levi'im have a number of other important privileges.

PRIVILEGES OF KOHANIM AND LEVI'IM

Rambam states as follows (*Hilchos Klei HaMikdosh* 4:2):

וצריך כל אדם מישראל לנהוג בהן כבוד הרבה ולהקדים אותם לכל דבר
שבקדושה לפתוח בתורה ראשון, ולברך ראשון.

With respect to the *Kohanim*, every Jew is obligated to accord them a great deal of deference, in any matter of *kedusha*, of holiness, so that they get the first *aliya* and they have priority for making *Berachos*. . . .

The Mishna Berura (201:2) points out that the Kohen's priority is derived from the word *v'kidashto* (Vayikra 21:8), meaning that you shall give the Kohen precedence in all matters of holiness. The Mishna Berura then learns from a different *pasuk* (Devarim 31:9) that the Levi has the next level of priority, superior to a Yisrael.

Aside from the priority for *aliyos*, with which we are all familiar, the status privileges of Kohanim and Levi'im apply in several surprising ways:

For example, the Mishna Berura (201:2, 13) goes so far as to refer to *poskim* who rule that a Kohen should even be the first to speak at a public gathering.

The Yoreh De'ah (*Hilchos Tzedaka* 251:9) states that if a person has a number of needy persons whom he is trying to help sustain, but he cannot take care of them all, then a Kohen has priority to a Levi and a Levi has priority to a Yisrael.

And the Mishna (*Horayos* 13a) states that the priority of a Kohen and Levi over a Yisrael applies even in the case of redeeming captives. This is quite remarkable. Who would have thought that when we are trying to decide whom – of multiple captives – to redeem, we must give priority to the Kohen and Levi?

So we see that halacha, based upon *pesukim* in the Chumash, has elevated the Kohen and Levi to a special status. Why did halacha create these privileges? What is so special about Shevet Levi? Many would probably answer that Shevet Levi deserved special status because they did not participate in the sin of the *egel*, the Golden Calf. This explanation is not entirely satisfactory, however, as it attributes great merit to not participating in the unthinkable transgression of idol worship. Although it is commendable that Shevet Levi did not participate in the sin of the *egel*, you could almost say that it was to be expected that they should not so participate, and not something for which their status would forever transcend all of the other eleven *sh'vatim*.

Moreover, and even more compelling, is the fact that Shevet Levi appears to have had a special status long before the incident of the *egel*. For instance, while Bnei Yisrael were still enslaved in Egypt, the Torah refers to Aharon as אהרן אחיך הלוי – Aharon, your brother, from Shevet Levi – implying that, even in Mitzrayim, Levi was a badge of distinction. And there is also at least one other example of this, which we will touch on later. So we see that the Torah, long before the incident of the *egel*, seems to be elevating Shevet Levi above the other tribes.

To try and understand the rationale for the special status of Kohanim and Levi'im, it would be helpful to briefly review the development of Shevet Levi in the Torah. The Torah gives us a clue as to the unique mission of Shevet Levi right from the outset of Levi's existence. When Levi was born, the *pasuk* says (Bereishis 29:34):

עַל כֵּן קָרָא שְׁמוֹ לֵוִי.

And that is why he was called Levi.

Rashi, noting the difference in the way Levi was named, compared with the manner in which all of the other *sh'vatim* were named, comments:

בכולם כתיב ותקרא, . . . וזה כתב בו קרא.

About all the other sons it is written "and *she* called,"
but in the case of Levi, the *pasuk* states "and *he* called."

In other words, each of Levi's eleven brothers was named by the boy's mother, but Levi was different. Rashi quotes a Midrash which states that Levi was named by Hashem. Moreover, the Rambam states the following (*Hilchos Avodas Kochavim* 1:3):

ויעקב אבינו למד בניו כולם והבדיל לוי ומינהו ראש והושיבו בישיבה
ללמד דרך השם ולשמור מצוות אברהם.

And Yaakov Avinu taught all of his children and appointed Levi the leader of them all and sat him in a Yeshiva to teach him the ways of Hashem, and the *mitzvos* of Avraham Avinu.

So it is apparent that Yaakov placed Levi in a special status, already grooming him for a unique role of leadership.

And we see a similar theme in the last *parsha* of the Torah. Moshe Rabbeinu, in Parshas V'Zos HaBracha (Devarim 33:10, 11), gives the following *bracha* to Shevet Levi:

יורו משפטיך ליעקב ותורתך לישראל ישימו קטורה באפך וכליל על
מזבחך. ברך ד' חילו ופעל ידיו תרצה מחץ מתנים קמיו ומשנאיו מן
יקומון.

They shall teach Your laws to Jacob and Your Torah to Yisrael; they shall place incense before Your presence; and burnt-offerings upon Your altar. Bless O Hashem, his possessions, and favor the work of his hands. Smite the loins of those that rise up against him and of those that hate him so that they rise not again.

So we see that Shevet Levi was destined from the beginning for spiritual leadership, in the special way he was named at birth and in the particular manner of his upbringing by Yaakov Avinu, and as confirmed by Moshe's eloquent *bracha* at the end of the Chumash. However, it appears as if there was a serious glitch along the way. Levi, at least for a time, as we will now discuss, took a very wrong turn.

❧ YAAKOV'S REBUKE TO LEVI

As we know, just before his passing, Yaakov Avinu addresses each of the *sh'vatim*. Yaakov's words to Levi, considering everything we have said so far, were surprisingly harsh (Bereishis 49:5):

שמעון ולוי אחים כלי חמס מכרותיהם.

Shimon and Levi are brothers; stolen tools are their weapons.

Rashi, on the words *klei chamas*, no doubt keeping in mind the notion that *"chamas"* has a connotation of theft, comments:

אומנות זו של רציחה חמס הוא בידיהם מברכת עשו היא זו.

This craft of murder [referring presumably to the revenge killings in Shechem], it is in their possession by theft, it is the character trait of Esav.

Yaakov's rebuke of Shimon and Levi then continues (49:6):

בסודם אל־תבוא נפשי בקהלם אל־תחד כבודי.

Into their counsel, may my soul not enter. With their congregation do not unite.

How do we reconcile Yaakov's harsh words to Levi with everything else we have said about Shevet Levi?

I believe that if we closely examine Yaakov's final words to Levi, we will find that Yaakov's message to Levi, unlike its apparent deep-seated negativity, in fact contains a fascinating and crucial insight into the special character of Shevet Levi. Let us examine the words one more time. Yaakov said to Levi (49:5):

שמעון ולוי אחים כלי חמס מכרותיהם.

Shimon and Levi are brothers; stolen tools are their weapons.

How do we understand the word *achim* in this context, since it seems to be redundant? I believe that a close analysis of the word *achim*, as it is used by the Torah in conjunction with members of Shevet Levi, can provide us with a deep insight into the character of this *shevet*. In fact, I would like to suggest that *"achim"* is a code word for the very essence of what is outstanding and unique about Shevet Levi.

When is the first time *"achim"* is used in connection with Shevet Levi? Let's examine the episode of Dinah's abduction. As we all know, Shimon and Levi acted in concert, in very dramatic fashion, to avenge their sister's violation, by tricking the people of Shechem into a position where Shimon and Levi were able to kill all of the males.

The Torah, describing Shimon and Levi arming themselves for the attack, states (Bereishis 34:25):

ויקחו שני בני יעקב שמעון ולוי אחי דינה.

The sons of Yaakov, Shimon and Levi, the *brothers* of Dinah, took their weapons.

Rashi, commenting on the words: אחי דינה, states as follows:

לפי שמסרו עצמן עליה נקראו אחיה.

Because they put themselves at risk for her, they were called *"achim"* (her brothers)

This Rashi deserves very close attention because it represents the first of several instances where the word *achim*, or its variation, is used in connection with Shevet Levi to represent something very significant and powerful, namely the readiness of members of Shevet Levi to risk their lives for the sake of their brethren.

Another instance where this code word appears in connection with members of Shevet Levi is when we meet Moshe Rabbeinu for the first time as an adult. As we read the *pasuk*, keep in mind that Moshe was raised in the privileged and protected environment of Pharaoh's palace and would have every reason to preserve his life-style and not jeopardize his privileged status. Nevertheless, the Torah wastes no time in revealing to us Moshe's special character, when the *pasuk* states (Shemos 2:11):

ויהי בימים ההם ויגדל משה ויצא אל אחיו וירא בסבלתם.

It happened in those days that Moshe grew up and went out to his *brethren* (אל אחיו) and saw their burdens.

Rashi refers to Shemos Rabba and comments as follows:

נתן עיניו ולבו להיות מצר עליהם.

He focused his eyes and his heart to be distressed over the plight of his enslaved and oppressed people.

Immediately afterwards, the Torah tells us, Moshe sees the Egyptian taskmaster beating *ish ivri me'echav* – once again, note the word *me'echav*. Moshe immediately kills the Egyptian and, in so doing, not only jeopardizes his lifestyle in the palace but puts his very life at risk. So again, we see the use of *achim*, or a variation thereof, to illustrate how a member of Shevet Levi was prepared to risk his life in order to protect his fellow Jews.

The code word *"achim,"* or its feminine variation, is used in two separate places in connection with Miriam. The first time occurs when Miriam goes to check on Moshe while he is in the bulrushes. In this episode, the Torah does not even call Miriam by her name, but states (Shemos 2:4):

ותתצב אחותו מרחוק.
His *sister* stationed herself at a distance.

Now, it is not obvious how Miriam, by merely observing Moshe, was placing herself in any danger. However, Rav Shimshon Raphael Hirsch comments that the word ותתצב is an active form of the word which implies a determination on Miriam's part to take some action to assist Moshe. In the face of Pharaoh's decree to throw Jewish boys into the river, Miriam must have placed herself at considerable risk of being accused of a plot to rescue Moshe. Nevertheless, she ignored the risk.

The second use of the code word in connection with Miriam occurs after Bnei Yisrael had successfully crossed the Red Sea. After Moshe led the men in song, symbolized by *Az Yashir*, Miriam led the women in song. The Torah uses the following words to describe Miriam's actions (Shemos 15:20):

ותקח מרים הנביאה אחות אהרן.

Rashi (quoting the Mechilta), no doubt wondering why the *pasuk* bothered to use the seemingly irrelevant expression אחות אהרן (it should have merely said ותקח מרים הנביאה), offers the following explanation:

דבר אחר, אחות אהרן, לפי שמסר נפשו עליה כשנצטערה נקראת על שמו.
Another explanation of *achos Aharon* is because Aharon acted in a self-sacrificial manner with respect to Miriam when she was in pain [presumably when Miriam was stricken with *tzaraas*].

This is yet another instance where Rashi associates a variation of the word *achim*, as used in connection with Shevet Levi, to denote self-sacrifice.

Now the manner in which Aharon demonstrated self-sacrifice

for Miriam requires some detailed analysis.[1] Suffice it to say that we again see a nexus between use of *ach* or *achim* to denote self-sacrifice and, as we have seen, the word *ach* is used by the Torah, first with Levi and then with Moshe, Miriam, and Aharon, to denote a willingness by a member of Shevet Levi to put his or her very life at risk for a fellow Jew. Moreover, this character trait appears to be the hallmark of Shevet Levi. And it is credible that this is precisely why halacha elevated Shevet Levi to such a special status, meriting the highest form of respect from everyone else.

So, in view of our hypothesis that Yaakov used the word *achim* as a code word to denote that Shevet Levi's members were ready to risk their own safety in order to benefit their fellow Jews, why did Yaakov otherwise rebuke Levi so harshly? I suggest that Yaakov may have been concerned that Levi was carrying his *ahavas Yisrael* too far by being much too quick to resort to the deadly violence of revenge killings, which Yaakov felt was a trait characteristic of Esav and therefore unbefitting of Shevet Levi. Yaakov perhaps felt that retribution alone was not a proper motive for mass killings.

Shevet Levi, unlike Shevet Shimon, which deteriorated to the point that it did not even receive a *bracha* in V'Zos HaBracha, apparently took Yaakov's rebuke to heart. Shortly after Yaakov's rebuke, in the midst of the enslavement in Mitzrayim, members of Shevet Levi began to use the noble character trait, symbolized by the word *achim*, in an extremely positive (and not a trigger-happy) way. Moshe killed the Egyptian taskmaster in self-defense of his fellow Jew, which was certainly a justified killing. And when the Levi'im killed 3,000 Jews after the incident of the *egel*, it was in response to Moshe's call, presumably approved by Hashem, of מי לד׳ אלי.

Parenthetically, I believe that the character of *ahavas Yisrael* which Shevet Levi demonstrated to such an extreme degree, helps us understand why *Birkas Kohanim* is the only *bracha* which is to be said *b'ahava*, with love. You cannot really command someone to bless another with

---

1. In brief, perhaps Aharon was spared the punishment of *tzara'as* because it would be unbefitting for the Kohen Gadol, so Miriam took the "hit" for both of them. By praying for Miriam to be healed, Aharon was taking a risk that Hashem would cure Miriam, and then Aharon would be next in line for punishment. And we know that a person with *tzara'as* is considered as a dead person, as evidenced by Aharon's own words in the same episode (Bamidbar 12:12).

love, unless the person making the blessing naturally loves the other person. Shevet Levi was so qualified.

◦§ DISTINCTION BETWEEN KOHEN AND LEVI

Now that we understand which character trait, symbolized by the word *achim*, makes Shevet Levi so special and worthy of honor, I would like to explore why, within Shevet Levi, the Torah found it necessary to create the separate categories of Kohen and Levi (we do not find such multiple categorization within any other *shevet*). What was the point of setting up separate classes of Kohen and Levi?

In an effort to answer this question, let us examine the first time in the Torah that we see a distinction between a Kohen and a Levi. The answer is actually in the Midrash, and not in the text itself.

As we all know, Hashem appeared to Moshe Rabbeinu in Mitzrayim in the guise of a burning bush. A lengthy and, in many ways mysterious, dialogue ensues in which Hashem relates to Moshe the severe oppression of Bnei Yisrael and urges Moshe to go to Mitzrayim and spearhead the rescue. Moshe, astonishingly, declines. Hashem then appears to try every trick in the book to persuade Moshe to go on this mission. But nothing works – Moshe offers up one excuse after another until Hashem promises to send Aharon to assist Moshe, and Moshe's resistance then abruptly ends.

I would like to focus on one of the most famous portions of the dialogue between Hashem and Moshe. When Moshe says "no" to Hashem for the last time (Shemos 4:10, 13), Moshe's excuse is:

לא איש דברים אנכי . . . שלח נא ביד תשלח.

"I am not a man of words . . . send whomever You prefer."

The Torah then tells us (Shemos 4:14) that Hashem "got angry" (*va-yichar af*) and appointed Aharon to assist Moshe.

Now, how do we understand Moshe's excuse of לא איש דברים אנכי? According to a common line of reasoning, Moshe declines the mission to redeem Bnei Yisrael on account of his speech impediment, whereupon Hashem appoints Aharon to act as Moshe's spokesman. This explanation, taken literally, seems problematic, for various reasons, including the following:

First of all, it makes no sense that Moshe would be arguing with Hashem, in view of the fact that Hashem so clearly wanted Moshe to go on this mission – we are talking about a mission to get Bnei Yisrael out of Mitzrayim, arguably the most important event in our history. Even if Moshe had a speech impediment, did he not have enough faith that Hashem would help him overcome this handicap?

But more to the point, if we believe that Aharon was appointed as spokesman on account of Moshe's speech impediment, let's remember who it was that ultimately spoke to Pharaoh. Of all the instances where the Torah tells us about a dialogue between Moshe, Aharon, and Pharaoh, not once that I am aware of do we ever find Aharon speaking to Pharaoh by himself. In almost every occasion, it is Moshe alone doing the speaking and on one or two occasions, both of them are speaking to Pharaoh, at it says ויאמרו אליו, but never Aharon alone.

And if we believe that Moshe was hesitant to confront others on account of his speech impediment, consider the following:

- Who spoke to Dasan and Aviram in a very forceful manner when they were about to attack each other – ויאמר לרשע למה תכה רעך?

- Who spoke to Korach – וידבר אל קרח ואל כל עדתו – to set up the test which would result in the downfall of Korach and his followers?

- Who repeatedly spoke to Bnei Yisrael, as we are told in Sefer Devarim, with strong words of rebuke?

- Who successfully and eloquently pleaded with Hashem that He spare Bnei Yisrael from total destruction when Bnei Yisrael strayed with the *egel* and again following the incident of the *meraglim*?

- And who sat as a judge over every matter, large and small, brought to him by Bnei Yisrael, until Yisro intervened?

So, we must find another interpretation for לא איש דברים אנכי, other than it referring to Moshe's speech impediment. I would like to sug-

gest an explanation which is based upon a Rashi at the very end of
the dialogue between Hashem and Moshe at the burning bush. Two
pesukim after Moshe says לא איש דברים אנכי, we are told that Hashem
got angry at Moshe and then appointed Aharon to assist Moshe. The
pasuk states (Shemos 4:14):

> ויחר־אף ד' במשה ויאמר הלא אהרן אחיך הלוי ידעתי כי דבר
> ידבר הוא.
>
> And Hashem got angry with Moshe and said, "Aharon
> your brother, I know that he will speak."

Let's examine a fascinating Midrash which Rashi quotes on this *pasuk*:

> רב יהושע בן קרחה אומר כל חרון אף שבתורה נאמר בו רושם וזה לא
> נאמר בו רושם, ולא מצינו שבא עונש על ידי אותו חרון.
>
> Rav Yehoshua ben Karcha said, "Each time the words
> *charon af* (Hashem's anger) are found in the Torah, we
> find a related consequence, but this time there is no
> stated consequence."

> אמר לו רבי יוסי אף בזו נאמר בו רושם, הלא אהרן אחיך הלוי
> שהיה עתיד להיות לוי ולא כהן, והכהונה הייתי אומר לצאת ממך, מעתה
> לא יהיה כן, אלא הוא יהיה כהן ואתה לוי.
>
> Rebbe Yosi responded, "No, there is a consequence in
> this incident as well, as we can derive from the words
> הלא אהרן אחיך הלוי (here comes your brother Aharon the
> Levi, implying that the word *haLevi* is meaningful) – until
> this moment, the *kehuna* was destined to emanate from
> you, Moshe, and Aharon was to be the Levi, but now the
> roles will reverse: Aharon will be the Kohen and you will
> be the Levi."

How do we understand this enigmatic Midrash? On the surface, Rebbe
Yosi is saying that Moshe angered Hashem by not signing onto the
sacred mission of going to Mitzrayim for the purpose of redeeming
Bnei Yisrael, and that Hashem became angry at Moshe and demoted
Moshe from Kohen to Levi. Now, as we have seen earlier, Levi is a
very important and prestigious position – not exactly a position to
which one gets banished for angering Hashem. Furthermore, when

one looks just two *pesukim* later, we find that Hashem promises that He will be supportive of both Moshe and Aharon and we also find the following words (Shemos 4:16):

וְהָיָה הוּא יִהְיֶה לְךָ לְפֶה וְאַתָּה תִּהְיֶה לּוֹ לֵאלֹהִים.
Hashem says to Moshe that "Aharon will be your mouth-piece and you, Moshe, will be to Aharon as an '*elohim.*'"

So, as a result of Hashem's "anger," not only did Moshe get the prestigious position of Levi, and not only did Hashem promise to be supportive of both of them, but Moshe is also designated by Hashem to be an "*elohim*" to Aharon. Whatever "*elohim*" means in this context, it doesn't sound like Moshe received much of a punishment, or indeed any punishment, for angering Hashem. So how do we understand the Midrash we quoted above?

I would like to try to resolve all of these questions with what, so far as I am aware, is a completely novel interpretation of לא איש דברים אנכי. I believe that Moshe Rabbeinu, far from being reluctant to go on this crucial mission to redeem Bnei Yisrael, was at all times ready, willing, and able to go. However, Moshe understood that redemption of Bnei Yisrael could only be accomplished through a *shevet* (namely Levi) which demonstrated total self-effacing love for Bnei Yisrael, and Moshe, of course, was a member of Shevet Levi.

If so, why did Moshe resist so strongly Hashem's repeated requests that Moshe go on this mission? I believe that Moshe, in his prophetic wisdom, realized that within Shevet Levi there are two distinct types of character traits – men of words and men of action – and that it would not be possible to successfully accomplish Hashem's objective of taking his people out of Mitzrayim unless both types were leading the mission.

The first personality type, a man of words, was represented by Aharon who, in Moshe's view, was the consummate *ish devarim* which, in this context, does not mean an eloquent spokesman or negotiator, but rather a man of peace; a man who, through words, reconciles the anger of one Jew towards another; and a man who, when he brings *korbanos*, offers prayers for the atonement of his fellow Jews. Moshe Rabbeinu realized that it would not be possible for Bnei Yisrael to be redeemed unless the redemption were spearheaded by a person, exemplified by Aharon, who, through words and prayers, created *shalom* between people and who had the power to pray for forgiveness of their sins.

The second personality type within Shevet Levi – the man of action – was represented by Moshe. This is Levi the warrior, who, unlike the Kohen, is ready to kill when necessary (as Moshe did to the Egyptian and as Shevet Levi did to thousands of their fellow Jews after the incident of the *egel*) in order to deal with an internal or external threat. Just as redemption cannot happen without leadership from an *"ish devarim,"* who unites people in peace and who prays for their welfare, so too is it not possible to have redemption without leadership from a warrior who is ready to kill if necessary, in Hashem's Name, in order to deal with an internal threat (as in the *chet ha'egel*) or an external threat (as in the case of the Egyptian taskmaster who was beating the Jewish slave).

So when Moshe said לא איש דברים אנכי, he did not mean that he was a stutterer – Moshe knew full well that he could and would be a strong spokesman for Bnei Yisrael and that, in any event, Hashem would help him overcome any physical handicaps he may have had.

What Moshe meant was that he did not possess the Kohen's character of quiet dedication to Hashem through *avoda*, prayer, and reconciliation of people's anger and hostility to others – through words. Unlike Levi the warrior, the Kohen does not kill people who rebel against Hashem's Torah (see Shabbos 32b).[2] As we know, Moshe Rabbeinu, prior to his dialogue with Hashem at the burning bush, had already killed the Egyptian taskmaster. This demonstrated the character trait of Levi the warrior. In order to be successful in the mission to redeem Bnei Yisrael, Moshe needed the Kohen, the other indispensable trait of Shevet Levi.

And now we understand Rav Yosi's statement as to why the sole consequence of Moshe's discussion with Hashem was that Moshe was designated a Levi instead of a Kohen. This wasn't a punishment. What we have is Hashem's acknowledgment of Moshe's statement

---

2. Pinchas is a special exception, as we can see from Nachshoni (*Studies in the Weekly Parsha*) who states, in his commentary to Parshas Pinchas as follows:

Chizkuni, Riva, and *Zohar* hold that the mention of the priesthood here serves to cleanse Pinchas of the taint of killing, which invalidates one from being a Kohen. Pinchas jeopardized his life, and his chances of ever becoming a Kohen, for the sake of Hashem's glory. Yet, the very fact that he did not flinch at sacrificing his priestly status to sanctify Hashem, purged and purified him, winning him reinstatement.

of דברים אנכי איש לא, namely that Moshe was a man of action and not a man of words, and therefore could not fulfill the role of the Kohen, as Aharon certainly could.

And this is why none of Hashem's other tactics in this lengthy dialogue with Moshe would convince Moshe to go on the mission – not the miracles of turning the stick into a snake, and not the assurance that Moshe's mission would be successful. Nothing worked until Hashem appointed Aharon and Moshe to go together. It was only at that point that Moshe was satisfied because he knew that Hashem had supplied the crucial component which Moshe was missing.

And this is also why, I believe, the *pasuk* states, in this same section, that Moshe would be as an *elohim* to Aharon. *Elohim* signifies *middat hadin*, the trait of meting out judgment, and this was Levi's role, the role of the warrior in defense of the Torah's holy principles.

As one very interesting proof of this novel interpretation of לא איש דברים אנכי, Hashem's initial response to Moshe's statement of לא איש דברים אנכי is to tell Moshe: מי שם פה לאדם – who gives man the power of speech, etc. Rashi interprets Hashem's words as follows: מי למדך לדבר כשהיית נדון לפני פרעה על המצרי – which means, Moshe, who taught you to speak when you were being judged before Pharaoh when you killed the Egyptian? Now, think about it. Moshe, since he was sentenced to die by Pharaoh's court, obviously did not make a very effective argument during this trial. So what does Rashi mean by the words: "Who taught you to speak at this trial?" Clearly, the word "speak" does not mean speak to the judges in Pharaoh's court, but it must surely mean speak to Hashem in prayer. So we see that *ish devarim* has nothing to do with speech from one person to another but rather deals with prayer, *korbanos*, and reconciliation.

This still leaves us with a couple of related questions. First of all, if Kohen and Levi are complementary, and if Moshe, when he said לא איש דברים אנכי, was simply asking Hashem for assistance by a person who, by virtue of his personality, could fulfill the role of the Kohen, why does the *pasuk* use the words *vayichar af* (G-d became angry) to describe Hashem's reaction to a perfectly reasonable request from Moshe? Also, what is the rationale for the Kohen's priority to a Levi with respect to *aliyos* and other matters of *kedusha*?

In response, I would suggest that, even though both personality types exemplified by Kohen and Levi are necessary to the mission of leading Bnei Yisrael, the Kohen's trait of not killing is ultimately the ideal. This is why, I believe, a Kohen has priority to a Levi. And this may also be the reason for the words *vayichar af* as a response to Moshe – the Torah may be teaching us, symbolically, that Moshe, by stating that he was not an *ish devarim* (i.e., Moshe, who had already killed the Egyptian taskmaster, was not an *ish devarim* by temperament), was bringing himself down one notch to a level which is less than the ultimate ideal (reminiscent of Israeli Prime Minister Golda Meir's comment that the one thing for which she cannot forgive our Arab enemies was for turning our soldiers into killers).

KOHANIM AND LEVI'IM AS COMPLEMENTARY

There is an interesting Midrash which supports the complementary roles of Aharon and Moshe, as we have just explained them. In Shemos (6:26), the *pasuk* says:

הוא אהרן ומשה – This was Aharon and Moshe.

Rashi, referring to the Mechilta, says:

יש מקומות שמקדים אהרן למשה, ויש מקומות שמקדים משה לאהרן, לומר לך ששקולין כאחד.

There are instances where Aharon's name precedes that of Moshe and there are instances where Moshe's name precedes that of Aharon, to teach us that they are considered as one.

Note that this Midrash does not say that Moshe and Aharon are of equal status, but rather that they are considered as one. The point, I believe, is that they are a team – each representing distinct personality types within Shevet Levi (the man of words and the man of action), each of which is indispensable.

To illustrate this same theme of necessary teamwork between the Kohen and the Levi, the Levi washes the Kohen's hands before *Birkas Kohanim*, even though the Kohen is halachically permitted to wash his own hands (which can be inferred from the fact that halacha permits Kohanim to say *Birkas Kohanim* when no Levi'im are present). I believe this is symbolic of the fact that Kohen and Levi are an indispensable partnership and that neither can function effectively without the other.

And the need for the Kohen and Levi to function in tandem also helps to explain why Aharon himself, without Moshe's assistance, was so ineffective in his efforts to prevent the *chet ha'egel*.

✍ SUMMARY

To summarize, I believe that Kohanim and Levi'im have a special status in halacha (which goes so far as to give the Kohen and Levi priority as recipients of *tzedaka* and in redemption of captives, among other things), precisely because of their trait symbolized by the code word *achim*, namely their readiness to put their own lives at risk for the sake of their fellow Jews. Halacha wants us to forever recognize and place upon a pedestal of honor a *shevet* which demonstrates this very noble character.

Shevet Levi redeemed itself, following Yaakov's sharp rebuke in Vayechi, by demonstrating, over and over again, the brotherly love symbolized by the word *achim* and by not resorting to killing unless it was clearly appropriate or sanctioned by Hashem, as it was following the *chet ha'egel*.

Moreover, Shevet Levi needs to be subcategorized by Kohen and Levi because these represent two distinct personality types. The man of prayer and reconciliation, on the one hand, and the man of action, on the other hand, are both indispensable to the redemption of Bnei Yisrael and, in fact, for any matter of *kedusha*.

We suggested that Moshe Rabbeinu never resisted the holy mission of redeeming Bnei Yisrael; it is just that Moshe knew in his heart that both personality types exemplified by Shevet Levi were indispensable to the mission. Moshe, having already killed the Egyptian taskmaster, did not view himself as an *ish devarim*. Hashem agreed and appointed Aharon to represent the *ish devarim*. From that point on, Aharon was the Kohen and Moshe the Levi.

And it is also worth noting that Hashem, Who we know punishes and rewards people *midda k'neged midda*, measure for measure, rewarded Shevet Levi's extreme *ahavas Yisrael* by performing logic-defying, lifesaving miracles for Shevet Levi in Mitzrayim, such as Shevet Levi being exempt from the horrors of slavery; such as Moshe being saved from the executioner's sword; such as the nursemaids not being harmed, even though they defied, with the flimsiest and most transparent of excuses, one of the country's most important decrees;

and such as Moshe and Aharon not being harmed by Pharaoh, even though they were the apparent causative factors in the ten plagues which caused Pharaoh and his people extreme grief.

Indeed, allowing Shevet Levi to roam free was completely illogical from Pharaoh's standpoint, considering that it was Shevet Levi, not that long before, which had been involved in the mass killings in Shechem, and it was also Shevet Levi who were the spiritual leaders of Bnei Yisrael and therefore the most likely to lead a rebellion.[3]

❧ CONCLUSION

To conclude, I would suggest that the lesson for us is to understand how the trait of *ahavas Yisrael*, taken to great extremes, gained Shevet Levi the everlasting prestige and respect which is embodied in the many *halachos* granting Kohanim and Levi'im special priorities and privileges; and which trait caused Hashem to select members of Shevet Levi to spearhead *Yetzias Mitzrayim*, one of the most significant events in our history as a people, and to designate Shevet Levi for the ultimate honor of serving Hashem in the Beis HaMikdosh.

Each time we pay homage to Kohanim or Levi'im – whether by giving them the first *aliyos* or in the other ways institutionalized by halacha – we should be reminded of the overriding importance of *ahavas Yisrael* to our fate and destiny as a people. Just as we remember the unmitigated *ahavas Yisrael* of Shevet Levi which pulled us out of the depths of Egyptian bondage, so too may these thoughts cause us to emulate Shevet Levi and, in so doing, lead us speedily to the final *geula*.

---

3. We probably do not give enough thought to how amazing it was that Moshe and Aharon could warn Pharaoh about an impending plague, and after the plague occurs just as they predicted, be able to walk into the palace undisturbed to warn Pharaoh about the next plague, and so on, ten times.

THE STRIKING UNIQUENESS OF THE SEDER NIGHT AND THE INTERPLAY OF *GEULA* AND *TEFILLAH*

❧ MA NISHTANA HALAILA HAZEH MI'KOL HALEILOS?

Most of us, when we hear the above words, focus on the first two: *"Ma Nishtana"* – what is different about this night? But there are two other words in this phrase, *"mi'kol haLeilos,"* which, although easy to overlook, have very great significance. I believe that these words intend to distinguish the Seder night not only from the other non-Pesach nights of the year *but even from the other days and nights of Pesach* [we note that three of the four *Ma Nishtana* questions, relating to leaning, dipping, and *maror*, deal with practices carried out only on the first night of Pesach, and the fourth question relates to the mitzvah of eating *matzo*, which has halachic requirements unique to the first night of Pesach]. How do we understand why the Seder night is so different, not only from the other nights of the year but, more significantly, from the other days and nights of Pesach itself?

Before we delve any further into *why* the Seder night is so uniquely different, let us review *how* the Seder night practices are in fact different. In no particular order, here is a top ten list (and there surely are others) of completely unique *halachos* and *minhagim* of the Seder night:

(1) Haggadah
(2) *Arba kosos*
(3) Involvement of children; starting as quickly as possible; getting them to ask questions
(4) Limitless discussion (*kol hamarbeh harei zeh meshubach*)
(5) Visualizing yourself as if you just left Mitzrayim

(6) Displaying our best *keilim*

(7) *Leil Shimurim* and not saying *Kriyas Shema Al HaMita* (except for the first *parsha* of *Shema*)

(8) *Hallel* at night

(9) Eliyahu's cup

(10) Declaring *L'Shana HaBa'a B'Yerushalayim*

Clearly, none of these *halachos* or *minhagim* apply to any other part of Pesach, night or day or, for that matter, to Sukkos, which also commemorates *Yetzias Mitzrayim*. Yet, logically, it is not at all apparent why this is so. To illustrate our puzzlement, let us focus for a moment on *Shvi'i Shel Pesach* – the very significant seventh day of Pesach – the day of *kriyas Yam Suf*. The Torah tells us (Shemos 14:31) that, after the events of *kriyas Yam Suf*:

ויאמינו בד' ובמשה עבדו.

Bnei Yisrael believed in Hashem and in Moshe His servant.

This was a state of faith which apparently even the ten plagues alone did not generate. Furthermore, there is a *minhag* to stand for the Torah reading of *Az Yashir* whereas we do not stand for any other portion of the Torah reading relating to *Yetzias Mitzrayim*. So, if amongst the events of *Yetzias Mitzrayim*, *kriyas Yam Suf* is clearly of such tremendous significance, then why do we not, on *Shvi'i Shel Pesach*, engage in any of the Seder night acts whereby we celebrate and demonstrate our freedom, such as *arba kosos*, *haseiba*, or Haggadah?

And what about Sukkos, which symbolizes our survival against impossible odds in the desert, wherein our survival also represents a part of the great miracle of *Yetzias Mitzrayim*? Let us remind ourselves of some of the awesome miracles in the desert which enabled Bnei Yisrael to survive. The *manna* gave Bnei Yisrael food. Miriam's well gave Bnei Yisrael water. Their clothes did not wear out the entire forty years, as the Torah tells us. Moreover, Bnei Yisrael were protected from the impossibly harsh climate and from dangerous animals and insects by the Clouds of Glory. Does all this not warrant any of the Seder night symbols of freedom?

We also take note of the fact, as we will demonstrate, that the Seder night, as distinct from the other days or nights of Pesach, includes a significant number of supplications (in the Haggadah) for our final *geula*. And so we ask what it is about the Seder night that dictates our focus, to a unique and significant degree, upon our final *geula* and how do we understand the close connection (as manifested on the Seder night) between the events of *Yetzias Mitzrayim* and our hopes and prayers for the final *geula*?

With these introductory questions, let us now launch into a discussion of *geula* and *tefillah*, which will hopefully culminate in answers to our questions and provide us with some original insights into the hidden significance of the Seder night.

◆§ UNDERSTANDING THE GLORIFICATION OF YETZIAS MITZRAYIM

Before we proceed to understand just what is exactly the essence of the Seder night commemoration of *Yetzias Mitzrayim*, it is helpful to note that the concept of *Yetzias Mitzrayim* clearly occupies an unusually prominent place in our tradition, as illustrated by the following examples:

(1) At the very formation of our nationhood, Hashem's covenant with Avraham Avinu contains a prediction of the slavery of Mitzrayim and the subsequent redemption.

(2) The very first *pasuk* of the *Aseres HaDibros* commands us to believe in G-d who took us out of Mitzrayim.

(3) Shabbos is a mitzvah which is so significant that it is one of a select group of *mitzvos aseh* [others are *yishuv Eretz Yisrael* and *Talmud Torah*] which are classified by our tradition as equivalent to all of the other *mitzvos*. And so it is instructive that, in the Friday night *Kiddush*, Shabbos is very closely intertwined with *Yetzias Mitzrayim* and is in fact stated to be a *zecher* (remembrance) of *Yetzias Mitzrayim*. In any event, this interrelationship of Shabbos and *Yetzias Mitzrayim* demonstrates once again how the notion of *Yetzias Mitzrayim* is bound up with so many fundamental concepts in our tradition.[1]

---

1. The explanation of the connection between Shabbos and *Yetzias Mitzrayim* is discussed in "The Hidden Essence of Shabbos" *d'var* in this *sefer*.

(4)   And finally, halacha makes it very clear to us that *Yetzias Mitz-
       rayim* is of paramount significance since (completely aside
       from the extremely important mitzvah of והגדת לבנך on the
       Seder night) we are obligated to remember *Yetzias Mitzrayim*
       morning and night of each day of the year, as we do in the
       Shema of *Shacharis* and *Maariv*.

But while it is apparent that *Yetzias Mitzrayim* is a very dominant
theme in our tradition, we need to understand why we glorify *Yetzias
Mitzrayim* to such a great extent, particularly on the Seder night. Specifically, what is so significant about a redemption, awesome miracles
and all, which was almost immediately followed by an unrelenting
continuum of suffering and tragedies for us as a nation? Rabbi Moshe
Sternbuch picks up on this question when he comments on the following statement in the Haggadah:[2]

> ואלו לא הוציא הקדוש ברוך הוא את אבותינו ממצרים הרי אנו ובנינו
> ובני ובנינו משועבדים היינו לפרעה במצרים.

If Hashem had not taken our forefathers out of Mitzrayim, then we and all our descendants would have
continued to be enslaved to Pharaoh in Egypt.

Rabbi Sternbuch then asks the following astute question with regard
to the praise embodied in this passage:

> ואלו לא הוציא : כאן הבן שואל מה הבדל יש בין שיעבוד מצרים לשיעבוד
> מלכיות ואדרבה בזמנינו ראינו שנשחטו ונטבחו באכזריות רבי רבבות
> מאחינו בני ישראל, ועדיין היום נמצאים במצוקה וייסורים רבי רבבות
> מאחינו בני רוסיא ועוד ארצות, ומחורבן והלאה בכל דור ודור מנת
> חלקינו רק שיעבוד צרות הריגות וא״כ היאך אנו מתפארים שאלו לא
> הוציא הקב״ה אבותינו ממצרים היינו אנו משועבדים והלוא בעוי״ה גם
> אחר היציאה מצבינו לא הוטב בזה היום?

What is the distinction between the enslavement of Mitzrayim and that of subsequent enslavements and exiles?
On the contrary, in our own days, were countless of our
brothers not slaughtered in the most vile and repulsive
manner? . . . And from the days of the *churban*, did we

---

2. Rabbi Moshe Sternbuch, *Mo'adim U'Zmanim*, Vol. 3 (Jerusalem), 129.

not encounter, in each generation, slavery, severe persecution, and murder? And if such is the case, how can we
state with such glory and pride that if Hashem had not
taken us out of Mitzrayim, then we would have continued to be slaves to this very day?[3]

Rabbi Sternbuch answers his own question by insightfully noting that
the effect and significance of *Yetzias Mitzrayim* reaches far beyond the
event itself, through its very profound and permanent effect on our
national psyche. To quote his words:[4]

> It seems to me that, prior to the time when we experi-
> enced the wondrous miracles of *Yetzias Mitzrayim*, our
> faith was entirely intellectually-based. However, after
> the events of *Yetzias Mitzrayim*, when we witnessed with
> our own eyes Hashem's all-encompassing and limitless
> power, our faith became tangible and real. The signifi-
> cance is that faith which is only intellectually-based will
> not withstand adversity, whereas faith which is tangible
> and real is everlasting. And this is the privileged status
> we reached only after we personally witnessed the in-
> credible wonders of *Yetzias Mitzrayim*, . . . the net effect of
> which was to imbue us with a feeling and emotion which
> remained with us forever.

This concept can probably be best understood on an individual level.
A crucial component of our *bitachon* is the memories, which each one
of us has, of the occasions upon which Hashem clearly intervened on
our behalf in some way which made a powerful impression upon us.
Accordingly, when we pray to Hashem in connection with a particular matter, it is our prior experiences which make it so much easier
to believe that Hashem may again come to our assistance when we
need Him.

---

3. In contemporary terms, we have all heard about the heroic secret Seders
conducted in concentration camps. How do we understand the ואלו לא הוציא said
by the inmates? Do we visualize the inmates saying: "If Hashem had not taken us
out of Mitzrayim, then we would really be in big trouble?"

4. Sternbuch, *Mo'adim U'Zmanim*, Vol. 3, 129.

Similarly with *Yetzias Mitzrayim*. I believe it follows logically from
the analysis of Rav Sternbuch that, when we glorify *Yetzias Mitzrayim*,
as we do on the Seder night, we are doing far more than focusing on
a single event in our history. Yes, it is true that *Yetzias Mitzrayim* was
followed by unrelenting and severe tragedies for our people. But in
the very midst of these tragedies, our glorification of *Yetzias Mitzrayim*
represents a declaration of our profound faith that Hashem will once
again demonstrate His supreme command of the forces of nature
when He miraculously leads us to the final *geula*.

And, incidentally, this may also explain why Hashem arranged
it so that the events of *Yetzias Mitzrayim* occurred almost at the outset
of our becoming a nation – perhaps our Creator intended that, in the
midst of the deep and depressing exile which Hashem knew would
follow *Yetzias Mitzrayim*, the spectacular nature-defying miracles of
the seminal event of *Yetzias Mitzrayim* would stand for us as a perpet-
ual bastion of hope of future redemption.

❧ THE FINAL GEULA AND THE SEDER NIGHT

If our proposition is correct, namely that the glorification of *Yetzias
Mitzrayim* is inextricably linked with our eternal hope for our final
geula, then we would expect that the Seder night would be infused,
to a significant degree, with the theme of the final *geula*. Let us now
demonstrate that this is in fact the case.

The final-*geula* dimension of the Seder night can be found in a *pasuk*
(Shemos 12:42), which refers to the Seder night as *"Leil Shimurim"* – a
night of protection. In the *pasuk*, the word *shimurim* is stated twice,
seemingly redundantly. The *pasuk* reads:

> ליל שימורים הוא לד' להוציאם מארץ מצרים הוא הלילה הזה לד'
> שימורים לכל בני ישראל לדורותם.

> It is a night of protection when He took Bnei Yisrael out
> of Mitzrayim; this is a night on which G-d protects Bnei
> Yisrael throughout the generations.

The first reference to *shimurim* in the *pasuk* is with respect to *Yetzias
Mitzrayim*, while the second reference is to a שימורים לדורותם – for the
generations. The Gemara (*Rosh Hashana* 11b), apparently picking up

on the duplicate reference in the *pasuk* to *shimurim*, and the fact that the second mention of *shimurim* is framed by the word לדורותם, informs us that *Leil Shimurim* is not simply a concept applicable to *Yetzias Mitzrayim*, but has a much broader connotation. The Gemara states:

[מהו ליל שימורים?] ליל המשומר ובא משֹשֹת ימי בראשית [לגאולה].

What does the *pasuk* mean when it says that it [the eve of the fifteenth of Nisan] is a night of protection? Rav Yehoshua states, "It means that this night is protected and designated from the time of the Creation of the world as a night of redemption."

In fact, the Gemara in *Rosh Hashana* goes on to say that Rav Yehoshua interprets this *pasuk* to mean that Moshiach will come on the first night of Pesach.[5] And the Midrash Rabba, on the *pasuk* of "*Leil Shimurim*," states that if a purported redeemer arrives and makes an effort to redeem us on a night other than the fifteenth of Nisan, we should take that as a clear sign that he is an impostor.

If we may digress for a moment, it is worth noting how the concept of *shmira* plays out on the Seder night. To illustrate, we find in Shemos (12:17) the command of ושמרתם את המצות. The Mechilta comments:

א"ר יאשיה: אל תקרא ושמרתם את המצות, אלא ושמרתם את המצוות. כדרך שאין מחמיצין את המצה, כך אין מחמיצין את המצוה אלא אם באה מצוה לידך עשה אותה מיד.

Rav Yoshiya says, "We should not read the text as 'guard the *matzos*' but rather 'guard the *mitzvos*' – just as time is of the essence in the leavening of *matzos*, so too should we be careful with the time element as it relates to *mitzvos*, so that an opportunity to perform a mitzvah should be taken advantage of immediately."

I believe that this Midrash exemplifies the dual dimension (i.e., past *geulos* and the final *geula*) of *Yetzias Mitzrayim* which we have been discussing. By our punctilious *shmira* of *matzos*, we demonstrate our unbounded gratitude for the events of *Yetzias Mitzrayim*. And by our equally scrupulous observance of *mitzvos*, we do our part to bring about the final *geula*. In this regard, we note the elegant symmetry of the image of *shmira* – we are *shomer* both the *matzos* and the *mitzvos*, and Hashem in return makes the Seder night into a *"Leil Shimurim"* for us throughout the generations, as He eagerly anticipates the opportunity to lead us to our final redemption.

So the picture of the Seder night now begins to emerge. We glorify *Yetzias Mitzrayim* not merely for its own sake. Indeed, if *Yetzias Mitzrayim* were the sole object of our praise, it is a sad fact that the exultation of our freedom from the slavery of Mitzrayim has long since been dissipated by thousands of years of severe persecution. Rather, we glorify *Yetzias Mitzrayim* in large part because its enormous miracles remind us of the great miracles through which Hashem will lead us to the final *geula*. This is the magic of the Seder night, when we can taste the feelings of liberty as if we had just been redeemed, and as we will soon be again redeemed – this time, permanently.

And the Seder night is the time during which the theme of the final *geula* is more dominant than on any other day or night of the year, primarily because our Father in Heaven established the Seder night as a ליל שימורים לדורותם, eternally designated as a night of redemption for our people.

ঙ্গ THE FINAL GEULA AND THE HAGGADAH

If our proposition is correct, namely that the glorification of *Yetzias Mitzrayim* is very closely linked with our eternal hope for our final *geula*, we would anticipate that the theme of the final *geula* is prominently reflected in the Haggadah and its *halachos* and *minhagim*. In fact, Rav Yitzchak Mirsky and others point out that, about half-way through the Haggadah, the text transitions from an almost exclusive focus on *Yetzias Mitzrayim* to a significant concentration on the future *geula*.

In fact, the Haggadah is replete with references to the ultimate *geula*, particularly from the *bracha* on the second cup and thereafter. For example:

(1)   The *bracha* on the second cup begins by praising Hashem

for taking us out of Mitzrayim and then continues with the following request:

כן ד' אלקינו ואלקי אבותינו יגיענו למועדים ולרגלים אחרים הבאים
לקראתנו לשלום שמחים בבנין עירך וששים בעבודתך.

So too may Hashem bring us to future holidays and festive celebrations on which we will rejoice at the rebuilding of Hashem's city and in the *avoda* [presumably referring to the Beis HaMikdosh].

(2) The *bracha* over the third cup is immediately followed by *Shefoch Chamoscha*, in which we implore Hashem to vent His wrath on the nations which do not know Him, to obliterate our enemies from under the heavens and to send Moshiach to redeem us.

The Ramoh commentary to the Orach Chaim discusses *Shefoch Chamoscha* (480:1):

הגה וי"א שיש לומר שפוך חמתך וכו' קודם לא לנו ולפתוח הפתח כדי
לזכור שהוא ליל שימורים ובזכות אמונה זו יבוא משיח וישפוך חמתו על
המכחשים בד'. וכן נוהגין.

And there are those who say that we should say *Shefoch Chamoscha* and open the door in order to remind ourselves that the Seder evening is a *Leil Shimurim* and, as a reward for this faith, Moshiach will come and vent his wrath on those who deny G-d. Such is the custom.

The Chafetz Chaim, in his Mishna Berura commentary upon this halacha, states the following (note 10):

ואין מתייראין משום דבר ונוהגין באלו מדינות למזוג כוס אחד יותר
מהמסובין וקורין אותו כוס של אליהו הנביא לרמוז שאנו מאמינים
שכשם שגאלנו השי"י ממצרים הוא יגאלנו עוד וישלח לנו את אליהו
לבשרנו.

And we are not afraid of anything. It is the practice in these countries to mix one additional glass of wine than is needed for the diners. This glass is called the glass of the prophet Eliyahu. The purpose of this glass is to indicate that we have faith that just as Hashem redeemed us from Egypt, He will again redeem us and will send us Eliyahu to inform us of the redemption.

(3)   Then, in *Adir Hu*, we sing:

אדיר הוא יבנה ביתו בקרוב, במהרה, בימינו בקרוב.

May the Glorified One build His house, soon, in our day.

(4)   And, finally, we conclude the Haggadah with *L'Shana HaBa'a B'Yerushalayim*.

These references, and there are others, are illustrative, I would suggest, of the fact that our aspiration for the final *geula* permeates the second half of the Haggadah.

Indeed, I believe that the Haggadah is in fact intended to be, at least in part, a profound, communal *tefillah* for our final *geula* and that many of the unique practices of the Seder night are specifically designed to enhance the effectiveness of this *tefillah*. In order to understand how this works, however, it is critical to understand the process of how we go about making requests of Hashem through *tefillah*. So let us now shift gears and focus on the *tefillah* portion of our discussion.

But first, let us briefly recap. We began by asking why the many *halachos* and *minhagim* of the Seder night are unique to this night and do not even apply on any other day or night of Pesach. We reviewed a number of ways in which the notion of *Yetzias Mitzrayim* is so pervasive and fundamental in our tradition, but then wondered why this should be so in view of the terribly bitter persecutions which followed.

We then concluded that *Yetzias Mitzrayim* means far more than just commemorating a historic event and that it is the forward-looking aspect of *Yetzias Mitzrayim* which makes the Seder night so special. In furtherance of this notion, we noted how both the Seder night and the Haggadah itself are infused with the notion of our final *geula*. We suggested that the Haggadah consists, in many ways, of a deeply significant *tefillah* for our final *geula* and that the unique *halachos* and *minhagim* of the Seder night are intended to enhance the effectiveness of this *tefillah*. In order to better understand how this works, we will now analyze the process of making a *bakasha* (request) in *tefillah*.

◈ BAKASHA (MAKING A REQUEST THROUGH TEFILLAH)

There is perhaps no better role model for the study of *tefillah* than Moshe Rabbeinu, who spoke with Hashem *panim el panim* (face-to-face), and so, for the purpose of gaining valuable insights into the process of *tefillah*, we turn to the very first *pasuk* in Va'Eschanan, where Moshe begins his plea to be permitted to enter Eretz Yisrael. Moshe uses the word *va'eschanan* to characterize the form of his plea. Rashi, in a comment which I believe is critical to an understanding of the most appropriate manner in which a person should relate to our Creator in *tefillah*, states as follows (Devarim 3:23):

> אין חנון בכל מקום אלא לשון מתנת חנם. אע"פ שיש להם לצדיקים
> לתלות במעשיהם הטובים אין מבקשים מאת המקום אלא מתנת חנם.
> The word חנון (as in ואתחנן) invariably means מתנת חנם,
> literally, a gift given without return consideration. Despite the fact that *tzaddikim* have sufficient merit to be able to base their requests to Hashem upon their good deeds, they do not do so and request from Hashem only a *matnas chinam*.

The first and most obvious question that we can direct at this Rashi is why is it inappropriate for a righteous person to base his or her requests to Hashem upon prior good deeds? In fact, all of us would probably have thought just the opposite. I would suggest three explanations.

Firstly, no person knows the rewards for particular *mitzvos*, and certainly not whether the reward will be granted in this world. In fact, there are numerous statements by our Sages to the effect that there is no direct correlation in this world between good deeds and reward (שכר מצוות בהאי עלמא ליכא) (*Pirkei Avos* 2:16).

Secondly, there is an intriguing Midrash in Vayikra Rabba which states (36:3):

> א"ר פנחס : כל מי שעושה מצוה ומבקש ליטול עליה שכרו מיד ליד לא
> ינקה רע רשע הוא ואינו מניח לבניו כלום.
> Rav Pinchas stated, "Anyone who performs a mitzvah and seeks instant reward for it is called a *rasha*, because

such person does not leave a legacy of *zechus avos* for his
children."

So we see from this Midrash that it is unseemly, at best, to desire and
expect immediate rewards for the *mitzvos* that we do.

Thirdly, if a person bases his *bakasha* upon prior good deeds, it
would appear as if the person performed these *mitzvos* not selflessly
but rather for the purpose of a reward, something which is not permitted (except for *tzedaka*).

Accordingly, it is entirely inappropriate for a righteous person
to base a *bakasha* upon his prior performance of *mitzvos*. But now
we are still searching for the answer as to the proper way to make a
bakasha. Turning back to the Rashi we quoted earlier, Rashi notes that
a righteous person's *bakasha* should be based not upon his prior good
deeds but rather upon *matnas chinam*, words which seem to imply a
free pass – a grant of a favor from Hashem with no *quid pro quo* on the
righteous person's part.

But this cannot be the meaning of *matnas chinam*. Firstly, how
could a righteous person request something for nothing from His
Creator? Moreover, if Hashem were to dispense freebies, then why
should one person be so graced, and not another? How would we
understand Hashem's system of perfect justice if there were no relationship at all between a person's deeds and the favors granted to
that person by Hashem?

So, what indeed is the basis upon which we ask things of our
Creator? In order to answer this question, we must turn back to the
second *pasuk* in Parshas Va'Eschanan, wherein Moshe, prior to his
plea to be permitted to enter Eretz Yisrael, refers to the initial miraculous conquests by Bnei Yisrael, and makes the following declaration
(Devarim 3:24):

> ד' אלקים, אתה החלות להראות את־עבדך את־גדלך ואת־ידך החזקה,
> אשר מי א־ל בשמים ובארץ אשר יעשה כמעשיך וכגבורתך.
> Hashem, You have just begun to show Your servant Your
> greatness, Your strong hand, and that there is no god in
> heaven or on earth who could accomplish Your feats.

The Gemara (*Berachos* 32a) derives the following vital lesson from the
manner in which Moshe made his case to Hashem. The Gemara states:

לעולם יסדר אדם שבחו של מקום ואח"כ יתפלל.

A person should always praise Hashem and then pray for his needs.

It should be noted that this is in fact the way in which *Shemoneh Esrei* is structured. The first three *berachos* of *Shemoneh Esrei* are called *berachos* of *shevach* (praise), the middle *berachos* wherein we make various personal requests are called *bakasha* (requests), and the final three *berachos* are called *hodaa* (thanks). It is apparent from the Gemara in *Berachos*, as well as from the ordering of the *berachos* in *Shemoneh Esrei*, that *shevach* should always precede a *bakasha*. The following halacha takes this concept even further and, in effect, illustrates just how critical *shevach* is to the *tefillah* process. The Shulchan Aruch states the following (Orach Chaim 101:1):

המתפלל צריך שיכוין בכל הברכות ואם אינו יכול לכוין בכולם לפחות יכוין באבות ואם לא כיון באבות אע"פ שיכוין בכל השאר יחזור ויתפלל.

Ramoh:

הגה והאידנא אין חוזרין בשביל חסרון כוונה שאף בחזרה קרוב הוא שלא יכוין, אם כן למה יחזור.

A person who davens *Shemoneh Esrei* is obligated to have *kavana* with respect to all of the *berachos*, but if that is not possible then at least on the first *bracha* [of *shevach*]. If a person has *kavana* on all of the *berachos* other than the first one, then such person must repeat *Shemoneh Esrei*.[6]

This *halacha* appears to have an astonishing implication, namely that if a person is, G-d forbid, in poor health and then, while davening *Shemoneh Esrei*, pours his heart out saying *Refa'einu*, or if a person needs a job desperately and sincerely cries out for help with the *bracha* of *Mevarech Hashanim*, then such person is nevertheless not *yotzeh Shemoneh Esrei*, and has to daven all over again, simply because such person did not have *kavana* in the first *bracha* – the *shevach* part of *Shemoneh Esrei*. How do we understand this halacha, which seems to confound all logic?

---

6. The Ramoh says, however, that we no longer force a repeat of *Shemoneh Esrei* on account of deficient *kavana* because who is to say that the *kavana* will be any better the second time around.

In response, I would submit that the best chance we have of receiving a favorable response to a *bakasha* is if we clearly demonstrate to
Hashem, through our sincere *shevach*, that we truly believe in His limitless power and that we appreciate to the fullest the extent to which
He controls events in the world and, individually, in each of our lives.
When Hashem sees that we recognize our total dependence upon
Him, and particularly if we do so prior to the time that we have even
begun to make a *bakasha* of Him, it will then be quite apparent that
we will use the benefits we receive from the granting of the *bakasha*
for a worthy purpose (for example, if a person who needs and prays
for good health promises to use such health to perform more *mitzvos*).
This is why sincere *shevach* is so crucial to the granting of our *bakashos*.

This idea is nicely reflected in the following Gemara (*Sotah* 14a):

> דריש רבי שמלאי, מפני מה נתאוה משה רבינו לכנס לא"יי? וכי לאכול
> מפריה או לשבוע מטובה הוא צריך? אלא אמר, הרבה מצוות נצטוו
> ישראל ואין מתקיימין אלא בא"יי, אכנס אני כדי שיתקיימו על ידי.
>
> Rav Simlai stated, "Why did Moshe want to enter Eretz
> Yisrael? Was it to taste the good fruit and other delicacies
> of Eretz Yisrael? No. Moshe Rabbeinu said that there are
> many *mitzvos* which are dependent for their performance
> on being in Eretz Yisrael. Moshe said: 'Let Bnei Yisrael
> perform these *mitzvos* as a result of my efforts.'"

Here, we see clearly that Moshe Rabbeinu's ultimate *bakasha* was
founded not on his prior good deeds, but rather on the mass performance by Bnei Yisrael of מצוות התלויות בארץ (*mitzvos* whose performance
is dependent upon possession of the Land) which would be engendered by the fulfillment of Moshe's request to enter Eretz Yisrael.[7]

We refer to Hashem as *Avinu she'BaShamayim* (our Father in
Heaven) and perhaps we can better understand the fundamental
function of *shevach* when we examine our relationship with our own
children. We all share a basic desire to give of our time and resources
to our children but it is also true that this desire is immeasurably
stronger in the case of a child who deeply appreciates what we do for

---

7. Chana, who prayed that if Hashem granted her a son, she would dedicate
him to Hashem, is another example of a *bakasha* being based upon a promise to put
Hashem's favorable response to a good use.

him or her. Such a child will not view the gift from us to him or her as an entitlement and will therefore not squander the gift and, indeed, is likely to use such gift for a worthy purpose.

The critical importance of *shevach* as a prelude to *bakashos* is also quite apparent from the following *halacha* (Orach Chaim 112:1):

אל ישאל אדם צרכיו בג' ראשונות.

We may not make private requests in the midst of the three *berachos* of *shevach* [at the very beginning of *Shemoneh Esrei*].

It seems that any personal requests made in the midst of the *berachos* of *shevach* would irretrievably adulterate the expressions of appreciation (and the implied future promise to perform good deeds with the fruits of Hashem's bounty) inherent in such *shevach* and would therefore completely undermine its purpose.

And it is precisely for the reasons we just discussed that Rashi states that a righteous person bases his or her *bakasha* on *matnas chinam* – this does not mean, I would submit, a gift in return for zero consideration, but rather that the person praying has, as evidenced by his or her expressed *shevach*, made an implied future promise as to the manner in which such person will use the fruits of Hashem's blessings and has therefore not yet earned the granting of the request. Hashem then relies on the sincerity of the person's *shevach* and strong belief in Hashem's control and power, to grant such person an "advance," and it is almost as if the granting of the request has already been earned.

✺ INSIGHTS INTO HALACHOS AND MINHAGIM OF THE SEDER NIGHT

We stated earlier that one of our objectives would be to achieve a deeper understanding and appreciation of a number of *halachos* and *minhagim* of the Seder night. Now that we have analyzed the process of making a *bakasha* in *tefillah*, we can understand that the purpose of these *halachos* and *minhagim* is to maximize our *shevach* of Hashem's incredible miracles which brought about our redemption from Mitzrayim and, through this *shevach*, we enhance our *tefillos* for the final *geula*. To illustrate:

CHAYAV ADAM

The Rambam, in *Hilchos Chometz U'Matzo* (7:6), recites the following obligation pertaining to the Seder night:

בכל דור ודור חייב אדם להראות את עצמו כאילו הוא בעצמו יצא עתה
משעבוד מצרים, שנאמר "ואותנו הוציא משם וגו', ועל דבר זה צוה
הקב"ה בתורה: "וזכרת כי עבד היית", כלומר, כאילו אתה בעצמך היית
עבד ויצאת לחירות ונפדית.

In each generation, a person is obligated to demonstrate himself as if he was just freed from the slavery of Mitz-rayim, as it says in the Torah: "And remember that you were a slave," and as it says "G-d took *us* out," which means that each person must visualize that he [or she] was a slave and was just redeemed.

This seems like a very nice idea but why does the rest of Pesach, or Sukkos, not have this obligation? For example, why, on שביעי של פסח are we not obligated to view ourselves as if we just witnessed the splitting of the Red Sea and why, on Sukkos, although we sit in *sukkos* as a reminder of the Exodus, are we not obligated to visualize ourselves as if we were sitting in *sukkos* on our way out of Mitzrayim?

The answer, I would suggest, is consistent with our proposition that an important theme of the Seder night is a request, via *tefillah*, for the final *geula* and that *shevach* is a prerequisite to the effectiveness of such request. We suggest that our powerful demonstration of *she-vach* on the Seder night, involving men, women and, to an unusual degree, children, is designed to enhance the effectiveness of our *Leil Shimurim tefillos* for our final *geula*. As we know, it is human nature to gradually forget the impact of a major event, good or bad. Time blurs our memory.

Accordingly, it is for the very purpose of counteracting this tendency to forget, and so as to maximize our *shevach*, that we imagine ourselves as just having been freed from the slavery of Mitzrayim. I believe that this obligation of *chayav adam* is part of a concerted effort by halacha to maximize our *shevach*, on the Seder night, for our *geula* from Mitzrayim, and thus enhance our *tefillah* for the final *geula*.

On the other days of Pesach, where prayers for the final *geula* are not a dominant theme, it is not necessary to generate this very high level of *shevach* and that is why there is no obligation of *chayav adam* on the other days or nights of Pesach.

OTHER HALACHOS AND MINHAGIM

Along the same lines, the other unique *halachos* and *minhagim* of the Seder night, such as *arba kosos*, *haseiba*, displaying our finest *keilim*, involvement of the children, the obligation to feel as if we were just redeemed, the Haggadah itself, *Hallel*, the desirability to re-tell the miraculous events of *geulas Mitzrayim* until sleep overtakes us, as well as other practices of the Seder night, seem to be also designed, for the very same reason, to generate tremendous *shevach* of our Creator on the Seder night.

✣ IMPORTANCE OF ANTICIPATING AND DESIRING THE FINAL GEULA

The *Me'am Loez*, in his commentary to Shemos,[8] refers to a Gemara (*Shabbos* 31a) which sets forth a short list of the first questions which a person will be asked upon arrival in the *olam ha'emes*. Among these questions, the Gemara includes צפית לישועה – did you eagerly anticipate the *geula*? The *Me'am Loez*, based on this Gemara, infers that "anticipating" the *geula* means, at least to a significant degree, doing so by our *tefillos*, and he goes so far as to conclude that a person who does not "fervently hope and pray for Moshiach" may actually not be worthy of תחיית המתים.

The very fact that the *Me'am Loez* would make such an apparently radical statement highlights the extreme importance of the concept of the final *geula* as well as the *tefillos* which are so instrumental in propelling us towards this *geula*. Despite the *Me'am Loez*'s extreme tones, we should acknowledge that *geula* is probably not that compelling a subject to most of us, and that it is just too easy to lapse into a *galus* mentality of comfort, particularly in countries of material prosperity.

I would like to offer up just one or two reasons why *geula* should be a very high priority to each of us. In this regard, there is a beautiful

---

8. *Me'am Loez*, p. 118, fn. 74.

passage in the Gemara (*Megilla* 29a), which comments on the *pasuk* of
ושב ד' אלקיך את שבותך (Devarim 30:3):

> תניא רבי שמעון בן יוחאי אומר בוא וראה כמה חביבים ישראל לפני
> הקב"ה, שבכל מקום שגלו – שכינה עמהן . . . ואף כשהן עתידין ליגאל
> שכינה עמהן, שנאמר: ושב ד' אלקיך את שבותך: והשיב לא נאמר, אלא
> ושב. מלמד שאף הקב"ה שב עמהן מבין הגליות.

Rebbe Shimon ben Yochai stated, "Come see how precious Bnei Yisrael are to Hashem. Because whenever we
are exiled, the Shechina accompanies us . . . As it says:
ושב ד' אלקיך את שבותך – the *pasuk* uses the word ושב and
not והשיב. This teaches us that when we are redeemed,
Hashem is also redeemed from *galus*."

What the imagery in this Midrash seems to suggest is that when we
are suffering the harsh conditions of *galus*, then Hashem feels our
pain, so to speak, as if Hashem Himself were exiled along with us.
And so, it is apparent that when we do our part to help speed the
geula, we not only help ourselves immensely but, כביכול, we are also
directly participating in the redemption of Hashem from *galus*, as
well as the eradication of G-d's great pain, engendered by our being
in *galus*.

Moreover, when we are in *galus*, Hashem's reputation among the
nations is seriously impaired. There are two instances in the Torah
(following the incidents of the *egel* and the *meraglim*) where Moshe,
in a successful effort to annul Hashem's severe decree against Bnei
Yisrael, makes the argument that if Hashem would inflict severe punishment upon Bnei Yisrael (even if such punishment were entirely
justified), the nations of the world would then view our suffering as
evidence of the inability of Hashem to assist us.

And the reverse is also true – when we are finally redeemed, the
Yad Hashem will be manifest for all to see. As we say in *Aleinu*: ביום
ההוא יהיה ד' אחד ושמו אחד – "on the day when Bnei Yisrael are finally
redeemed, Hashem's Name will at last be One among the nations."
And so, another compelling reason to desire the *geula* is because our
redemption would result in the immediate restoration of Hashem's
Name to its rightful place of universal reverence and glory.

It is with this understanding that I believe we can better appreciate why it is incumbent upon us to strive to the best of our abilities

to bring about the final *geula*, and why our *tefillos* for the final *geula*, and particularly on the Seder night (when the theme of the *geula* is, as we have seen, so dominant), must be particularly fervent and heartfelt.

The great importance of *tefillah* in bringing about the final *geula* is reflected in the very important halachic principle of *somech geula l'tefillah*, which is an absolutely fascinating topic but warrants a separate and detailed discussion (see Addendum). We should note, however, that the very close connection between *geula* and *tefillah* is beautifully reflected in the following statement in the Gemara (*Berachos* 4b):

אמר ר' יוחנן איזהו בן עולם הבא? זה הסומך גאולה לתפילה.

Rav Yochanan said, "Who is assured of *Olam HaBo*? A person who is *somech geula l'tefillah*."

❧ CONCLUSION

In summary, it is the intense focus on, and our hopeful and fervent *tefillos* for, the final *geula* which, I believe, distinguishes the first night of Pesach even from the other days and nights of Pesach, and which offers the rationale for the many unique *halachos* and *minhagim* of the Seder night.

We wondered about the significance of glorifying the events of *Yetzias Mitzrayim* – an event which was followed by endless persecution. We have seen, however, that *Yetzias Mitzrayim* instilled in us eternal hope for our final redemption. Indeed, without the incredible miracles of *Yetzias Mitzrayim*, it seems hard to imagine how we would have been able to gather the inner strength as a people, in light of our enduring the most severe and relentless persecution, to enthusiastically and confidently pray for the final *geula*. But now, however, that we are able to recall and re-live each year the experience of *Yetzias Mitzrayim*, as if these events just occurred, and demonstrate through the Haggadah and its related *halachos* and *minhagim* our boundless *shevach* of our Creator, we are able to proudly pray for the final *geula* in the firm knowledge that Hashem will again miraculously redeem us.

We conclude with another quote from the *Me'am Loez*,[9] who so beautifully elucidates the connection between *geula* and *tefillah*:

> There is another question that one might ask. We have a firm tradition that when a person worships with the congregation, such prayer is very precious to G-d and is accepted with love. If this is true, why are we not redeemed? Three times each day, Jews gather together and pray for the redemption. The *Amidah* is replete with prayers such as: תקע בשופר גדול לחרותנו; ולירושלים עירך ברחמים תשוב and וגאלנו מהרה למען שמך. A good part of the *Amidah* is a plea for redemption.
>
> Truthfully, these prayers are often said without feeling. But it is impossible to say that none are said with feeling. There were thousands upon thousands of sages and saints, from the time of the Temple's destruction until today who prayed with the utmost devotion. All this being true, why have we not been answered?. . . .
>
> With regard to the redemption, however, it is not sufficient that a portion of the Jewish community says the prayers with great devotion. When asking Hashem to redeem us, all Israel must worship with the greatest possible feeling. Moreover, one prayer alone is not enough. Since the final redemption will involve many great miracles, it will require many, many prayers [referencing Rav Moshe ben Yosef of Trani].

It is my sincere hope that our detailed analysis of the enormous importance of anticipation for our final *geula*, and the critical interplay of *geula* and *tefillah*, particularly on the Seder night, as well as the crucial importance of *shevach* to the *tefillah* process, will not only improve the quality of our davening but will also make our Seders and *tefillos* for the *geula* so much more meaningful.

And finally, there is another very important aspect of our Seder night *tefillos* which we need to keep in mind. Just as *tefillos* are most effective through a *tzibbur*, so too is the Seder night designed to be a communal event, at least on a small scale (evidenced in part, I would

---

9. *Me'am Loez*, Shemos commentary on *Leil Shimurim*, pp. 116, 117.

suggest, by the seemingly strange halacha of forbidding *korban Pesach* "leftovers," which seems designed to encourage larger Seder gatherings). When we daven in a *tzibbur*, we must particularly keep in mind not only the content of the *tefillos*, but also the enduring impact we have upon others when we sincerely and with great fervor offer our *tefillos* to Hashem.

So too is it the case on the Seder night – when we strive to maximize our *shevach* for the events of *Yetzias Mitzrayim*, in furtherance of our efforts to anticipate and pray for the final *geula* – that we must particularly bear in mind the impact we can have upon others in our Seder group and beyond. The Rambam (*Hilchos Chometz U'Matzo* 7:5), in discussing the command of *chayav adam*, uses the anomalous expression:

בכל דור ודור חייב אדם להראות את עצמו.
In each generation, a person is obligated to demonstrate
to others [his or her feeling of just having been redeemed
from Mitzrayim].

Many question why the Rambam uses the word להראות (rather than לראות, as stated in the Mishnah) but, in view of our understanding of the great importance of *tefillah b'tzibbur* whereby the enthusiastic *tefillos* of each person delivers strong encouragement to others, we can understand very well why it is not only necessary to feel as if we just left Mitzrayim but to do everything we can to impart this feeling to others.

May our powerful public demonstration of appreciation of, and fervent *tefillos* for, the *geula* at the Seder bring us much closer to a *geula shleima bimheira beyameinu*.

ADDENDUM

Relationship of Geula and Tefillah

We have now seen that much of what transpires at the Seder can be understood on a much deeper level if we appreciate the fact that our *tefillos* for the final *geula*, and the related Seder night practices which greatly enhance this *tefillah*, are a dominant theme of this night.

But to carry these insights even further, it is very important to perceive that, although sincere *tefillah* can help us achieve many goals (and not only our *geula*), there nevertheless appears to be an incredibly close connection between *tefillah* and *geula*, as we will see in a moment when we review some remarkable *halachos*. The question is why this is so?

I would suggest as a possible explanation that, because it is so easy to lapse into a *galus* mentality, whereby we are almost enjoying ourselves too much, it is extremely important that we demonstrate to Hashem, through our *tefillos*, that *geula* is very meaningful to us. The sincerity and intensity of our *tefillos* for the *geula* constitute the acid test of whether we really are eagerly anticipating the *geula*, or whether we are just going through the motions and, deep down inside, we would not mind if Moshiach would hold off just a bit longer so that we can continue to live our good life in *galus*.

In any event, it is quite apparent, as is beautifully reflected in several *halachos* and *midrashim* which we will now note, that our tradition goes to very great lengths to underscore the importance of *tefillah* in bringing about the *geula*. For example, the Orach Chaim states as follows (111:1):

צריך לסמוך גאולה לתפילה ולא יפסיק ביניהם אפילו באמן אחר גאל ישראל.

Geula and *tefillah* must be adjacent to each other in time, and not even an אמן may cause an interruption between them.

This *halacha* refers to the fact that no *hefsek* is permitted to intervene between (1) the *bracha* of גאל ישראל, which immediately precedes *Shemoneh Esrei*, and (2) the beginning of *Shemoneh Esrei*. In the context of what may or may not be said between the end of one *tefillah* and the beginning of another, this is a completely unique halacha[10] and, understandably, the commentators seem to struggle to define its purpose. However, I believe that this *halacha* beautifully demonstrates the critical importance of *tefillah* in bringing the *geula* closer.

We note that the *shevach* of the first three *berachos* of *Shemoneh Esrei* links the *bracha* of גאל ישראל (which immediately precedes *Shemoneh Esrei*) to that of גואל ישראל, which almost immediately follows the שבח of the first three *berachos*.[11] The words גאל ישראל are phrased in the past tense and therefore speak to the *geulos* of the past, while גואל ישראל, recited at the outset of the *bakashos* section of *Shemoneh Esrei*, is forward-looking and, I suggest, speaks to the final *geula*.

How do we transition from גאל ישראל? The answer is *shevach*. How beautiful it is to perceive that *shevach* acts as the direct link in our *tefillos* between the *bracha* of גאל ישראל and the *bakasha* of גואל ישראל.

In this regard, it is quite interesting to note that on Shabbos, when the *bracha* of גואל ישראל is not said and therefore there is no chain to be broken between the *geulos* of the past and the final *geula*, there is no requirement[12] to be *somech geula l'tefillah* (Ramo on Orach Chaim 112:1). On Yom Tov, however, there is a requirement to be *somech geula l'tefillah* (112:21). We note that on Yom Tov, we do implore Hashem, in *Yaaleh V'Yavo*, to bring Moshiach and it is apparent that the link between the *geulos* of the past and our final *geula* re-appears on Yom Tov, *albeit* in a different guise than during the weekdays. Accordingly, there is good reason to be *somech geula l'tefillah* on Yom Tov.

The incredible importance of the link between *geula* and *tefillah*

---

10. It is unique in the sense of prohibiting *any hefsek* between the end of one *tefillah* and the beginning of the next one. The issue with making a *hefsek* prior to the morning *Shema* results from an opinion that one may not make a *hefsek* between the *bracha* for a *tefillah* and the *tefillah* (rather than a *hefsek* between two entirely separate *tefillos*).

11. This chain is "broken" only by the *berachos* for knowledge and *teshuva*, since *teshuva* is a partner with *tefillah* in bringing about the *geula* – see *Encyclopedia Talmudit* discussion of *Geula*.

12. Although there may be a *chumra* to do so.

is also powerfully exemplified by the following halacha, found in
Orach Chaim (111:3):

> עד שלא קרא ק״ש מצא ציבור מתפללין לא יתפלל עמהם אלא קורא
> ק״ש ואח״כ יתפלל דמסמך גאולה לתפילה עדיף.
>
> If a person comes late to *shul* and the *tzibbur* is about to
> daven *Shemoneh Esrei*, and the person is forced to choose
> between saying *Shemoneh Esrei* with the *minyan* or saying
> *Shema* in the usual order (preceding *Shemoneh Esrei*) so
> that his *geula* and *tefillah* would be connected, then the
> person should not daven *Shemoneh Esrei* with the *minyan*,
> because connecting *geula* and *tefillah* is more important
> than saying *Shemoneh Esrei* with a *minyan*.

This is a remarkable halacha. *Minyan*, as we all know, is an extremely
important concept – it is therefore very meaningful that the obligation
to connect *geula* and *tefillah* would supercede the obligation of *minyan*
where there is a conflict between the two.

And finally, we note the following astounding statement (*Berachos* 4b):

> אמר ר׳ יוחנן איזהו בן עולם הבא? זה הסומך גאולה לתפילה.
>
> Rav Yochanan said, "Who is assured of *Olam HaBo*? A
> person who links *geula* to *tefillah*."

Who would have ever thought that the mere act of linking *geula* to
tefillah warrants a reward of *Olam HaBo*? Clearly, halacha is sending
us yet another very strong signal that *tefillos* for our final *geula* are of
overriding importance.

MEGILLAS ESTHER AND
PIRSUMEI NISA: THE OBLIGATION
TO PUBLICIZE HASHEM'S MIRACLES ৵ঌ

৵ঌ INTRODUCTION

Generally, the *mitzvos* of *arba kosos* and *neiros Chanuka* are virtually unique in respect of the expense to which a person must go, if necessary, in order to perform the mitzvah.[1] In the case of every other *mitzvas aseh*, a person is not obligated to spend his or her last penny on the performance of such mitzvah. The Ramoh states as follows (Orach Chaim 656:1):

> הגה ומי שאין לו אתרוג או שאר מצוה עוברת א"צ לבזבז עליה הון רב,
> וכמו שאמרו המבזבז אל יבזבז יותר מחומש.
>
> Someone who does not have money to purchase an *esrog* or some other object for a mitzvah whose time for performance will lapse, is not obligated to spend great fortunes in order to perform the mitzvah, as it says in the Gemara, do not spend more than a fifth of what you have.

However, in one of the most remarkable *halachos* in the Shulchan Aruch, the Mishneh Berurah states, with respect to the mitzvah of *arba kosos* (*Hilchos Pesach* 472:13):

> אפילו עני המתפרנס מן הצדקה ימכור מלבושו או ילוה או ישכור עצמו
> בשביל יין לארבע כוסות.

---

1. Lighting of Shabbos candles has a similar stringent requirement in mandating a person to go door-to-door in order to acquire the means to light these candles (Rambam *Hilchos Shabbos* 5:1).

> Even a person who is so poor that he is supported by
> charity is obligated to sell his clothing or hire himself
> out in order to purchase wine which he needs in order
> to perform the mitzvah of *arba kosos*.

An almost identical halacha is found with respect to the obligation to
light *neiros Chanuka*.

Now, many of us have learned this halacha of *mechor malbusho*
– the obligation to sell one's clothing in order to be able to perform
the *mitzvos* of *arba kosos* and *neiros Chanuka* – without giving it much
thought. Yet, I believe that this concept has very deep significance and
is worth exploring further.

Let us think for a minute about how unusual this halacha is. We all
know about the extreme lengths to which the Torah goes to encourage
us to support the destitute. We really do not need to dwell on this
notion since it is virtually self-evident. Accordingly, since halacha is
very concerned about the welfare of a destitute person, let alone one
who is so poor that he subsists entirely on *tzedaka*, it is remarkable
that it would require such a person to literally sell the shirt off his
back or hire himself out in order to perform the *mitzvos* of *arba kosos*
and *neiros Chanuka*.

To reinforce this mystery, it should be noted that the *mitzvos* of
arba kosos and *neiros Chanuka* are *mi'd'rabbanan* – of rabbinic origin.
We do not have the requirement of *mechor malbusho* for any *mitzvah*
d'oraisa, including those which we generally regard as very important
mitzvos, such as *mezuza*, *tefillin* and *tzizis*. For all these *mitzvos*, the
financial obligation is limited to one-fifth of a person's assets, as noted
earlier.

Before we launch into our discussion, we should note one fact
which turns out to have great significance, namely that the *mitzvos* of
arba kosos and *neiros Chanuka* share the characteristic of *pirsumei nisa* –
they are performed for the purpose of publicizing particular miracles.
We all know that this is so in the case of *neiros* Chanuka. However,
this fact is a bit less obvious in the case of *arba kosos*. The *Encylopedia*
Talmudit, on the topic of *arba kosos* (page 160), refers to the Maggid
Mishneh, and states as follows (Rambam *Hilchos Chanuka* 4:12):

הטעם שהחמירו [חכמים בדבר לפי שבארבע כוסות] יש משום פרסום נס.
The reason the Sages were so stringent with this mitzvah

of *arba kosos* is because of the aspect of *pirsumei nisa* associated with it. (See *Pesachim* 112b for the basis of this statement.)

What is left unsaid by the Maggid Mishneh, however, is why this aspect of *pirsumei nisa* should have such a powerful impact on the mitzvah of *arba kosos*. It is this relationship of *pirsumei nisa* and the mitzvah of *arba kosos*, and the resulting extreme and unusual requirement of *mechor malbusho*, which I would like to explore in this *d'var*.

We can shed some light on the intriguing requirement of *mechor malbusho* by analyzing certain portions of Megillas Esther, the reading of which is another mitzvah whose purpose is *pirsumei nisa*. If nothing else, if you choose to tell someone at the Seder table that you would like to tell him or her a Pesach *d'var Torah* which is based on an analysis of Megillas Esther, they might think you drank the *arba kosos* before the Seder started.

In any event, I hope that the reader will find the analysis to be both interesting and worthwhile.

◌ꜫ MEGILLAS ESTHER

After Esther was crowned as Queen, Mordechai communicated with Esther, as we know, through Hasach, who acted as an intermediary between them. [There is an opinion recited in the Gemara, although not relevant to our discussion, that Hasach may have been Daniel.] Shortly after the King's edict to kill all the Jews had been distributed throughout the Kingdom, Mordechai sends a message to Queen Esther through Hasach. The Megilla states (4:7):

ויגד לו מרדכי את כל אשר קרהו.

The literal translation of this *pasuk* is:

And Mordechai told Esther all that had transpired.

At first impression, this *pasuk* appears to tell us that Mordechai informed Esther about the King's decree against the Jews. However, several *pesukim* earlier (4:4), we read the following:

ותבואנה נערות אסתר וסריסיה ויגידו לה ותתחלחל המלכה.
Esther's maids came and told Esther what had happened
and she was very greatly distressed.

So, if Esther already knew the terrible news, what was Mordechai telling her when it says: ויגד לו מרדכי את כל אשר קרהו? In order to understand
Mordechai's response to Esther in *pasuk* 4:7, let us examine Esther's
question to him two *pesukim* earlier (4:5):

ותקרא אסתר להתך . . . . . . ותצווהו על מרדכי לדעת מה זה ועל מה זה.
Then Esther summoned Hasach . . . and ordered him to
go to Mordechai, to learn what this was about and why.

The Midrash Rabba (Esther 8:4) on this *pasuk* notes that Esther
sent a message to Mordechai to ask him whether Bnei Yisrael had
transgressed the Torah, wherein it is written, regarding the *luchos*
(Shemos 32:15): מזה ומזה הם כתובים. In other words, Esther was not
asking Mordechai *what* had happened – she already knew that – but
why it happened. Mordechai, who had been on the Sanhedrin, was
obviously extremely wise and was likely to possess deep insight into
how the behavior of Bnei Yisrael may have caused this impending
tragedy.

So now we need to try to understand how Mordechai's response
of ויגד לו מרדכי את כל אשר קרהו was responsive to Esther's question of מה
זה ועל מה זה.

The Midrash Rabba (Esther 8:5), on the words ויגד לו מרדכי את כל אשר
קרהו, states:

אמר ליה להתך, לך אמור לה של בן בנו של קרהו בא עליכם הדא הוא דכתיב
אשר קרך בדרך.
Mordechai told Hasach, "Go tell Esther that the grandson of Karahu attacked us," as it says in the *pasuk* אשר קרך
בדרך (Devarim 25:18).

How are we to understand this very enigmatic Midrash? First of
all, who is Karahu? Secondly, instead of Mordechai saying that the
grandson of Karahu attacked us, why didn't he just say that Haman
attacked us – after all, Haman was a prominent *rasha* in his own right?

Thirdly, what is the connection between the first part of the Midrash and the *pasuk* referenced at the end of the Midrash: אשר קרך בדרך?

Let us analyze this Midrash. The words at the end of this Midrash, אשר קרך בדרך, are found in Ki Tetzeh, in the story of Amalek, which we read on Shabbos Zachor. Rashi, on the words *asher karcha*, referring to the Sifri, says: "*lashon mikreh*," which means a random or coincidental event. The Sifri, quoted by the Torah Temima, on the words *asher karcha*, comments as follows:

> אין קרך אלא נזדמן לך.
>
> The word *karcha* must mean "something which occurred to you by chance."

So, according to the Sifri, when Amalek attacks Bnei Yisrael, the attack appears to us to be the result of some chance, random, coincidental event.

So we have to ask ourselves, why would the Torah go to the trouble of pointing this out? What is the significance of the fact that Amalek, our archenemy down through the ages, attacks us seemingly at random or coincidentally?

We can glean some additional insights into this question by examining the encounter of Bnei Yisrael with Amalek in Parshas Beshalach. Just prior to coming under attack by Amalek, Bnei Yisrael had complained about a lack of water. It was a very nasty incident during which Moshe Rabbeinu complained to G-d that the people were on the verge of stoning him. The *pasuk* says (Shemos 17:2):

> וירב העם עם־משה ויאמרו תנו לנו מים ונשתה.
>
> Bnei Yisrael fought with Moshe and said, "Give us water."

After Moshe, at Hashem's instructions, hit the rock and the water flowed, the Torah states (Shemos 17:7):

> ויקרא שם המקום מסה ומריבה על־ריב בני ישראל.
>
> Moshe called the place מסה ומריבה because of the strife of Bnei Yisrael and because they provoked Hashem by saying: היש ד' בקרבינו – "Is Hashem amongst us?"

Immediately thereafter, the Torah tells us that ויבא עמלק – Amalek came to attack Bnei Yisrael. Rashi states on this *pasuk*:

סמך פרשה זו למקרא זה לומר תמיד אני ביניכם ומזומן לכל צרכיכם,
ואתם אומרים היש ד' בקרבנו אם־אין, חייכם שהכלב בא ונושך אתכם
ואתם צועקים לי, ותדעו היכן אני.

These *parshios*, namely the complaining related to water and the incident of Amalek are adjacent to each other, in order to teach us the following lesson:

> Hashem says, "I am always among you to take care of all
> of your needs and yet you say היש ד' בקרבנו – as you live,
> I will bring Amalek along to bite you and then you will
> know where I am."

So we see that Bnei Yisrael, just before the encounter with Amalek in Beshalach, said היש ד' בקרבנו – "Is Hashem among us?" Now, think about this. Bnei Yisrael had just witnessed incredible miracles. And this was not in the distant past but it was still very fresh in their minds. So, if, despite the remarkable events which they had witnessed, Bnei Yisrael can say היש ד' בקרבנו, what were they thinking? Surely they must have felt that the enormous nature-defying miracles which they had witnessed were the result of natural events and not the result of Hashem's intervention.

And I believe that it was for this very reason that Hashem caused Amalek to "just happen" – לשון מקרה – אשר קרך בדרך. The *midda k'neged midda* represented by Amalek's attacks is that if Bnei Yisrael believe that the miracles which Hashem brings about for our benefit are במקרה, or random events, then Hashem will cause Amalek to just happen to attack the Jews, as if by some random, coincidental occurrence.

As a quick aside, the random attack of Amalek is indicated in the Torah by the fact that there is no build-up of Amalek as an enemy. Unlike the case of the Egyptians who, we are told, were afraid that the Jews would grow powerful and rebel, the Torah gives us no rhyme or reason for Amalek's attacks, but simply states: ויבא עמלק – and Amalek came, as if out of the blue. Similarly, in the Megilla, Haman's hatred of the Jews surfaces very suddenly, without any apparent rationale. So Haman's hatred of the Jews also appears to be a random occurrence.

Now, back to the main discussion, it should be noted that we, as a people, become vulnerable to the vengeance of Amalek not only when Bnei Yisrael view Hashem's redeeming miracles with an improper perspective but also when we react inappropriately to national tragedy. We see this in Megillas Esther.

In the Megilla, Bnei Yisrael had just recently been driven into *galus Bavel*. We know that when people suffer, they are theoretically much more inclined to turn to Hashem than when things are going very well. Nevertheless, we see at the beginning of the Megilla that all of Achashverosh's subjects participated in the party which the King had made and the Midrash tells us that the Jews not only participated but did so with enthusiasm – instead of turning to Hashem at a time of national tragedy and mourning, Bnei Yisrael said, "let's party."

As did the דור המדבר, the Jews in Achashverosh's day also seemingly proceeded on the notion of היש ד' בקרבינו – this is an attitude that our experience as a people (whether miraculous as in *Yetzias Mitzrayim*, or tragic, as in the exile which preceded the events in the Megilla) is made up of merely historical coincidences.

We see from all this that the attitude of אשר קרך is a grave failing which leads directly to being subjected to the attack of our archenemy Amalek.

Coming back now to the Midrash with which we began, the Midrash Rabba, on the words ויגד לו מרדכי את כל אשר קרהו, comments:

אמר ליה להתך. . . . . . בן בנו של קרהו בא עלינו.
"Tell Esther that the grandson of Karahu attacked us."

From our analysis so far, we are now able to understand the underlying meaning of this Midrash. The Midrash does not mean that the grandson of someone named Karahu attacked Bnei Yisrael, but rather that the very same attitude of *"karahu"* which caused Hashem to visit Amalek upon the Jews in Beshalach, had reappeared to threaten the very existence of the Jews during the reign of Achashverosh. And now we see that Mordechai was in fact responsive to Esther's request to understand מה זה ועל מה זה.

✣ TOCHACHA

Aside from the incident of Amalek, it is very interesting to note that the Torah, in the Bechukosai *tochacha*, also illustrates for us very dramatically the extremely serious danger of this attitude of viewing historical events as *b'mikreh*, as happenstance.

Now the *tochacha* is something which we read quickly and quietly and we don't pay too much attention to it because it's very unpleasant but, like everything else in the Torah, the words are there for a purpose, and we can learn important lessons from them. In Bechukosai, the Torah says, by way of warning (Vayikra 26:21):

ואם תלכו עמי קרי ולא תאבו לשמוע לי.

If you walk with Me in a manner of *keri*, and do not listen to Me, . . .

Now, what does ואם תלכו עמי קרי mean? Rashi, referring to the Toras Kohanim, explains the word *keri* as meaning *b'mikreh* – random or accidental. This is reminiscent of the Sifri's interpretation of the word קרך in אשר קרך בדרך.

I believe that the Torah is referring here to the same attitude of קרך which we have been discussing. So, in the Megilla and in Beshalach, we see that the attitude of קרך can bring on Amalek. And in the *tochacha*, at the end of the *pasuk* we quoted a moment ago, we are warned about the severe consequences of such an attitude.

SEVENFOLD PUNISHMENT

The full *pasuk* reads:

ואם תלכו עמי קרי ולא תאבו לשמוע לי ויספתי עליכם מכה שבע כחטאתיכם.

If you walk with Me in a manner of *"keri"* and do not listen to Me, I will punish you sevenfold times your sin.

The *tochacha* warns of a sevenfold punishment. And it is worth noting that the *tochacha* continues to drive this point home repeatedly. Two *pesukim* later in the *tochacha* (Vayikra 26:23, 24), we read:

ואם באלה לא תוסרו לי והלכתם עמי קרי והלכתי אף־אני עמכם בקרי
והכיתי אתכם גם־אני שבע על חטאתיכם.

Again, the attitude of *karahu* is connected to a sevenfold punishment.
And again, several *pesukim* later (26:27, 28):

ואם־בזאת לא תשמעו לי והלכתם עמי בקרי, והלכתי עמכם בחמת־קרי
ויסרתי אתכם אף אני שבע על חטאתיכם.

Obviously, the Torah is trying to get our attention with regard to what
the Torah clearly regards as an extremely serious issue.

BA'CHAMAS KERI

It is also interesting to note that, aside from the triple warning of
punishment on the scale of שבע על חטאתיכם, one of the *pesukim* in the
tochacha refers to Hashem punishing us *"ba'chamas keri,"* the anger of
keri. What is the "anger of *keri*?" It seems to be almost a contradiction
in terms – anger is purposeful while *keri* is random. What is the meaning of *"ba'chamas keri"* – the anger of randomness?

I believe that the Torah is emphasizing the grave threats to our
existence if Hashem is not exercising His protection over us. In other
words, if we, as a people, are subjected to the random forces of history, we may be alright for a while (since randomness, by definition,
means that we will experience some very good months or even years)
but then the odds inevitably catch up with us. For example, we may
rise to the intelligentsia and the highest levels of society and business
in Germany but then a Hitler comes along. Or we may be enjoying
the mother of all parties with Achashverosh but then Haman comes
along.

This is *"chamas keri,"* the anger and the very severe punishment of
keri. Hashem is telling us that if we think the events of the world are
just random coincidences and if we do not appreciate Hashem's intervention on our behalf for what it is, then Hashem will show us the
enormous national tragedies that true randomness can bring about.

ঙ RANDOMNESS AS A THEME OF MEGILLAS ESTHER

Now, coming back to Megillas Esther, it should be noted that this theme of apparent randomness is almost intrinsic to Megillas Esther. In fact, the word "Purim" itself comes from the word פור, or lottery. Moreover, there is no mention of Hashem's Name in the Megilla and it is the one holiday we have where we observe an event which was not an overt miracle – the entire Megilla is nothing but a story.

If someone wants to, they can read the story in the Megilla and interpret it as merely a series of coincidences, which just happened to work in the Jews' favor. Alternatively, a person can, if they wish, easily see right through the seeming randomness of events and perceive the *hashgacha* of our Creator.

THIS TIME HAMAN USES THE EXPRESSION את כל אשר קרהו

We can perceive a fascinating example of the attitude of *karahu* from a very different perspective if we examine a certain *pasuk* in the Megilla which occurs immediately after events had begun to shift in the Jews' favor. Haman had just finished parading Mordechai around the city and he had returned to his house אבל וחפוי ראש, totally despondent. The Megilla (6:13) then states as follows:

ויספר המן לזרש אשתו ולכל אוהביו את כל אשר קרהו.
Haman told Zeresh his wife and his confidantes everything that had transpired.

Haman tells his confidantes את כל אשר קרהו! Note that these are the very same words that Mordechai spoke to Esther and which we discussed earlier. I suggest that this repetition of the exact wording is very significant. Remember, at the beginning of the Megilla, the Jews were partying with the King, apparently having the attitude of *karahu*. We have seen the result of an attitude of *karahu* – that Hashem, in response, causes Amalek (Haman in the Megilla) to attack Bnei Yisrael.

Mordechai, by way of explanation, tells Esther את כל אשר קרהו – that the Jews' attitude of *b'mikreh* caused Hashem, in a like-kind response, to bring about the seemingly random attack of Amalek, which occurred only a few years after Bnei Yisrael were partying with the King and no doubt feeling quite secure. Finally, after the Jews do *teshuva* and fast for three days and pray to Hashem, and clearly discard the attitude of *karahu*, the entire process dramatically reverses itself.

In a wonderful example of ונהפוך הוא – of events being turned on their heads – it is Haman who then thinks that he is the victim of *karahu*, a series of bad breaks. After the Jews do *teshuva*, as did the Jews of Shushan during the three days of fasting and prayer (which, by the way, occurred on the first days of Pesach), and acknowledge Hashem's mastery over the world, then it is Amalek who thinks fate is against him and it is Haman who bemoans את כל אשר קרהו. When Haman tells his wife and confidantes את כל אשר קרהו, we imagine him telling them about all of the remarkable coincidences (see addendum – Partial List of "Coincidental Events") which led to Haman's being forced to parade Mordechai around town.

FURTHER ANALYSIS OF THIS PASUK

Now, the *pasuk* we quoted above where Haman tells his gang את כל אשר קרהו would be intriguing enough if for no reason other than its sharp and compact expression of the complete turning of the tables in the Jews' favor.

In addition, however, if we closely examine this entire *pasuk* (which on a superficial reading seems innocuous enough), we discover not only that the *pasuk* fits very nicely with our theme, but that the *pasuk* demonstrates how a tremendous wealth of insight and wisdom can be ingeniously embedded inside a single *pasuk* of our כתבי קודש. The *pasuk* reads in its entirety (6:13):

ויספר המן לזרש אשתו ולכל אוהביו את כל אשר קרהו ויאמרו לו חכמיו וזרש אשתו אם מזרע היהודים מרדכי אשר החלות לנפול לפניו לא תוכל לו כי נפול תפול לפניו.

Haman told Zeresh his wife and his confidantes everything that had transpired, and his *chachamim* responded to him that "If Mordechai is from the seed of the Yehudim, you have no chance against him, and you will definitely be defeated."

There are a number of questions we can ask about this *pasuk*. First of all, the Gemara (*Megilla* 16a) notes that Haman called his confidantes אוהביו but the Megilla calls them חכמיו. The Gemara states:

קרי להו אוהביו, וקרי להו חכמיו א"ר יוחנן, כל האומר דבר חכמה אפילו באומות העולם נקרא חכם.

Haman called them אוהביו (his loved ones) and the Megilla called them חכמיו (his wise men). Rebbe Yochanan commented that even an idol-worshipper who says something wise is called a *chacham*.

This Gemara seems very strange. First of all, what did Haman's advisers say that was so wise? Not to start up with the Jews? Everyone does it and most get away with it. And even if their advice was clever, why call them *chachamim*? Can we imagine Hitler, ימח שמו, being called a *chacham* by one of our כתבי קודש just because he said something wise? Secondly, if Haman's advisers really felt that Haman shouldn't start up with the Jews, why did they advise Haman to hang Mordechai in the first place? Thirdly, what does the *pasuk* mean by the following words:?

אם מזרע היהודים מרדכי אשר החלות לנפל לפניו לא תוכל לו כי נפול תפול לפניו.

The apparent translation of this *pasuk* is:

If Mordechai is Jewish, don't start up with him because you will surely be defeated.

Now, how could אם מזרע היהודים possibly mean "If Mordechai is Jewish?" The Megilla (3:4) earlier tells us expressly that Haman knew that Mordechai was Jewish – כי הגיד להם אשר הוא יהודי. Fourthly, why did Haman's advisers say אם מזרע היהודים – "if Mordechai is from the *seed* of the Yehudim"; they should have simply said "if he is a *Yehudi*" – what is the significance of the word *mizera*?

I believe that all these questions can be answered, and everything we said can be brought together, when we analyze what the word *Yehudi* really means. We know that Leah called her fourth son Yehuda because it represents *hodaa* to Hashem, in other words thanking Hashem for giving a person more than he or she deserves.

The ArtScroll Chumash in Vayechi, commenting on Yaakov Avinu's final words to Yehuda, states that Mordechai was known as a Yehudi, even though he was from the tribe of Binyamin, on account of Leah's motive in giving Yehuda his name.

In a different, but equally relevant explanation of the words *ish Yehudi*, the Torah Temima, in the Megilla, when Mordechai is first introduced as an *ish Yehudi* (2:5), quotes a Midrash Rabba, which plays on the similarity of the words *Yehudi* and *yechidi* (one who unifies):

למה נקרא שמו יהודי והלא ימיני הוא? לפי שייחד שמו של הקב"ה כנגד
כל באי עולם.

Why was he called a Yehudi, after all he was from the tribe of Binyamin? Because he bonded humanity with Hashem.

And there are other similar *midrashim* on the significance of the name Yehuda and why Mordechai was called *ish Yehudi*, including a Midrash which equates Mordechai's greatness to that of Moshe Rabbeinu. All of these commentaries contain the common theme of Yehuda symbolizing total faith and the exercise of leadership in bringing Bnei Yisrael closer to Hashem.

Now, we can better understand Haman's advisers' reference to זרע היהודים. Haman's advisers were not saying that Mordechai cannot be defeated if he is Jewish (we know sadly from history that this is not the case). What they were saying was that if Mordechai is מזרע היהודים, in other words, from the same gene as Yehuda, meaning that he relies on Hashem for his salvation and gives thanks to Hashem for all His kindnesses, and causes Bnei Yisrael to do the same, then you have no chance against him. They did not give Haman this advice originally because Bnei Yisrael then had the attitude of *karahu*, making them vulnerable to Amalek. It was only after Bnei Yisrael fasted and prayed and did *teshuva* that the threat of Amalek disappeared and Haman's advisers saw the handwriting on the wall.

And now we understand why the Megilla called Haman's advisers *chachamim* – the advisers' comments to Haman reflected an understanding that Amalek can successfully attack Bnei Yisrael only when we have an attitude of *karahu* and that, on the other hand, when we act as if we are מזרע היהודים, giving thanks and praise to Hashem, and doing *teshuva*, Amalek has no chance. This is a very deep insight indeed and even people of the ilk of Haman's advisers are called *chachamim* when they make this point.

❧ CONCLUSION

To conclude, we began this *d'var Torah* with the question of why even a destitute person must sell his clothes or hire himself out, if necessary, in order to perform the *mitzvos* of *arba kosos* and *neiros Chanuka*.

We have seen, through our analysis of Megillas Esther and the *tochacha*, that one of the worst things we as a people can be guilty of is an attitude of *karahu* – a perspective that our experience as a nation, ranging from the spectacular events of *Yetzias Mitzrayim*, to the enormous tragedies of our exile, consists of merely random, historical events.

We have discussed the almost overwhelming, sevenfold punishment set forth in the *tochacha*, as well as the attacks of our archenemy Amalek, with which we are threatened if we treat Hashem's kindnesses, or for that matter His collective punishment of Bnei Yisrael, as just historical accidents, as *karahu*.

The *mitzvos* of *arba kosos* and *neiros Chanuka*, as we have seen, each involve *pirsumei nisa*, a concept which is so critically important in halacha because it represents the complete antithesis to the attitude of *karahu*. By imposing the extreme requirement of מכור מלבושו for the performance of the mitzvah of *pirsumei nisa*, halacha is telling us that if we do not acknowledge the *chesed* which Hashem directs our way – if Hashem performs miracles for our benefit, and we make the severe error of misinterpreting what happened as nothing more than a lucky break, or the result of our own abilities – then nothing matters, not even the shirt on a destitute person's back.

And another possible reason for the unique requirement of *mechor malbusho* may be that the *chachamim*, who observed that we are כפויי טובה בני כפויי טובה[2] – exceedingly ungrateful to Hashem – felt it necessary to correct this characteristic by the drastic requirement of *mechor malbusho* in order to promote *pirsumei nisa*.

---

2. *Avoda Zara* (5:1) at the bottom of the *daf*.

Pirsumei nisa is our way of showing the world that we will never allow Hashem's miraculous acts on our behalf to be misconstrued – we proclaim to the world that there was enough oil, at the time of the Chashmonaim, to burn for only one day and no more, even though such a seemingly insignificant historical fact could easily be blurred with the passage of time; we proclaim to the world that even though Megillas Esther appears to be just a series of coincidences which happened to work out well for the Jews, and despite the absence of any overt miracles, or even a single mention of G-d's name, in the Megilla, we avoid any resulting temptation to deny the miraculous nature of the events described there; we proclaim to the world, as we retell on the Seder night the wonders of *Yetzias Mitzrayim*, that we will never again say היש ד׳ בקרבינו; and, in a modern context, we proclaim our gratitude to Hashem for the continuous miracle represented by the very existence of Medinas Yisrael.

When we prepare to sit down to the Pesach Seder and perform its *mitzvos*, particularly that of *arba kosos*, it is critically important that we fully appreciate the preciousness of this mitzvah involving *pirsumei nisa*, which halacha regards as having such overriding significance that even the clothing of a destitute person must give way, if necessary, in order for this mitzvah to be performed.

We recognize, in the *Modim* prayer, three times each day – הניסים שבכל יום עמנו – the miracles which are with us each and every day. When we raise the *arba kosos* at the Seder night in joyful acknowledgment and thanks to Hashem, and in commemoration of the four expressions of *geula*, let us remember that it is our solemn and fundamentally important duty to constantly remind ourselves and the world-at-large that the events in our lives, on both a national level and on an individual level, are anything but *b'mikreh* – mere coincidence – but rather the result of our Creator's ever-compassionate *hashgacha*.

As we conclude in *Modim*:

הטוב כי לא כלו רחמיך, והמרחם כי לא תמו חסדיך מעולם קוינו לך.
Your compassion, which never ceases, and Your kindness, which is ever-present, we will forever place our hope in You.

*

✥ PARTIAL LIST OF "COINCIDENTAL EVENTS" OCCURING PRIOR TO HAMAN'S RECITAL OF את כל אשר קרהו

Achashverosh just happened to decide to ask Vashti to appear naked at his banquet.

Vashti happened to be struck at this time with a skin or other disease which made her refuse to appear.

The King's advisers happened to advise the King that Vashti be given the death penalty.

The adviser who made this suggestion happened to be Haman (the King later hated him for this when he regretted killing Vashti and this made the King more amenable to taking revenge on Haman).

Haman was the one to suggest that Vashti be killed even though the King consulted with seven advisers and Haman (then called Memuchan) was the last of the advisers to be called upon but spoke out of turn.

Esther, Mordechai's adopted daughter or wife as the case may be, happened to be the one chosen by the King to replace Vashti.

Mordechai happened to advise Esther not to reveal her origin – if she had done so, Haman would not have suggested a general edict against the Jews and the events leading to Haman's downfall and the *teshuva* of Bnei Yisrael which preceded it, might not have occurred.

Mordechai happened to overhear the plot of Bigsan and Theresh to kill the King.

Esther happened to relate this plot in the name of Mordechai.

It just so happened, for whatever reason, that Mordechai was not immediately rewarded for his saving the King's life.

Haman just happened to build a gallows for Mordechai at the very time it was about to be used on him.

The King happened to get restless at just the right time and it was then read to him that Mordechai had not been rewarded for saving the King's life.

Haman just happened to pay a visit to the King at this time and got trapped into listing all of the honors which should be directed towards a deserving person, just when the King was disposed towards rewarding Mordechai.

A LIFESAVING MITZVAH:
AVRAHAM AVINU'S PERSPECTIVE
ON *HACHNASAS ORCHIM*

The *Encyclopedia Talmudit*, on the topic of *hachnasas orchim*, states as follows (column 127):

לעולם ישתדל אדם בהכנסת אורחים שאין לך מצוה גדולה מזו, והמשובח שבצדקה הוא הכנסת אורחים, ושכרה גדול עד מאד. ואמרו : בזמן שבית המקדש קיים מזבח מכפר על אדם, ועכשיו שאין בית המקדש קיים שולחנו של אדם מכפר עליו, והיינו הכנסת אורחים, שנותן פרוסה לאורחים, והרבה הפליגו חכמים במעלת מצוה זו, בתלמוד ומדרשות ובספרי המוסר.

A person should always make great efforts to perform the mitzvah of *hachnasas orchim* because there is no greater mitzvah (referencing the Meiri in *Shabbos* 127a). And its reward is very great. It is said that at the time of the Beis HaMikdosh, the altar atoned for man, but now a person's table represents the altar. And this refers to *hachnasas orchim*, a mitzvah whose importance our Sages much stressed, in the Talmud, Midrash, and books of *mussar*.

How can we understand the Meiri's remarkable declaration that there is no greater mitzvah than *hachnasas orchim*?

⊷ PARSHAS VAYERA

At the outset of Parshas Vayera, Hashem is visiting with Avraham Avinu. Suddenly, Avraham notices three travelers and very respect-

fully asks Hashem to wait while he attends to the needs of the travelers (Bereishis 18:3):

ויאמר, ד', אם נא מצאתי חן בעיניך, אל נא תעבר מעל עבדך.

Hashem, if I have found favor in Your eyes, please do not
leave Your servant.

The Gemara comments on Avraham's asking Hashem to wait while
he attends to the needs of the guests (*Shabbos* 127a):

גדולה הכנסת אורחין מקבלת פני השכינה.

Attending to guests is greater than greeting the Shechina.

The following questions can be asked on this Gemara:

(1) Why indeed does *hachnasas orchim* take precedence over
     the awesome privilege and responsibility of greeting the
     Shechina?

(2) Moreover, how did Avraham know this to be so? Our tradition
     tells us that Avraham arrived at his faith through observation
     and reasoning. What logical process led him to the above
     conclusion regarding the overriding importance of *hachnasas
     orchim*?

✒ WHAT IS HACHNASAS ORCHIM?

Many people believe that *hachnasas orchim* applies any time a person
has guests in his or her home, such as inviting friends over for a
Shabbos meal. However, this is apparently not the case. The *Encyclopedia Talmudit*, on the topic of *hachnasas orchim*, states as follows
(column 133):

אינו מקיים מצוות הכנסת אורחים אלא כשבאו אורחים מחוץ לעיר
ונתארחו בביתו, והוא הדין כשנתארחו אצל אחרים ומזמינים לסעודה
בביתו.

A person does not fulfill the mitzvah of *hachnasas
orchim* unless the guests came from outside the city, or

if intercity travelers are lodging elsewhere in the town
and are invited to such person's home for a meal.

The *Encyclopedia Talmudit* cites a number of sources in making the
above statement, including the Ramoh (Orach Chaim, *Hilchos Shabbos*
333:1), where there is a discussion of activities, otherwise prohibited
on account of *sh'vus*, which are permitted on Shabbos, provided they
are undertaken specifically for the purpose of a mitzvah.

For example, engaging in a great deal of exertion to access contain-
ers of grain or wine is normally rabbinically prohibited on Shabbos,
on account of *sh'vus*, but is permitted for the sake of *hachnasas orchim*,
provided such mitzvah is actually being fulfilled thereby. The Ramoh
notes that the mitzvah of *hachnasas orchim* is not fulfilled in the case
of an invitation extended to a friend (Orach Chaim, *Hilchos Shabbos*
333:1):

> אבל כשזימן חבירו לסעוד אצלו לא מקרי אורחים ואינו סעודת מצוה
> רק סעודת רשות.

> If a person invites friends over for a meal, this is not
> considered a *seudas* mitzvah but merely a *seudas reshus*.

To better understand why the great mitzvah of *hachnasas orchim* applies specifically to inter-city travelers, let us examine the Torah's
discussion of *eglah arufa* (Devarim 21:1–9).

EGLAH ARUFA

The Torah discusses the case of a person who was found murdered
"ba'sadeh" (in the field) and it is not known who committed the deed.
A rough translation of the relevant Torah passage follows:

> If a corpse is found in the field of the Land which Hashem
> gave to you [Eretz Yisrael] and the murderer is unknown,
> the *zekeinim* and judges shall go out and measure the
> distances to the towns which surround the corpse. The
> *zekeinim* of the nearest town shall then take a calf which
> has not previously carried a burden and shall slaughter
> the calf in the valley. The Kohanim then approach, while

the *zekeinim* of the nearest town wash their hands over the slaughtered calf and declare: "Our hands did not spill this [the victim's] blood and our eyes did not see." Please forgive Your people and let not innocent blood be spilled amongst Your people, and the blood of the calf shall serve to atone the spilt blood (ונכפר להם הדם).

A number of questions can be asked about the *eglah arufa* process:

(1)   Why are the elders of the nearest town (as opposed to the elders of some other town) required to undergo the *eglah arufa* ceremony?

(2)   What is it about the nearest town which causes the Torah to presume the guilt, rather than the innocence, of the people of this town?

(3)   The Torah requires that the elders of the nearest town, as part of the ceremony, declare (Devarim 21:7):

ידינו לא שפכו את הדם הזה ועינינו לא ראו.
Our hands did not spill this blood and our eyes did not see.

Why do we need both branches of the above declaration, since it seems that either one – our hands did not spill this blood, or, our eyes did not see – should be sufficient to exonerate the elders (and, by extension, the inhabitants of the town)?

(4)   Once the elders declare their innocence in shedding the blood of the murdered person, and that they never saw the victim, why do they still need atonement from the blood of the *eglah arufa*?

With respect to the first of our questions, one would think that we measure to the nearest town either because we assume that (a) this is where the traveler last visited, and that the townspeople must have failed to show the deceased proper *hachnasas orchim*, perhaps resulting in his death, or (b) the murderer resides in the nearest town. However, we will demonstrate that neither of these assumptions are correct, and then suggest a rationale for undertaking such measurement, all with the objective of developing a deeper understanding of the seminal mitzvah of *hachnasas orchim*.

Searching for the Last Town Visited by the Victim?

The purpose behind measuring to the nearest town cannot be an effort to determine which town was last visited by the victim, as evidenced by the following:

(1) The Torah states: לא נודע מי הכהו (the identity of the murderer is unknown) (21:1). Now, if the reason for measuring to the nearest town is because we are unaware of, and therefore trying to determine, the last town visited by the deceased, the Torah surely would have stated expressly that the last town visited by the victim was unknown, just as the Torah states that the identity of the murderer was unknown.

(2) Once the *zekeinim* declare that they never saw the victim (21:8), indicating that the victim did not visit their town, and if indeed we are trying to determine the last town visited by the victim, the search should then have been expanded to the second nearest town. But no such expanded search is conducted.

(3) No doubt, there are occasions when the actual itinerary of the victim can be readily determined and it may accordingly be known with certainty that the deceased did not visit the nearest town. The Torah makes no exception for this situation and accordingly, even under these circumstances, the measurement to the nearest town takes place, making it quite clear that the purpose of measuring to the nearest town is not to ascertain the town last visited by the victim.

Remarkably, it appears as if the nearest town must undergo the *eglah arufa* expiation ceremony even if we have actual knowledge or very good reason to believe that the victim never stepped foot in that town!

Searching for the town in which the murderer resides?

We will now demonstrate that the purpose of measuring to the nearest town cannot be an effort to determine the town in which the murderer resides. Consider the following:

(1) If indeed we seek out the nearest town because we assume that is where the murderer resides, then, if the murderer is

not found in that nearest town, the search logically should be expanded to the second nearest town. But no such expanded search is conducted.

(2) As will be discussed below, the Gemara tells us that in reality we do not even measure to the nearest town but rather to the nearest town which has a Beis Din, even if this entails skipping several more proximate towns which do not have a Beis Din. If the Torah's purpose was to focus on the town where the killer most likely resided, what would be the logic of skipping several towns nearer to where the victim was found than the town which has a Beis Din? All the more so because it seems far less likely that a killer would reside in a town which has a Beis Din, and hence a more institutionalized rule of law.

Accordingly, it seems that the Torah is telling us that even if the victim never visited the town nearest in distance to where the victim is found, and regardless of where the murderer resides, it is nevertheless the *zekeinim* of the nearest town (with a Beis Din) which undergo the *eglah arufa* procedure. But now we need to understand: (1) why such town should bear such great responsibility even if the victim did not pass through that town, and (2) why is the determination of the "nearest" town restricted to towns which have a Beis Din.

EGLAH ARUFA – MASECHES SOTAH

Eglah arufa seems to be such an important concept that an entire *perek* of the Talmud is dedicated to this topic (the ninth *perek* of *Sotah*). The Gemara introduces what seems to be an astounding and, at first glance illogical, *chiddush* with respect to the Torah's instruction to measure to the nearest town (*Sotah* 45b):

מנין שאם נמצא סמוך לעיר שאין בה בית דין, שמניחין אותה ומודדין
לעיר שיש בה בית דין.

How do we know that if the nearest town to the corpse has no Beis Din, we skip over that town and instead measure to the closest town which has a Beis Din? [The Gemara quotes a *pasuk* in support of the above principle.]

Regardless of the Gemara's rationale for the above statement (which rationale we will examine in a moment), the above Gemara offers further cogent evidence that we measure to the nearest town *not* for the purpose of determining either (1) the most likely town last visited by the victim, or (2) the town where the murderer most likely resides because, in either of these cases, it would make no sense to skip a town which does not have a Beis Din, as explained in detail above.

Although the requirement of skipping over a nearest town which does not have a Beis Din has created difficulty for some commentators, I would like to suggest a construct for the *eglah arufa* process which seems to nicely explain why it makes perfect sense to skip a town which does not have a Beis Din.[1]

We begin with the proposition that intercity travel is an inherently dangerous activity. The Gemara states that one should not transport children, for schooling purposes, from one town to another because intercity travel is dangerous (*Bava Basra* 21a):

לא ממטינן ינוקא ממתא למתא.

A child should not be transported from one town to another.

Rashi explains that this refers to schooling:

ללמוד מיום ליום, שמא יוזק בדרכים, שהשטן מקטרג בשעת הסכנה,
שנאמר פן יקראנו אסון.

[The warning against transporting children between towns applies], for purposes of daily schooling, because

---

1. Fn. 24 in the Schottenstein version of the above Gemara in *Sotah* states: Tosafos in *Bava Basra* (23b) . . . finds this law (skipping the closest town if it has no Beis Din) difficult. Although the town closest to the corpse does not contain a Beis Din, its proximity to the corpse nonetheless indicates the probability that the murderer came from there and not from any of the other surrounding towns. Why then is a town further away obligated to bring an *eglah arufa* because it is the closest town with a Beis Din? Because of this difficulty, Ritzba offers a different explanation (not relevant here).

However, from the silence of Rashi and Rambam (*Hilchot Rotzeach* 9:5) regarding this distinction, it appears that they do not accept it (i.e., the Ritzba's alternate explanation referenced above). *D'var Avraham* (1:4:6) therefore suggests that it is simply a Scriptural decree that the rule of following the "closest" is abrogated when that town does not have a court.

the child might encounter death or injury along the
way, since Satan promulgates his arguments at a time
of danger, as it states [in the case of Yosef's brothers not
wanting to transport Binyamin to Mitzrayim]: פֶּן יִקְרָאֶנּוּ
אָסוֹן – lest an accident befall him (Bereishis 42:4).

I would suggest that, precisely because intercity travel is inherently
dangerous, the Torah established the elaborate system of *eglah arufa*
to maximize the safety of such traveler. To illustrate, our modern air
traffic control system is based on control towers which monitor each
plane that is flying within a certain radius of such tower. Thus, there
is a circle of jurisdiction around each control tower. The next tower
over will also have a circle of jurisdiction and each of these various
circles intersect adjoining circles so that a plane is never outside
the jurisdiction of one tower or another. This is because air travel is
considered dangerous so that a plane needs to have a control tower
watching over it at all times.

So too does the Torah set up a system to protect a traveler every
step of his journey. The system requires that each traveler have a
"control tower" town which is morally and halachically responsible
for him every step of his travels, *whether or not he ever visited such town.*
Accordingly, each "control tower" town has a radius of responsibility
for travelers. Since, at each moment of a traveler's journey, there must
always, by definition, be a nearest town, a traveler always has a town
which is responsible for his safety.

However, the Torah recognizes that it is a very great responsibility
for a town to be charged with looking after the welfare of a traveler
even if such traveler never stepped foot inside that town. Accordingly,
the Torah does not impose such responsibility over every single town,
but only over a town which has a Beis Din. I would suggest that this
is so because a town with a Beis Din is presumed to possess an infra-
structure which has the ability to make itself aware of, and safeguard,
travelers in the area, even if they never entered the town.

And now it all makes sense. We measure to the "nearest" town
with a Beis Din, not because we presume the traveler visited that
town, nor because we are searching for the murderer, but because
the victim was, by reason of proximity, found within the "controlled
airspace" of that town. This proximity invests the town with an even

greater responsibility for the traveler than the more proximate town he or she may have last visited.

And only a town with a Beis Din can be charged with responsibility for a traveler who may never have visited that town. This rationale neatly explains why Rashi and the Rambam (as referenced in the above-referenced Schottenstein footnote) have no apparent problem with the notion of skipping over a closer town with no Beis Din in favor of a more distant town which possesses a Beis Din.

This also helps us understand why, to answer the second question we posed earlier, it is necessary for the elders of the town to declare not only that they did not see the traveler but also that they did not spill his blood. If they declare only that they did not see the victim, that is not sufficient to absolve them of responsibility because the Torah nevertheless makes the nearest town (with a Beis Din) responsible even if the inhabitants of that town never saw the victim. Therefore, it is necessary for the elders to declare not only that they did not see the traveler but also that they did not spill the victim's blood, i.e., they were not remiss in watching over the welfare of travelers within their "control tower" jurisdiction.

Moreover, the converse is also true. Accordingly, it is not sufficient for the *zekeinim* simply to declare that they did not spill the victim's blood (i.e., they must also declare that they did not see the traveler) because, if the people of the town saw the victim, then they are automatically invested with an entire set of responsibilities related to *hachnasas orchim* (e.g., food, accommodations, and accompaniment when the person leaves). If the people of the town did not do these things, then they are culpable even if they were not actually complicit in spilling the victim's blood.

Our third question was: why the *zekeinim* need atonement from the blood of the *eglah arufa*, even if they are able to declare both that they did not see the victim, or spill his blood? It seems, however, that the very fact that the murder took place is *per se* a serious indictment of the town responsible for such traveler. By requiring the sacrifice of the *eglah arufa*, no matter how innocent the townspeople can declare themselves to be, the Torah imposes a system of strict liability whenever a murder has occurred. Atonement is required because, ultimately, the very existence of the corpse within the boundaries of a town's jurisdiction testifies to the deficiency of the town's vigilance.

⋙ CONCLUSION

We can now understand why *hachnasas orchim* is greater than greeting the Shechina. Since *hachnasas orchim* applies to intercity travelers, and since we have seen from the Gemara (*Bava Basra* 21a) that such traveler is considered to be in a situation of danger, then the mitzvah of *hachnasas orchim* can be said to be in a category of its own, amongst *mitzvos* of *gemilus chassadim,* because of its lifesaving nature. Surely, G-d does not want Avraham to greet Him while His creatures are in physical danger. And it makes perfect sense that Avraham was able to deduce this notion through logic – he understood that the possible saving of a life takes priority, in Hashem's eyes, to greeting G-d. Indeed, saving a life is the ultimate way to show respect towards Hashem and His handiwork.

And to buttress our proposition that the reason for the extreme importance of the mitzvah of *hachnasas orchim* is its lifesaving nature, we refer to the Rambam where he states as follows (*Hilchos Avel* 14:2):

כל שאינו מלוה כאילו שופך דמים.

Any host who does not accompany his guest upon the guest's departure, it is considered as if the host has spilt blood.

The underlying rationale for *hachnasas orchim* also explains why its reward is so great. The Torah, in its infinite wisdom and justice, balances enormous rewards with enormous responsibility. And we can also understand why inviting a neighbor within a person's own town does not constitute *hachnasas orchim.* The tremendous responsibility of *hachnasas orchim,* together with commensurately great reward, cannot logically apply to a simple invitation to a neighbor.

Let us hope that these insights into *hachnasas orchim* help us all observe this mitzvah with greater enthusiasm and dedication.

The following article, dated February 16, 2012, is from the website of Arutz Sheva.[2]

BIBLICAL CEREMONY HELD FOR SLAIN SOLDIER
Rabbis hold a biblical-style ceremony for soldier killed in traffic accident. "Our hands did not shed this blood."
By Maayana Miskin

The death of a female soldier in a car accident last Friday has led to an unusual response – the revival of an ancient ceremony described in the Bible. The ceremony was traditionally used in cases where a person was murdered by an unknown killer.

Rabbis belonging to the Tzohar organization held the "egla arufa" ceremony on Thursday morning in response to the death of Manesh Yazachu, a 19-year-old soldier who was killed in a hit-and-run accident near the town of Yokneam.

The driver who hit Manesh abandoned the scene, leaving her in the road, where she was hit by subsequent cars.

Rabbis met at the gas station at the entrance to Kibbutz Zorea, and said the ancient prayer, "Our hands have not shed this blood, neither have our eyes seen it. Forgive, oh Lord, Thy people Israel, whom Thou hast redeemed, and suffer not innocent blood to remain in the midst of Thy people Israel."

They did not conduct the traditional sacrifice of a calf at the site of the death.

Rabbi David Stav, head of Tzohar, explained that the ceremony was intended to draw attention to the responsibility the community bears to keep its members safe. "One could ask, how can the people of the city who did not know, did not hear, and did not see be guilty? We see here an uncompromising moral view, a determination that all of us – religious, traditional, secular – must adopt: we are responsible for spilled blood.

"We are responsible for the blood spilled in traffic accidents, for the blood of youth shed in pointless fighting, for the women murdered by their husbands. We are responsible for the blood spilled in the murders we read about in the papers. When it comes to human life, there is no escaping responsibility."

"Indirect responsibility is still responsibility," he added.

The ceremony is as relevant today as it was in the past, said Rabbi Rafi Feuerstein. "If every time a woman were murdered by her husband, the heads of social services, the family court judges, and the local rabbi would come and say, 'We did everything possible to prevent this,' reality would look better," he said.

---

2. http://www.israelnationalnews.com/News/News.aspx/152838

LESSONS FROM ADAM AND CHAVA
ON *SHALOM BAYIS*   פּ

It is generally believed that Adam's first sin was his eating
from the *eitz hada'as*. I believe, however, it can be demonstrated that
Adam had previously sinned. Moreover, based upon our novel interpretation, we can derive a very important and practical moral lesson
from this episode.

Let us begin by asking two questions:

(1) On the phrase עזר כנגדו (Bereishis 2:18), Rashi comments, refer-
     encing the Gemara which attempts to reconcile the seemingly
     opposite expressions of עזר (a helpmate) and כנגדו (a force of
     opposition). The Gemara states (*Yevamos* 63a):

     זכה עזר, לא זכה כנגדו להלחם.
     If he [the husband] merits it, she [the wife] is a source of
     constructive assistance; if he does not merit it, she will
     be an opposing force in strife and quarrels.

Now, if we assume that Adam had never sinned prior to eating from
the *eitz hada'as*, then (according to the above Midrash) Adam deserved
for Chava to have been an *ezer* to Adam. But, if such is the case, how
could she possibly have enticed Adam into eating from the *eitz hada'as*? Is this not a classic example of *k'negdo*?

(2) After Adam ate from the *eitz hada'as*, Hashem said to him
     (Bereishis 3:17):

     ולאדם אמר כי שמעת לקול אשתך ותאכל.

This is typically translated as: And to Adam, Hashem said: "Because you listened to your wife and you ate . . ." However, this translation is very problematic. First of all, for Adam to listen to his wife was not *per se* a sin; after all, Chava was expressly given to Adam as an *ezer*. Secondly, the above interpretation presents us with a striking lack of parallelism between the way Hashem rebukes Chava and the way He rebukes Adam. Hashem's rebuke of Chava is found in Bereishis 3:13:

ויאמר ד׳ אלקים לאשה מה זאת עשית.

Hashem said to the woman [Chava], "What did you do?"

We note that Hashem (unlike His comment to Adam about Adam's listening to his wife) said nothing to Chava about her listening to the snake. Why did Hashem not say to Chava כי שמעת לקול הנחש, just as He said to Adam, כי שמעת לקול אשתך?

As a result of the above questions, I would like to suggest a very different explanation of the *eitz hada'as* episode. In fact, Adam's first sin was not his eating from the *eitz hada'as*, but rather his not stopping Chava from eating from the *eitz hada'as*. Adam had the opportunity to stop Chava because she did not suddenly walk over to the *eitz hada'as* and begin eating – she first discussed it with the snake (3:2):

ותאמר האשה אל הנחש מפרי עץ הגן נאכל.

The woman [Chava] said to the snake: "Let us eat from the *eitz hada'as*."

Moreover, it appears as if Adam was in the vicinity at the time (and it is therefore quite plausible that he heard the entire conversation between Chava and the snake), evidenced by the fact that, just a few *pesukim* later, we are told that Chava gave the fruit of the *eitz hada'as* to Adam.

Accordingly, the alternate translation of ולאדם אמר כי שמעת לקול אשתך ותאכל would be as follows: "To Adam, Hashem said: Because (1) you heard your wife's voice [discussing, with the snake, eating from the *eitz hada'as*]; (2) you accepted her rationale, and (3) you then did not stop her from eating the forbidden fruit . . ."

Now, it seems to all fit together: Adam's first sin was in not stopping Chava from eating from the *eitz hada'as*. Once he failed to stop her, he was no longer free of sin. As a result of Adam's sin, Chava became a *k'negdo* instead of an *ezer* and enticed Adam to eat as well. Hashem then rebukes Adam (3:17):

ולאדם אמר כי שמעת לקול אשתך ותאכל.

> You heard your wife's voice [discussing, with the snake, eating from the *eitz hada'as*, i.e., you had an opportunity to stop her], and she nevertheless went ahead and ate[1]. . . .

As further evidence of the above interpretation, let us examine the continuation (emphasized) of the above words:

ולאדם אמר כי שמעת לקול אשתך ותאכל מן העץ אשר צויתיך לאמר
לא תאכל ממנו.

> And to Adam, Hashem said: . . . because you heard your wife's voice, yet she ate from the tree about *which I com-manded you* not to eat from it.

If, according to the standard interpretation of the above *pasuk*, Hashem was faulting Adam for taking bad advice from Chava, and thereby eating from the *eitz hada'as*, there would be no need for Hashem to remind Adam of the prohibition against eating from the *eitz hada'as*. After all, Adam had only received one commandment. On the other hand, if Adam's first sin was in not preventing Chava from eating from the *eitz hada'as*, then it makes sense that Hashem needed to remind Adam that it was Adam (and not Chava) who received this commandment[2] and of his consequent responsibility for his wife's actions; Hashem was informing Adam that Adam should have under-

---

1. Note that ותאכל has a dual meaning and could mean "and she ate," as well as "and you ate."

2. In fact, Chava had not even been created at the time that the commandment to Adam not to eat from the *eitz hada'as* was given:

ויצו ד' אלקים על האדם לאמר מכל עץ הגן אכל תאכל ומעץ הדעת טוב ורע לא תאכל.

Hashem commanded Adam: You may eat from every tree in the Garden, but you must not eat from the *eitz hada'as* (Bereishis 2:16–17).

It is only several *pesukim* later Bereishis (2:22) that we are told of Chava's creation.

stood, even if Hashem never expressly so stated, his responsibility for his family's observance of G-d's commandments.

In summary, as soon as Adam violated Hashem's commandment by failing to stop Chava, she became a *k'negdo* and then enticed him to eat as well. The very important moral lesson here is that, not infrequently, a wife may act as a *k'negdo* and get in her husband's way. The typical reaction of the husband is to blame his wife for acting in a destructive manner, just as Adam did (3:12):

> ויאמר האדם האשה אשר נתתה עמדי היא נתנה לי מן העץ ואכל.
> And Adam said to Hashem: "This woman that You gave me, she enticed me to eat [from the *eitz hada'as*]."

The Gemara (*Avoda Zara* 5b) comments that Adam, by improperly blaming his wife for his situation, was being ungrateful for Hashem's gift to him in the form of Chava. On the surface, this Gemara is not understandable because, after all, the Torah explicitly states that Chava gave Adam fruit from the *eitz hada'as* and she therefore apparently was blameworthy for Adam's cardinal sin, and for Adam's resulting banishment from the Garden of Eden. However, now that we have explored the root cause of Adam's downfall, which seems to be his own sin in not preventing his wife from transgressing Hashem's commandment, we can better appreciate Adam's instrumental role in his own demise.

Accordingly, whenever a person is tempted to blame his wife for what he perceives to be his wife's destructive behavior or divisive strife, it is most appropriate to remember the very valuable lesson of Adam and Chava and the fact that, whether or not a wife acts as an *ezer* or a *k'negdo* is very often within the power of the husband to influence and control, through his observance or transgression of Hashem's commandments.

BEHIND THE OBLIGATION TO RECITE
ONE HUNDRED *BERACHOS* DAILY   ৵৩

Most of us are aware that there is an obligation to make one hundred *berachos* each day. What is less commonly known is that this obligation is derived from a *pasuk* in Ekev (Devarim 10:12).

> ועתה ישראל מה ד׳ אלקיך שואל מעמך כי אם־ליראה את־ד׳ אלקיך ללכת
> בכל־דרכיו ולאהבה אותו ולעבוד את־ד׳ אלקיך בכל־לבבך ובכל־נפשך.
> And now Israel, what does Hashem ask of you, but merely to fear your G-d, to walk in all His ways, and to love Him, and to serve Him with all your heart and all your soul.

What is even less commonly understood is how and why the *pasuk* in question teaches us this principle. The Gemara states as follows (*Menachos* 43b):

> תניא היה רבי מאיר אומר, חייב אדם לברך מאה ברכות בכל יום, שנאמר
> ועתה ישראל מה ד׳ אלקיך שואל מעמך . . .
> Rav Meir said that a person is obligated to make one hundred *berachos* each day [quoting the above *pasuk*]

Rashi explains that Rav Meir's opinion is based on the word מה in the *pasuk*, which Rav Meir believes should be read, not literally as מה, meaning "what," but rather as מאה – one hundred, which Rav Meir then extends to mean the mitzvah of saying one hundred *berachos* each day.

According to Rashi's explanation of Rav Meir, we wonder why Rav Meir would have selected this particular *pasuk* upon which to base his statement, since this is the seventy-seventh instance that the word מה appears in the Torah.

Tosafos helps explain why Rav Meir chose this *pasuk* over all of the other instances where the word מה appears. Tosafos notes that this *pasuk* has ninety-nine letters. When you read מה as מאה, as Rashi suggests, a letter א is added and we then have one hundred letters in the *pasuk*.

Now, all of this works out nicely numerologically, but there appears to be a significant substantive problem associated with Rav Meir's statement, namely that there is absolutely no mention (not even a hint) in our *pasuk*, about *berachos*, nor does the *pasuk* refer to frequency of performing an act nor does the *pasuk* even refer to a specific mitzvah.

We know that Rav Meir was brilliant and would not dream up an analysis which seems to be so devoid of logic. So in fact it must be that Rav Meir had independently reached the conclusion, from reading and analyzing our *pasuk*, that a person is obligated to make one hundred *berachos* each day. The textual support (whether it involves adding one to the ninety-nine letters or changing the word מה to מאה), is merely an *asmachta*, or literally something to lean on, or a memory aid, but is not the primary basis for the halacha.

Which brings us back full circle – how does this *pasuk* lead us to the conclusion that a person is obligated to make one hundred *berachos* each day?

I suggest that a careful reading of the *pasuk* will help us find the answer. The *pasuk* starts off with the words: ועתה ישראל מה ד' אלקיך שואל מעמך כי, which means "What am I asking of you – merely . . . ." So, if we read the opening words of the *pasuk*, we would think that the *pasuk* would conclude by reciting something which is very easy to do. And then we get the surprise ending:

> ליראה את־ד' אלקיך ללכת בכל־דרכיו ולאהבה אותו ולעבוד את־ד'
> אלקיך בכל־לבבך ובכל־נפשך.
> . . . to fear Hashem your G-d, to walk in all of His ways,
> to love Him and to serve Him with all your heart and all
> your soul.

"To fear Hashem your G-d, to walk in His ways, to love Him, and to serve Hashem with all your heart and all your soul." Is that all? What happened to the easy request we were anticipating? So we have an apparently difficult contradiction within the *pasuk* itself.

I believe it is the reconciliation of the two parts of the *pasuk* which led Rav Meir to his conclusion about the mitzvah of making one hundred *berachos* each day. And I would like to suggest that his reasoning works as follows:

If Hashem told us in the Torah, out of the blue, that we are obligated to "fear Hashem, and to love Him, and to walk in His ways, and to serve Him with all our heart and all our soul," this would be a very difficult task for anyone to accomplish. So how do we get to the stage where it is an easy thing to do, as the first part of the *pasuk* implies? I believe the answer is making one hundred *berachos* a day.

When we properly perform the mitzvah of making *berachos*, we express, one hundred times each day, our appreciation for all of the benefits which Hashem constantly and mercifully grants to us, and also recognize G-d's awesome presence in this world.

And so, we make a blessing, in appreciation and thanks, for the delicious foods that we eat (each with its own distinct taste), for the new clothes that we wear, for the beauty of nature, for the smell of a fragrant flower, for the blessing of peace, for the precious gift of Eretz Yisrael, for the incredibly sensitive and humanitarian laws and ethics as embodied in the Torah, for the ingathering of the exiles, for healing the sick, for sustaining us through good times and bad, for saving us from a life-threatening situation, for lifting our spirits when we're down, and for so many other things.

And we also make *berachos* in recognition of G-d as the Creator and the source of all natural phenomena, as when we make *berachos* for the awesome power of Hashem embodied in thunder and lightning, and upon seeing majestic mountains and other spectacular natural sights such as comets and meteors.

Now, if we make these *berachos* and *mean them*, one hundred times a day, this works out to more than 36,000 *berachos* per year and over one million *berachos* in thirty years. If we do all this, and we do it sincerely, and with proper focus, then it will become second nature for us to love Hashem and to be totally and absolutely dedicated to Him.

So the Rabbis of the Talmud understood very well that Hashem, in the *pasuk* we have been discussing, was directing us towards the only formula which ultimately makes it almost effortless to accomplish those seemingly unattainable objectives listed in the second half of the *pasuk.* If we make *berachos* and express and feel appreciation for the countless benefits with which Hashem has blessed each and every one of us, then it is only natural and almost effortless that we will come to love G-d and walk in His ways.

We as a people are called "Yehudim," which very name symbolizes gratitude. When Leah gave birth to Yehuda, her fourth son, she realized that Hashem had blessed her with more than her proportionate share of three sons [twelve sons divided by four mothers]. She named him Yehuda, because of the *hoda'a* which she directed towards Hashem in gratitude. So too are we called "Yehudim," the nation which expresses its gratitude in prayer. When Hashem grants us His blessings, we should be grateful not only for the blessing itself, but we should also have the attitude of Leah, namely that we have received more than our share.

We are always looking for new and more effective ways to improve our behavior. Let us hope that through understanding the purpose of the obligation to make one hundred *berachos* each day, we will focus that much more intensely on the meaning and purpose underlying each *bracha* we make. In doing so, we will surely develop a deeper appreciation for everything we have to be thankful for and for the infinite power of our Creator who rules over the wondrous, awesome, and beautiful world in which we live.

If we do so, the *pasuk* promises us, our love and devotion towards our Creator will become second nature to us and, as the beginning of the *pasuk* says, it will seem easy for us to be devoted to Hashem and His *mitzvos.* May we all accomplish this worthy objective.

TZEDEK TZEDEK TIRDOF AND B'TZEDEK TISHPOT AMISECHA: TWO STANDARDS OF JUSTICE AND THE RELEVANCE TO OUR CLAIM TO ERETZ YISRAEL ৵৶

Parshas Shoftim begins with the command to set up judges and police in every settlement. Then, in the third *pasuk*, the Torah commands: צדק צדק תרדוף – we must pursue justice (Devarim 16:20). In Parshas Kedoshim, the Torah seems to convey a similar message – בצדק תשפוט עמיתך, you shall judge your fellow with צדק (Vayikra 19:15).

A review of both *pesukim* leads to several questions:

(1) Firstly, why do we need both *pesukim*?
(2) Why does one *pasuk* use the word תשפוט, which implies a definitive decision, and one *pasuk* uses the word תרדוף, which seems to refer to a decision which is more elusive, which has to be pursued?
(3) Why the double *lashon* of צדק צדק in Parshas Shoftim?
(4) The *pasuk* in Parshas Shoftim ends with the words: למען תחיה. וירשת את הארץ. What is the connection between צדק צדק תרדף and ירושת הארץ? And why is no such connection made in the case of בצדק תשפט עמיתך of?

The Gemara (*Sanhedrin* 32b) gives us some insight into the difference between the two *pesukim*. The Gemara indicates that the *pasuk* in Parshas Kedoshim relates to דין, a judgment, whereas the *pasuk* in Parshas Shoftim refers to פשרה, a compromise.

The Gemara gives the following example of the type of case which can only be settled by a compromise or פשרה:

Two ships approach a narrow channel through which only one can safely pass at one time and there is a dispute over who goes first. The Gemara says:

טעונה ושאינו טעונה, תדחה שאינו טעונה מפני טעונה.
If one ship is carrying a heavier load, then that ship goes
first.

קרובה ושאינו קרובה, תדחה קרובה מפני שאינו קרובה.
If one ship is nearer the channel, then that ship goes first

היו שתיהן קרובות שתיהן רחוקות הטל פשרה ביניהן ומעלות שכר זו
לזו.
If they are equidistant from the channel, then they should
work out a compromise between them and they will be
rewarded.

We see from the above examples that there is a category of disputes
which are not capable of a clear-cut judgment or decision in the usual
sense. In these cases, we are not dealing with a situation where one of
the litigants is completely in the right and the other is in the wrong (in
which case the Beis Din determines which party is right and judges
accordingly), but the situation is one where both parties are at least
partially right and sometimes equally right.

In the Gemara's example, no-one can say that the ship which is
further away or the ship which has a lighter load has no right to use
the channel. Both ships have some right to use the channel. Therefore,
when the Beis Din is asked to decide who goes first, it does not issue
a משפט – a decision which states that A is completely right and B is
completely wrong.

Instead, the Beis Din has to conduct a careful examination of the
facts (e.g., which ship is closer; which has the heavier load and any of
dozens of other possible factors) and then come up with an equitable
solution. Sometimes, the scale is evenly balanced (as where the ships
are equidistant) and the Beis Din may try to work out a compromise
where one goes first and the other is compensated for the disadvan-
tage of going second.

Now we understand why in Kedoshim, the word תשפוט is used,
whereas in Parshas Shoftim, which refers to a פשרה situation, the word

תרדוף is used. Where more than one party has a right to something, then the correct decision is very elusive, you have to chase it. You examine the facts very carefully in order to achieve a resolution which is equitable. Beis Din does not decide who is right and who is wrong but rather what is fair.

Let us now explore the connection between observance of the command of צדק צדק תרדוף and the end of the *pasuk* – למען תחייה וירשת את הארץ.

As an introductory matter, we should explore a passage in Parshas Ekev, where Hashem makes it very clear that it is not because of our merits that we inherited Eretz Yisrael, but because the other nations are worse than we are (Devarim 9:5):

> לא בצדקתך ובישר לבבך אתה בא לרשת את ארצם כי ברשעת הגוים
> האלה ד' אלקיך מורישם מפניך ולמען הקים את הדבר אשר נשבע ד'
> לאבותיך לאברהם ליצחק וליעקב.

> It is not because of your righteousness that you come to inherit their Land, but rather it is because of the sheer wickedness of the [seven] nations that Hashem drives them away from you, and also in order to fulfill the promise which Hashem made to your Forefathers.

What happens when the Jewish people come to the Heavenly Court to make a claim for Eretz Yisrael? We know that Hashem deals with us *midda k'neged midda*, measure for measure. So, when we begin to make our case, Hashem says to us that we will be treated according to the manner in which we conduct our courts.

So, when we say to G-d that we are careful to observe בצדק תשפוט עמיתך, i.e., we judge people properly in cases where right and wrong are clear-cut, then He says, "Okay, try to make a case for Eretz Yisrael based upon clear-cut right and wrong." But we cannot, because we see that the *pasuk* says לא בצדקתך, you cannot make your case based upon clear-cut right and wrong – on your own merits, you do not deserve it.

So we try another tack. We argue that the other nations are worse than we are – they are evil. We also ask Hashem to go back hundreds of generations and remember His promise to our Forefathers. So Hashem says, Okay, you want Me to compare relative merits with respect to the other nations? You want Me to go back hundreds of generations? You want Me to dig deep, look carefully into all of the relevant facts and give you Eretz Yisrael because you deserve it more than the other nations? For this, you have to demonstrate that you are careful about צדק צדק תרדף – that you, Bnei Yisrael, are also careful to dig deep to pursue justice where neither party has an absolute right.

What moral lesson can each of us learn from these *pesukim*? We all know that whenever anyone does anything which we find contrary to our interests, we are often very quick to conclude that the other person is all wrong and that we are all in the right. We are then quick to issue our personal משפט accordingly. The Gemara learns the following from בצדק תשפט עמיתך (*Shevuos* 30a):

הוי דן את חבירך לכף זכות.

We have to give the other person the benefit of the doubt, in other words, attribute צדק to the other person. Of course, if after doing so, we still feel that we are at least partially in the right, then the תורה tells us צדק צדק תרדוף. If the facts are not so simple and everyone has some rationale for his position, then we have to actively pursue the right result; we have to work hard to understand all of the facts and to come up with the most equitable solution under the circumstances.

Let us all be more diligent in giving other people the benefit of the doubt and, by working very hard to pursue the just and equitable outcome in all situations, we will clearly demonstrate to Hashem that we deserve ירושת הארץ.

THE RELATIONSHIP OF *PARA ADUMA* AND *EITZ HADA'AS:* THE IMPACT OF SCRUPULOUS OBSERVANCE OF *CHUKIM* ❧

The Midrash, in explaining the meaning of a *chok*, differentiates between *mishpatim* – those laws which, had they not been written in the Torah, human understanding would have in any event demanded, such as the prohibitions against stealing and murder – and those laws called *chukim*, such as *para aduma*, *sha'atnez* and others, whose underlying meaning and purpose we simply do not understand. The Midrash Tanchuma states that the *yetzer hara* and the nations of the world rebel against *chukim* (Rashi, Bamidbar 19:2).

The Torah does not provide a rationale for *chukim*, and our commentators take different approaches. Some, such as the Rambam, maintain that we should attempt to ascribe reasons for a *chok*, even though we are not certain as to what the true reasons are. The purpose of coming up with our own reasons is to assist us in performing the mitzvah, since human nature is such that we are motivated by a purpose and rationale, even if this purpose and rationale may not be accurate.

Other commentators, such as Rav Yehuda HaLevi (*Sefer HaKuzari*) feel strongly that we should not try to come up with the reasons underlying a *chok*. These commentators feel that, since a man-made reason may not be accurate, we may eventually disagree with the reason, and will then stop doing the mitzvah altogether.

In any event, all agree that a *chok* is a mitzvah whose real reason is hidden from us and that we are obligated to perform these *mitzvos* for no reason other than our unconditional faith in Hashem.

Yet, despite the fact that we do not understand the purpose behind the *chukim*, or perhaps because of it, the Torah seems to go out of its way to emphasize the importance of observing these types of *mitzvos*.

Two separate *parshios* – Bechukosai and Chukas – begin with reference to *chukim* in their very names and, moreover, in Vayikra (26:3), the Torah seems to add otherwise unnecessary words to make the point: אם בחוקתי תלכו ואת מצוותי תשמרו – the Torah is not satisfied with stating only ואת מצותי תשמרו – "if you keep all my *mitzvos*" – but goes out of its way to add a statement about performing the *chukim*. Why such an emphasis on *chukim*?

Parshas Chukas (Bamidbar 19:1) opens with the words זאת חקת התורה – which means: "This is the decree of the Torah," and then goes on to discuss the laws of *para aduma*. There are numerous *chukim* in the Torah, many of which preceded *para aduma* in the Torah's order, so why does this *parsha* begin with the words זאת חקת התורה, with חקת expressed in the singular, and then goes on to single out the laws of *para aduma*, as if this were the only *chok* in the Torah. It appears as if the Torah is presenting *para aduma* as the paradigm, or the classic example, of a *chok*. Why is this so?

Many have suggested that the reason for the extraordinary focus on *para aduma* is that this mitzvah contains an element of even greater mystery than the other *chukim*. Whereas *chukim* in general have no apparent rhyme or reason, *para aduma* goes further in that it seems to actually defy reason – on the face of it, *para aduma* is a mitzvah with an inherent paradox. *Para aduma* was a completely red cow, without physical blemish, whose ashes and blood were used to purify certain persons who had become ritually unclean – but, perplexingly, its ashes are *metameh ha'tehorim* and *metaher ha'temaim* – although they purify a person who is ritually unclean, they also contaminate a person who is pure, namely the person preparing the ashes.

Can any of us make sense out of this? It defies our sense of rational reasoning. Perhaps this is the reason why the Torah selected *para aduma* from among all of the *chukim*, to tell us *zos chukas HaTorah* – this is the *chok* and we are obligated to obey it.

The opening Rashi in this *parsha*, on the words *zos chukas HaTorah*, quotes the Midrash and states as follows:

> Because Satan and the nations of the world taunt Israel, saying, "What is this commandment and what reason is there in it," the Torah calls it a *chok*, implying that it is a decree from Hashem and we have no right to criticize it.

So we have seen that the Torah, at the beginning of Parshas Chukas, tells us in a very direct way that we are obligated to observe the *chukim*, without questioning their rationale. However, in line with the concealed nature of the *chukim*, I believe that there is a very subtle but instructive allusion, later in the *parsha*, to the very great rewards in store for us if we are scrupulous in our observance of the *chukim*.

After Bnei Yisrael complained about a lack of water, Hashem punished the complainers by sending poisonous snakes into the camp and many Jews died. In order to stop this plague, Moshe, at G-d's command, placed a snake made of copper on a pole and whoever looked at the snake was miraculously healed from any otherwise fatal snakebites (Bamidbar 21:8).

In a parallel incident in Parshas Beshalach (Shemos 17:11), when the Jews were fighting their first battle with Amalek (the archenemy of the Jews throughout history), Moshe went up to the top of a nearby hill with Aharon and Chur and, with their assistance, Moshe held his hands raised in the air during the battle. The Torah tells us that so long as Moshe's hands stayed up in the air, the Jews were victorious over Amalek and that when Moshe let his hands down, Amalek prevailed.

The Mishnah in *Rosh Hashana* discusses these two incidents as follows (29a):

"והיה כאשר ירים משה ידו וגבר ישראל" וגו' (שמות, יז, יא). וכי ידיו של משה עושות מלחמה או שוברות מלחמה? אלא לומר לך : כל זמן שהיו ישראל מסתכלים כלפי מעלה ומשעבדים את לבם לאביהם שבשמים – היו מתגברים, ואם לאו – היו נופלין. כיוצא בדבר אתה אומר (במדבר כא, ח) : "עשה לך שרף ושים אותו על נס והיה כל הנשוך, וראה אותו וחי". וכי נחש ממית, או נחש מחיה? אלא בזמן שישראל מסתכלין כלפי מעלה ומשעבדין את לבם לאביהם שבשמים – היו מתרפאים, ואם לאו – היו נימוקים.

The *pasuk* states: "When Moshe raised his hands, Bnei Yisrael prevailed, and when Moshe lowered his hands, Amalek prevailed." Do the hands of Moshe wage war or lose the battle? Rather, the *pasuk* is there to tell us that as long as Bnei Yisrael look towards their Creator and subjugate their hearts to their Father in Heaven, they prevail in battle, and if not, the opposite it true. Similarly, the *pasuk* in Chukas says that G-d commanded Moshe to place a copper snake on a staff and anyone who was bitten by a snake would gaze upon the staff and snake and would be healed. Does gazing upon a snake cause one to live or die? Rather, when Bnei Yisrael look towards their Creator and subjugate their hearts to their Father in Heaven, they would be healed.

Now, in the midst of this expression in the Mishnah of the importance of faith, how do we understand the symbolism used in these two incidents? What is the message and the relevance of Moshe's hands raised in the air or the snake curled on a pole?

I would like to suggest that the hands in the air and the snake in these incidents are an allusion to Adam and Chava eating from the *eitz hada'as*. The hands in the air remind us of the hands which reached into the tree to take the fruit which was not permitted to Adam and Chava and the snake represents the animal which originally stirred things up. If so, however, what is the connection of *eitz hada'as* to Parshas Chukas?

I believe that we can understand this a little better when we see the parallels between the commandment not to eat from the *eitz hada'as* and the laws of *para aduma*. The commandment not to eat from the *eitz hada'as* was the first *chok* in the Torah and, just like *para aduma*, it was not only devoid of any rationale, but it actually defied logic. After all, the Garden of Eden contained the best of everything – it was truly a Paradise and everything in it was wonderful for humans to consume and enjoy.

Therefore, when Hashem came along and told Adam not to eat from the *eitz hada'as*, this commandment made no sense. How could a fruit from the Garden of Eden be harmful or dangerous? Of course, as soon as Adam and Chava began to question the reasoning behind the commandment, they stumbled and sinned. Then, on account of disregarding one simple *chok*, they lost everything.

So far, this is a negative and depressing message. But there is a deeper and much more hopeful message in the two incidents discussed in the Mishnah in *Rosh Hashana* mentioned above. In both of these situations – the battle with Amalek and the search for water in the desert – logic would tell us that Bnei Yisrael should not have made out too well. For instance, how could Bnei Yisrael, fresh out of 210 years of slavery, possibly have managed to defeat Amalek? Where were their weapons, their armed forces, their battle experience, or their morale? Also, in the second incident, how could the desert possibly have provided sufficient water for the needs of two million people?

When the Torah tells us that Bnei Yisrael, despite overwhelming (and in reality impossible) odds, defeated Amalek and were also able to get all the water they needed in the desert, the message is that our human rationale can only take us so far. There is a great deal we do not, and cannot understand, and must rely on our faith in Hashem. Just as we are called upon to perform the *chukim*, even though they appear to us totally illogical or at least devoid of logic, we must realize that, as a nation, we are often the beneficiary of Hashem accomplishing things for us which, on a purely logical basis, we have no right to expect.

In a modern context, we see an illustration of this idea in the case of Medinat Yisrael. When we read about the problems with the Palestinians and all of our other archenemies in the region, we sometimes feel as if the struggle is too difficult and that logically we have no chance to overcome the countless and seemingly insurmountable problems.

The lesson of Parshas Chukas and the *para aduma* is, however, that our intellect is limited and that faith has to take over where logic seems to reach a dead end. Just as we demonstrate our faith by observing the *chukim* which appear to have no logic, so too will Hashem perform for us great miracles which logically are completely beyond our reach.

May we, as the Mishnah in *Rosh Hashana* states, subordinate our hearts to our Father in Heaven so that we will observe even those commandments whose logic defies our understanding and, in turn, Hashem will enable us to prevail over our enemies and benefit from His countless blessings.

THE TORAH'S HIGHLY SENSITIVE
STANDARD OF CHARITY

Those who spend time in the business of law or the giving of tax advice, and who have had the questionable pleasure of studying our twentieth-century laws, know very well that laws written by man can go on for pages and pages and make very little sense, even though they are often written by teams of experts assisted by the tools of modern technology. In sharp contrast, our Torah can pack infinite sensitivity, compassion and insight into two or three short words. Such is the case with Parshas Re'eh.

Towards the end of the Parsha, the mitzvah of *tzedaka* is discussed. The Torah states that when there is a person amongst us who is in need, we should not refrain from assisting such person and we must give such person די מחסורו אשר יחסר לו (Devarim 15:8), which literally means "what such person is missing, what he is missing" (seemingly repeated twice, with similar words).

The last three words of this phrase appear to be superfluous. Once the Torah tells us that we have to give the person די מחסרו – what he or she is missing, why is there a need to state again אשר יחסר לו, which seems to mean the same thing? Rashi comments:

> אפילו סוס לרכוב עליו – which means even a horse to ride on, if such is what the person was used to previously [although, Rashi adds, there is no obligation to assist the person to get a better horse than he had before].

In modern terms, if a person is used to living in a five-bedroom house in a high-end zip code, and he or she falls upon hard times, or has a bad year, the Torah tells us that the mitzvah of *tzedaka* commands us to enable such person to maintain the standard of living which such person is accustomed to. We should not take the position that such person can move to a one-bedroom apartment in a low-income area and why should we be obligated to enable such person to maintain his or her more comfortable lifestyle.

The Torah, in its infinite wisdom and compassion, tells us that you have to look at the person's pain – particularly the pain which a person feels when they are experiencing financial problems and are faced with the possibility of being forced to drastically reduce the standard of living to which they are accustomed. This is why the Torah uses the words אשר יחסר לו – in other words, you have to *consider what the person suffering a financial setback is missing* – not what *you think* is good enough, or should be good enough, for him or her.

In practical terms, it should be noted that there are today, more than a few people in our communities who are out of a job, or whose business is not what it was the year before, and whose financial situation may be in jeopardy. The pain that these people feel is no doubt compounded by the fact that they are suffering in the midst of what they may perceive as general affluence.

How important is it for us to try to assist these individuals? The Rambam, in a famous teaching, placed the mitzvah of *tzedaka* in eight categories: the lowest category is when we give reluctantly or grudgingly; next is when we give with a good attitude but the amount is inappropriately low; next is to give adequately but only after the needy person asks; next is to give the needy person before he asks; next is when the needy person knows the identity of the giver but the giver does not know who the recipient is; next is the reverse – when the giver knows who the recipient is but the recipient does not know who the giver is; the second highest category is when neither knows who the other is.

Finally, the highest category of all is to help someone become independent, as when you help them find a job because, whereas giving someone a gift of money helps for a little while, getting someone a job helps for a long time and, more importantly, maintains that person's pride and dignity.

Interestingly enough, the Rambam, in this highest category, does not mention the desirability of helping out anonymously, perhaps because when you assist someone to obtain a position, the person you assist has pride of self-sufficiency and is far less likely to be embarrassed by knowing the identity of the person who assisted him than if he received an outright monetary donation.

Many communities have one or more members who make it their business to try to place people who need a position. Unfortunately, more often than not, these people fight a very lonely battle. Even those in otherwise very generous communities sometimes overlook those individuals who from time to time could use a hand in finding a position or making a business contact. Often, we are not even aware of those individuals who have a great need, as it is very awkward for such persons to publicize their own situation. This is why it is so important for each of us to take the initiative in this area.

We are blessed with many successful people in all kinds of professions and businesses. It is this very success, and the many business contacts we make, which gives us the ability to refer and direct people who need a placement or a business contact. When Queen Esther was initially reluctant to approach King Achashverosh on behalf of the Jewish people, Mordechai reminded her (Esther 4:14):

ומי יודע אם לעת כזאת הגעת למלכות.

> Who knows if it was not precisely for the purpose of assisting Bnei Yisrael that you were elevated to such a lofty position.

So too each career and business success which we experience brings with it the challenge and opportunity of placing us in a position where we may be able to give someone a valuable and much appreciated assist.

It should also be noted that there are ways to perform this mitzvah even if we are not in a position to directly help someone find a job or make a business contact. Halacha states that a person who is unable to help someone directly should at least offer a kind word. Certainly, this lifts the other person's morale and has many other beneficial effects. So if we go to someone who is looking for a position and we give them encouragement and comfort, we have done something very worthwhile and important.

Parshas Re'eh also contains the words עשר תעשר, in connection with the mitzvah of *tzedaka*. The Midrash reads this double word to mean

עשר בשביל שתתעשר – give *tzedaka* so that you will become wealthy.[1] This Midrash has actually become embodied into halacha.

Normally, *mitzvos* must be performed for their own sake and not for the sake of receiving reward. There is one exception – the mitzvah of *tzedaka*, where it is not only permissible to perform the mitzvah of *tzedaka* with the intent of receiving reward, but the Shulchan Aruch goes so far as to say that it is actually permitted to test G-d with the mitzvah of *tzedaka*.

In other words, halacha tells us that not only will a person never lose money by giving *tzedaka*, the person giving *tzedaka* is permitted, so to speak, to challenge G-d to return the money with a profit. If this is true for the giving of money, then we can certainly appreciate the great importance of assisting someone to make a living, which is the highest form of *tzedaka* according to the Rambam.

Clearly, to help a person find a position or to make a good business contact could literally turn such person's life around. If each one of us resolves to make a good-faith attempt to help at least one person with their career or business, especially those who may have suffered a temporary setback, we can collectively make a difference. If we do so, hopefully Hashem will look upon us as a people and community which truly cares.

---

1. This mitzvah, as with virtually every other positive commandment, has an upper limit beyond which a person is generally not permitted to go, i.e., a person must not expend more than twenty percent of a person's wealth on this mitzvah.

LIBEL AND SLANDER:
HALACHA VS. SECULAR LAW

A person's reputation is a very precious commodity. In Ecclesiastes (Koheles), King Solomon tells us that a good reputation is more valuable than good oil (i.e., wealth). Unfortunately, our modern legal system, in comparison to halacha, is not very protective of a person's reputation. In fact, there are many ways in which our modern laws permit a person to be libeled or slandered, and his or her reputation destroyed, without any legal consequence.

A few examples would help to illustrate the above point. In the first place, truth is an absolute defense to a claim of libel. If a person maligns another, but is telling the truth, then the communication is always excused, even if it is prompted by malicious motives. Another example is a newspaper or journal which publishes a story which is based upon incorrect facts and, as a result, is injurious to someone's reputation. In such a case, the newspaper is not liable if it based its report on a source which it reasonably considered reliable, even if other readily accessible sources could have been used to determine the falsity of the report. The newspaper has no obligation to investigate any further than the first "reliable source."

It is also true, although most people would find this hard to believe, that almost any statement made in the course of litigation, whether such statement is made in legal papers or in open court, cannot be attacked as libelous, provided only that such statement has some relationship to the litigation at issue. A false statement made in the course of legal proceedings, even if maliciously made, is excused. And it is also very difficult and rare to convict the person making such false statement of perjury.

There are many other communications which are privileged despite their being both false and injurious to someone's reputation, such as statements made by certain public officials and politicians.

Jewish law, by contrast, goes to very great lengths to protect a person's reputation. It should be noted that not all of these laws are enforceable by a religious court in an action for monetary damages; however, the laws of libel and slander are presented in halacha as being extremely serious and the moral message is accordingly very clear.

For example, in halacha, the truth of a statement is no defense, unless it is made under very carefully controlled conditions, and in order to warn someone of a perceived danger, e.g., where there is potential for physical or financial harm. Moreover, there is never any defense for a false statement, whether such statement is made in reliance upon a "respectable" source or if it is made in the heat of a legal battle.

Our tradition tells us that those people who are not careful with their speech or written words "destroy the world," even if they said nothing untruthful (Rambam *Hilchos De'os* 7:2). A review of the very detailed halachic codes governing libel and slander makes it very apparent how extraordinarily sensitive is our tradition in safeguarding a person's reputation. May we all have the moral strength to be faithful to these guidelines and not be misled by the false signals of our "modern" laws.

AN *AUFRUF D'VAR* I: THE VOICES OF *SIMCHAS CHASAN V'KALLA*

This *d'var* focuses specifically on the theme of *simcha* as it relates to *chasan* and *kalla*. The Gemara in *Berachos* (6b) states as follows:

אמר רב הונא : כל הנהנה מסעודת חתן ואינו משמחו, עובר בחמישה
קולות, שנאמר קול ששון וקול שמחה קול חתן וקול כלה קול אומרים
הודו את ד'.

Whoever benefits from the *seuda* of a *chasan,* and does not make the *chasan* happy, transgresses five *kolos: kol sasson v'kol simcha*, and so on.

At first glance, the terminology of this Gemara seems strange. We know what it means to transgress a positive or negative commandment, but what does it mean to transgress a קול (sound)?

A second question, which I heard was asked by Rabbi Yisroel Reisman in his *motzaei* Shabbos *shiur*, is: Why in general is it so important to be *mesame'ach chasan v'kalla* (to generate additional joy for the groom and bride)? After all, we assume that the *chasan* and *kalla* are getting married because they have very strong feelings for each other. That alone should generate considerable *simcha* between *chasan* and *kalla*. Why then is it necessary for us to go out of our way to make them happy?

In order to gain some insight into these questions, we need to explore and understand the role of *simcha* in the performance of *mitzvos* generally, and how this operates specifically in the case of a *chasan* and *kalla*.

✣ SIMCHA IN THE PERFORMANCE OF MITZVOS GENERALLY

In Ki Savo, towards the end of the *tochacha*, after we read about all the terrible things which may come upon Bnei Yisrael, the Torah tells us that the cause of these tragedies is our failure to serve Hashem with joy when things are going well for us (Devarim 28:47):

תחת אשר לא עבדת את ד' אלקיך בשמחה ובטוב לבב מרב כל.

And so we see that it is not enough just to perform the *mitzvos* – it is extremely important that we do so with great enthusiasm. Why is this so? Partly, I believe, in recognition of the fact that when Hashem helps us, He similarly does so with great enthusiasm. We see this notion in the following *pasuk*, also in Ki Savo (28:63), which I believe has tremendous importance:

והיה כאשר שש ד' עליכם להיטיב אתכם ולהרבות אתכם כן ישיש ד'
עליכם להאביד אתכם ולהשמיד אתכם.
And just as Hashem rejoices to do good for you and to cause you to increase in numbers, so too will He rejoice when He [figuratively] destroys you.

Although the end of this *pasuk* may appear somewhat depressing, we can learn a very valuable lesson from this *pasuk*, namely that when Hashem helps us, it is as if it gives Him great joy, כביכול, to do so. This means that, at the very least as a matter of *hakaras hatov*, we absolutely need to show similar joy in the manner in which we serve Hashem.

The Gemara in *Arachin* helps us understand what it means to serve Hashem with joy. On the *pasuk* of תחת אשר לא עבדת את ד' אלקיך בשמחה ובטוב לבב (Devarim 28:47), the Gemara (*Arachin* 11a) comments:

מניין לעיקר שירה מן התורה, ... א"ר מתנה דכתיב, תחת אשר לא
עבדת את ד' אלקיך בשמחה ובטוב לבב, איזו עבודה שהוא בשמחה
ובטוב לבב, הוי אומר זו שירה.
How do we know that the primary source of the *shira* which the Levi'im sang in the Beis HaMikdosh is from the Torah? Because it says:

תחת אשר לא עבדת את ד' אלקיך בשמחה ובטוב לבב.

"Because you did not serve Hashem, your G-d, with gladness and goodness of heart, when everything was abundant." What type of *avoda* is considered *avoda* with *simcha* and gladness of heart? The answer is *shira*, or song.

No doubt, the songs of the Levi'im in the Beis HaMikdosh greatly enhanced the joy with which Bnei Yisrael served Hashem. Similarly, in the context of the *bikkurim*, in Ki Savo (Devarim 26:11), the *pasuk* says ושמחת בכל הטוב – that we have to be joyful when we bring the *bikkurim*. The Gemara learns from a *gezeira shava* that the person who brings the *bikkurim* and makes the recital of *"Arami Oved Ovi,"* etc., must do so in song.

And we see in Beshalach (Shemos 15:1) that when Bnei Yisrael experienced the culmination of the enormous miracles of *Yetziyas Mitzrayim* at the splitting of the Sea, they broke out in song and with instruments.

This does not mean that every mitzvah we perform has to be accompanied by song. But it does mean that we should feel as if each mitzvah is a precious gift from Hashem and, for this reason alone, we should be ecstatic to perform such mitzvah. For example, when we kiss our *tzizis* each morning, it is clear that we should do so in a manner which indicates our great love for the mitzvah, and not in a manner of someone who is just trying to fulfill an obligation. This illustrates the general notion of *simcha shel mitzvah* (joy in performing a mitzvah).

❧ ADDITIONAL ASPECT OF SIMCHA IN CERTAIN MITZVOS

As we will explain in a moment, aside from the general notion of *simcha shel mitzvah*, it seems that there is a category of *mitzvos*, such as *bikkurim*, Yom Tov and *chasan v'kalla*, where halacha mandates an additional layer or heightened level of *simcha*. The common theme among this category of *mitzvos* appears to be that the very opportunity to perform each such mitzvah is caused by the kindness and *hashgacha* of Hashem, and we demonstrate our appreciation for this kindness and *hashgacha* by ratcheting up our level of *simcha* when we perform these *mitzvos*.

For example, *bikkurim* could not be brought without Hashem's generosity in creating favorable conditions for the fruits of the Land to grow. In recognition of this fact, there appears to be a requirement for an extra dose of *simcha*, in addition to the *simcha shel mitzvah* of bringing the *bikkurim*. The Torah passage on *bikkurim* tells us (Devarim 26:11): ‏ושמחת בכל הטוב.

And we all know that on Yom Tov, aside from the *simcha shel mitzvah* of *arba kosos*, *lulav*, etc., the Torah's statement of ‏ושמחת בחגך (you shall be joyous on your holiday) superimposes a requirement of *simcha* over the entire *chag*. On Yom Tov, it is self-evident that the requirement of ‏ושמחת בחגך is based on the incredible miracles represented by *Yetziyas Mitzrayim* and *Matan Torah*.

In the case of the *chasan* and *kalla*, there is similarly an added requirement for *simcha*, and we have seen, in the Gemara in *Berachos*, the very unusual requirement that, aside from the *simcha shel mitzvah* itself, others are obligated to be *mesame'ach* the persons performing the mitzvah. Why is this so?

Once again, I believe that the heightened emphasis on *simcha*, in the case of a *chasan* and *kalla*, constitutes our collective acknowledgement of the powerful *hashgacha* which led to the *simcha*. But how does this *hashgacha* operate in the case of a *chasan* and *kalla*? On the one hand, this seems like an obvious question. We are all familiar with the notion of *bashert* and we have all witnessed, many times, the absolutely remarkable way in which events unfold so that *chasan* and *kalla* are drawn to each other. However, there is another very important aspect of *hashgacha* which is very important but not nearly so apparent.

The Gemara, at the very beginning of *Sotah* (2a), states:

אמר רב יהודה אמר רב: ארבעים יום קודם יצירת הוולד בת קול יוצאת
ואומרת, בת פלוני לפלוני.

> Rav Yehuda said in the name of Rav: "Forty days before a child is created, a Heavenly voice goes forth and announces: The daughter of so-and-so is destined for so-and-so."

A question to be asked on this Gemara is: Why does Hashem begin the matchmaking process forty days before the *chasan* and *kalla* are first created? What is the rush, considering that the couple will not meet for another twenty years or so?

To answer this question, I would suggest that the notion of *bashert* lies not only in the incredible manner in which Hashem makes sure that a man and woman each meet the one who is predestined for them, but it also means that Hashem actually forms the *chasan* and *kalla* in a way which makes them uniquely suited for each other, and this process begins all the way back at the moment when a person's unique traits and personality are formed by the injection of the *neshama* into the infant's body.

With this construct, we can better understand the special requirement to be *mesamayach chasan v'kalla*. Yes, we assume the couple have a very strong attraction to each other and, in that respect, perhaps they do not have a particular need for us to make them happy. However, it is extremely important for us to demonstrate the second dimension of *simcha*, which is the recognition of, and appreciation for, the tremendous lengths to which Hashem has gone to make this moment happen.

We asked at the outset what the Gemara in *Berachos* means when it says that failing to bring joy to the *chasan* means that we transgress in five sounds. But now that we have learned the Gemara in *Sotah*, we can understand this concept much better. The בת קול (Heavenly voice) which announces, before a child is even born, that the daughter of פלוני is destined for פלוני – this is the בת קול which loudly and clearly announces to us that Hashem very long ago began the remarkable process of making this *shidduch* happen. This בת קול, many years later, is transformed into the *kol* of ששון, the *kol* of שמחה, the *kol* of the חתן, and the *kol* of the כלה.

These are the קולות produced by Hashem and these are the קולות which we transgress if we do not properly celebrate with the *chasan* and *kalla*. On the other hand, if we are *mesamayach chasan v'kalla* with enthusiasm, we demonstrate our recognition and *emuna* that the בת קול produced the *kol* of *simcha* and the *kol* of the *chasan* and *kalla*.

It only takes a moment of meeting our *chasan* and *kalla* to perceive the great miracles of the *Yad Hashem* in not only bringing them together despite a distance from each other of hundreds, and even thousands, of miles, which is an amazing feat all by itself, but also in forming their personalities from the very beginning in a way which makes them so remarkably suited to each other.

May the spirit of *shira* of this special Shabbos inspire us to celebrate the incredible *hashgacha* of Hashem which makes us want to celebrate this wonderful *simcha* with such great joy.

AN AUFRUF D'VAR II: THE CONCEPT OF *B'MIKREH* (COINCIDENCE) AND THE BUILDING OF A JEWISH HOME ८०

The *tochacha*, which we read in Bechukosai, illustrates very dramatically the extremely serious danger of an attitude of viewing events in our lives as במקרה (as happenstance). As the Torah states (Vayikra 26:21):

ואם תלכו עמי קרי ולא תאבו לשמוע לי.
If you walk with Me in a manner of קרי, and do not listen to Me, . . . etc.

Rashi, relying upon the Midrash, explains the word קרי as meaning במקרה – random or accidental, meaning that we treat events, good or bad, as merely chance, rather than the results of G-d's ever-present *hashgacha*. The Torah goes on to state the consequences of doing so. The conclusion of the aforementioned *pasuk* reads:

ויספתי עליכם מכה שבע כחטאתיכם.
I will punish you sevenfold times your sin.

In fact, there are a number of indications in the Torah and in Megillas Esther that, on a national level, the retribution for Bnei Yisrael's regarding events as happenstance or coincidence is the immediate attack by our archenemy Amalek. We are told that Amalek attacks us suddenly and without rhyme or reason, as if to underscore the fact that our attitude of במקרה, or randomness, caused Amalek's attack to occur, מידה כנגד מידה, measure for measure.

The *tochacha*'s warning of punishment for the attitude of במקרה is driven home with a threefold repetition, within just a few *pesukim*, of the same message. Why do we need to hear this three times? Although the Torah is clearly trying to get our attention with regard to an apparently very serious issue, would we not have understood this point very well if the Torah had stated, merely once, that the punishment is seven times the magnitude of the sin?

I would suggest, however, that the significance of the Torah's emphasis upon punishment in the magnitude of seven times our sin is the reciprocal, namely the boundless rewards which are in store for us if we perceive G-d's guiding Hand in seemingly random events – events which most people are quite ready to ascribe to coincidence.

To illustrate the role of *hashgacha* in the context of a *chasan* and *kalla*, there is a fascinating statement in the Talmud (*Sotah* 2a) about how, forty days before a child is born, it is decided in the Heavens who is destined to be paired with whom, which is no doubt where the concept of *"bashert"* originated. In the context of this Midrash, we can better appreciate the almost magical way in which bride and groom seem to be so often propelled towards each other, almost as if there were a predestination.

In fact, the pairing-off of husband and wife is probably one of the most remarkable examples of an event which superficially appears to be just a random occurrence but yet anyone who cares to look at the event more closely can readily perceive the incredible underpinning of *hashgacha*. We all have great stories to illustrate this point.

The exuberant manner in which we celebrate G-d's orchestration of human affairs, as exemplified by the union of man and woman in marriage can, I believe, be viewed in part as our triumphant response to the stark message of the *tochacha*. Yes, the sevenfold punishment noted in the *tochacha* is a dire warning, but it is also true that, in sharp contrast, seven is also a precious number in our tradition, exemplifying special gifts from Hashem. For example, "seven" plays a prominent role in the marriage ceremony and also represents the special gift Hashem gave to us in the form of Shabbos, whose observance, just like the celebration of marriage, represents a powerful counterpoint to the notion of במקרה, or randomness.

Much of the world believes that the world was created by a random accident. And so we observe Shabbos to demonstrate to one and all that G-d created the world in six days before resting on the seventh. Shabbos represents a proud declaration of G-d's ever-present guidance and control of human affairs.

And just as we demonstrate on Shabbos, the seventh day of the week, that the notion of במקרה is an illusion, it is not surprising that we also demonstrate our deep gratitude for Hashem's union of bride and groom with the number seven. The bride circles the groom seven times under the *chuppah*; the ceremony is consecrated with seven special blessings and then, after the wedding, we engage in seven special days of celebration, which celebration is greatly enhanced by our appreciation of Hashem's careful orchestration of the union of *chasan* and *kalla*. I would suggest that these traditions represent the *tochacha's* hidden message of hope which lies in store for us if we utterly reject the notion of במקרה.

To the *Chasan* and *Kalla*, it is our prayer and blessing to both of you that, just as we know you perceive and appreciate G-d's guidance and love in bringing you together, so too may you always perceive and be grateful for the Hand of Hashem in your lives so that you will accordingly be blessed with everything you wish for, seven times over.

Thomas Furst, a descendant of the Chasam Sofer, is a son of Holocaust survivors. The author attended Yeshivat Kerem B'Yavneh, is a business graduate of McGill University, received an MBA from the University of Michigan and a law degree from the University of Toronto. He is a real estate attorney in Manhattan. The author lives with his family in Great Neck, New York, where he is currently an active member of the Great Neck Synagogue. Born in Czechoslovakia, he is named after Thomas Masaryk, a three-time President of Czechoslovakia who was a great friend of the Jewish people.

The author can be contacted through his website:
www.thomasfurst.com.